About the author

Edward Thomas has lived and worked in Sudan and South Sudan for over eight years. He worked as a teacher, researcher and human rights worker for Sudanese and international organizations. Over the past five years, he has written numerous books, reports and articles about South Sudan and its neighbours.

T0314860

SOUTH SUDAN
A SLOW LIBERATION

Edward Thomas

Zed Books
LONDON

South Sudan: A slow liberation was first published in 2015 by Zed Books Ltd, 7 Cynthia Street, London N1 9JF, UK

www.zedbooks.co.uk

Set in Monotype Plantin and FontFont Kievit by Ewan Smith, London
Index: ed.emery@thefreeuniversity.net
Cover image (c) Sven Torfinn/Panos
Cover designed by www.roguefour.co.uk

A catalogue record for this book is available from the British Library

ISBN 978-1-78360-405-0 hb
ISBN 978-1-78360-404-3 pb
ISBN 978-1-78360-406-7 pdf
ISBN 978-1-78360-407-4 epub
ISBN 978-1-78360-408-1 mobi

To KD with love

CONTENTS

Figures and tables | viii Acknowledgements | ix
A note on terminology | xi

INTRODUCTION: Gabriel Anyang remembers his
childhood 1

PART ONE: SOCIETY AND STATE

1 The social landscape 33
2 South Sudan's encounter with modernity 53
3 Development and representation 82
4 Theories of revolution 106
5 State and society in Jonglei after the Comprehensive
Peace Agreement 126

PART TWO: JONGLEI'S MUTINIES

6 The life and death of Hassan Ngachingol 169
7 The civil wars in Jonglei 178
8 The geography of conflict in Jonglei after the
Comprehensive Peace Agreement 211

PART THREE: SOCIAL TRANSFORMATION

9 Raiding and eating. 243
10 Nyaburjok 260

CONCLUSION: Slow liberation 278

Bibliography | 293
Index | 309

FIGURES AND TABLES

Figures

1.1 South Sudan's main ecological zones 35
1.2 Ethnic groups of the Greater Upper Nile 43
2.1 John Petherick's sketch of a Murle or 'Djibba' warrior . 74
3.1 Government per capita current expenditures 2011 or
    last available year. 83
7.1 Counties and population density in Jonglei, 2008 . . .181
8.1 Reported abductions 2009–11 in eight selected counties
    of Jonglei. 219
8.2 Reported killings 2009–11 in eight selected counties of
    Jonglei. 219

Tables

1.1 Responses to the 1955/56 census question 'What
    language do you speak at home?' for the nine largest
    languages in the Southern provinces of Sudan 40
5.1 South Sudan budgets in Sudanese pounds, 2005–11 . 142
7.1 Losses in the 1992–94 Lou–Jikainy war 193
8.1 Reported cattle lost to raiding 2009–11 in eight selected
    counties of Jonglei 220
8.2 Number of raids in eight selected counties of Jonglei in
    2010 221
9.1 Herd dynamics for an average household with a herd of
    sixty-five cattle. 246
10.1 Ethnicity and fertility in the 1955/56 census. 268
C1 South Sudan's military budget, 2011–13 280
C2 GDP and GNI, East African countries 289

ACKNOWLEDGEMENTS

This book is based on several hundred interviews with people in South Sudan. Most interviews were conducted between 2011 and 2013, in Juba, Upper Nile, Jonglei and Eastern Equatoria. But only a handful of interviewees are identified by name. At the time of publication, the political situation in South Sudan had become very polarized, and I was concerned that using names might complicate things for people. It feels unfair not to credit interviewees by name, though, because the book was made possible by their generous willingness to share with me stories of their lives; or testimonies about historical events that have not made it into written records; or their attempts to engage with fundamental questions about the state and liberation.

The book was the idea of Mareike Schomerus. I had been commissioned to conduct and analyse the interviews as an independent researcher, and she suggested that I turn it into a publication. Not only that, but she supported my application to become an associate of the Justice and Security Research Programme, an international research consortium led by the London School of Economics and Political Science, which commissioned me to complete this book and allowed me the use of their facilities. Alex de Waal gave his strong backing to the project and connected it to the publishers. Both he and Mareike read through successive drafts of the manuscript and their comments have greatly improved it. I am sincerely grateful to them, and to Wendy Foulds of the JSRP, for all that support.

I would also like to thank the many people who reviewed all or part of the book. Hiruy Amanuel, Gabriel Anyang, Mike

Arensen, Daniela Baro, Zoe Cormack, Diana Felix da Costa, Khairun Dhala, Magdi El Gizouli, Indrajit Ghosh, Lydia Green, Avery Hancock, Ferdinand von Hapsburg, Liz Hodgkin, Douglas Johnson, Niall Kishtainy, John Kumen, Mawan Muortat, Brigid O Connor, Henry Radice, John Ryle, James Sharrock, Miri Weingarten and Hazel de Wet all gave up their time to read through drafts and provide valuable (and, even better, speedy) comment. Liz Hodgkin provided patient commentary and angelic encouragements for not one but several drafts, and Douglas Johnson generously shared otherwise unobtainable primary sources on which Chapter 8 is based.

A NOTE ON TERMINOLOGY

Since 2011, South Sudan has been a republic and its citizens are called South Sudanese. The territories making up South Sudan began to be delineated in the mid-nineteenth century. At that time, foreign administrators called different parts of the South names like 'Fashoda' after a Shilluk settlement, 'Bahr al-Ghazal' after the Arabic name for a river, or 'Equatoria' after a line on a map. Sometimes Southern Sudan had a unified administration – a Regional Government or a Coordinating Council. But sometimes it was just three Southern provinces, which became three Southern regions, and then became ten Southern states. Governments sometimes viewed these provinces/regions/states as a single political unit, but only in the sense that they were part of the Southern Question, which was sometimes also the Southern Problem, which they sometimes believed had been caused by Southerners in the South. It was confusing, because there was no political entity called Northern Sudan, and northerners from the north were seldom called Northerners from the North. This book generally embraces anachronism by using the terms South Sudan and South Sudanese for Southerners and Sudan and Sudanese for the people of the rest of Sudan. But here is a sequence of names that outsiders applied to the territory of present-day South Sudan.

Pre-colonial period (to nineteenth century) South Sudan had state systems in a few areas, most notably the kingdoms in Shilluk areas (late seventeenth century to late nineteenth century) and Zande areas (eighteenth century to 1900).

The Turkiya (1820–85) and the Mahdiya (1885–98) 'The interior'
becomes the 'southern provinces': In 1820 Turco-Egyptian
(Turkiya) armies conquered the Funj and Taqali sultanates in
present-day Sinnar and Kordofan. In 1841, the Ottoman sultan
assigned the *vali* or viceroy of Egypt the heritable government
of Nubia, Sinnar, Kordofan and Darfur, without defining their
boundaries. South Sudan was a slave-raiding hinterland for
Turkiya expeditions (1840s) and then private entrepreneurs
under Turkiya protection (1850s–70s). The creation of administrative structures was linked to the movement for the abolition
of slavery. The White Nile district was set up in Shilluk lands in
1855 as a measure for interdicting the slave trade, and the Shilluk
kingdom withered. From the late 1860s, districts (*muḥāfiẓas*) and
then provinces (*mudīrīyas*) were set up in Equatoria and Bahr al-
Ghazal, but their borders were not defined. In 1885, the Turkiya
fell to the Mahdist state. Mahdist and Turkiya governors, Belgian
and French colonialists and Ethiopian slave traders sporadically
occupied areas of the southern provinces.

The Anglo-Egyptian Condominium (1898–1956) 'The Southern
Provinces of the Sudan': Southern Sudan was made up of three
provinces with defined borders. It was treated as a culturally
and linguistically distinct zone, one of several 'closed districts' in
Sudan. Between 1894 and 1910, the Lado enclave around Juba
was under Belgian occupation.

Independent Sudan (1956–2011) 'The Southern Provinces' or
'Southern Sudan': Independent Sudan inherited the Southern
provinces of Equatoria, Bahr al-Ghazal and Upper Nile, and
with them the Southern Question. In 1973, the three provinces
were unified under a single Southern Regional Government. In
1976, Jonglei, the vantage-point for much of this book, became a
province, as the three big old provinces were divided up into six
smaller new ones. In 1983, the Southern Regional Government
was abolished, and the three big old provinces of Equatoria,

Bahr al-Ghazal and Upper Nile were reconstituted. But this time, they were called regions, and Jonglei remained a province of Upper Nile region. In 1994, the three regions were divided into ten states. Upper Nile region was divided into three: Jonglei state, Unity state and Upper Nile state – in this book the phrase 'greater Upper Nile' refers to the larger region or province, and 'Upper Nile state' to the post-1994 state. Three years later, a new all-south political structure was established, as a result of the 1997 Khartoum Peace Agreement. It was called the Coordinating Council in Southern States. In 2005, the Comprehensive Peace Agreement established the autonomous Government of Southern Sudan, which governed the country in the run-up to a referendum on self-determination.

The Republic of South Sudan (2011–) The 2011 referendum led to an overwhelming vote for South Sudanese independence, which was declared on 9 July 2011.

INTRODUCTION: GABRIEL ANYANG REMEMBERS HIS CHILDHOOD

At the end of December 2011, an armed column of about ten thousand young men attacked Pibor county in Jonglei state, the largest of ten states in the new republic of South Sudan. County officials said that they killed 3,000 people; they stole thousands of cattle, and abducted women and children. The young attackers did not belong to an organized armed force: they bought their own small arms and announced their intentions through blood-curdling press releases written by Jonglei migrants in places like Nebraska or New South Wales. The press releases said that the attacks were in revenge for a series of child abductions, cattle thefts and massacres whose intensity had increased over the previous seven years.

Those seven years had witnessed the implementation of a 2005 peace agreement which ended a long civil war between Sudan's government in Khartoum and rebels based in South Sudan. Until 2011, South Sudan had made up the southernmost third of the territory of the Republic of Sudan, whose boundaries had been established by Turco-Egyptian and British colonialism. Twentieth-century Sudan was Africa's conflicted behemoth: a landmass of 1 million square miles; societies rich with interconnections and contradictions; and a highly unequal economic and political system that set those societies against each other. The 2005 Comprehensive Peace Agreement between the Khartoum government, led by the National Congress Party – a Khartoum-centred alliance of security men, Islamists and finance and merchant capital – and the southern-based rebels of the Sudan People's Liberation

Movement/Army (SPLM/A) brought an end to decades of civil war in South Sudan, then Sudan's most diverse, least developed and most violent region. The peace deal brought the SPLM into a Government of National Unity in Khartoum, and established an SPLM-led autonomous Government of Southern Sudan in Juba, which was financed from the South's oil wealth. In the last few years of the twentieth century, the Khartoum government had turned subterranean wealth into export revenue, through a mix of astute trade diplomacy in East Asia and ferocious warfare that depopulated the muddy Upper Nile pastures of present-day South Sudan, to tap the oil deposits that lay beneath them. At first, new oil revenues helped to escalate the war, but in 2005 they financed the peace deal, with revenues split between governments in Juba and Khartoum. The aim of the peace deal was to reinvent Sudan as a more inclusive, more equal country. But it also allowed for South Sudanese voters, who had borne the brunt of the country's long wars, to pass judgement on that reinvention in a referendum that gave them a choice between unity and independence. The vote was unexpectedly peaceful, solemn and joyous. Over 98 per cent of voters chose independence, and the new Republic of South Sudan was born in July 2011.

Lubricated by oil rents, the Comprehensive Peace Agreement ended the war between Sudan's two biggest armies. But peace and South Sudanese independence reframed the many contradictions of South Sudan's societies rather than resolving them, and the violence in Jonglei state continued. Jonglei is a place where wars are more likely to start than they are to finish – in late 2013, after the research for this book was completed, a political crisis in Juba morphed into a civil war once it reached the mutinous periphery of Jonglei.

Most of Jonglei's wars have gone unremarked. In 2011, the young attackers in Pibor county made the news in part because they began marching out for the massacre on Christmas Eve. International news outlets briefly picked up the Christmas massacre story. The raiders were from the Nuer ethnic group and most of the casualties were from another ethnic group called Murle, and many journalists on the holiday shift explained the violence as 'tribal', a handy catch-all for indecipherable African motivations. The attackers' Nebraskan propagandists likewise favoured ethnicity-first explanations: their 25 December press release said that the youth army had decided to 'wipe out the entire Murle tribe on the face of the earth'. Attackers who torched a health centre near Pibor scrawled words to that effect on its walls.

Newswires had covered the child abduction story for some years, and activists raised the problem at the highest levels. In a 2008 interview, South Sudan's president, Salva Kiir, gave his version of events to an American activist:

> [Abduction has been going] on for a very long time. That the Murle will come to Dinka land, or they go to Nuer land, or they go to Anuak, or they go to Toposa land, to take children and come and adopt them [Dinka, Nuer, Anuak and Toposa are neighbouring ethnic groups]. They adopt them as their children. It is not an enslavement, except that they take them by force. Because there is a problem in the Murle land, that there is infertility of the people, that they don't produce the way others are producing. And I said this in America when I was there. I said – if this problem is to be resolved once and for good, we need a hospital, a big hospital in Pibor, the town of these people, with specialist doctors, to find out exactly what sort of venereal diseases that these people have, and so they are treated. To bear their own children. Instead of going to look for other people's children.[1]

The president's views on the origin of the problem are commonplace in South Sudan: Murle people's ethnic vulnerability to

---

1 Interview available at www.youtube.com/watch?v=FhsQb8UR7AQ, accessed 25 May 2013.

sexually transmitted disease lowers their birth rates and Murle raiders steal children from neighbouring ethnic groups to make up for it. In any society, it would be hard to assemble evidence supporting this clunky sequence of simplifications: in South Sudan there are no reliable studies correlating fertility and ethnicity. Although concerns about Murle infertility date back to colonial times, South Sudan's rudimentary census series, from 1955 to 2008, gives little suggestion that population growth rates in Pibor are lower than those of neighbouring counties. And the government's own records of 700 abductions in Jonglei between 2009 and 2011 suggest that Murle women and children were abucted in greater numbers than were women and children from any other ethnic community in Jonglei.

Gabriel Anyang's story

Research on abducted children is full of ethical traps. Researchers can complicate things for interviewees, and have little to offer except perhaps the satisfaction of telling a story. One way to 'do no harm' is to interview adults with a childhood experience of abduction about their histories. What a relief it was, then, to encounter the warm, self-assured voice of Gabriel Anyang, who gently dismissed concerns that talking about his experiences might awaken unhappy memories. He's in his early thirties, and studying for a degree in public administration, and when I called to check whether I could use his name in a publication, he said he had just got a job in a foreign humanitarian organization: as a food security officer. Gabriel is from a Dinka community near Bor, which lies on the White Nile near where it reaches Jonglei on its route north from Africa's Great Lakes. I interviewed him in 2012, when Bor was a fast-growing market town. Twenty years before, Murle raiders abducted him when he came to Bor town, looking for food during one of Bor's worst famines.

People tried to take food from the UN in the town. I start coming

here to get food. I came here with my mum. Came two gentle-
men carrying guns, people ran away, I tried to run, the aim was to
get a small child, the target was me. (Interview 136/2012)

Most of Jonglei's population are Nuer or Dinka, and most of
them live near two all-season White Nile tributaries, the Bahr
al-Jebel and the Sobat, that approximately trace the western and
northern borders of the state. Murle people live in a hinterland around smaller seasonal rivers, which lie to the south-east,
beyond an arid expanse about one hundred kilometres wide.
Gabriel's abductors took him across that expanse, to a settlement on the Nanaam river, just on the edge of the arid belt.
They kept him at home, where he helped with the family herd.
He sensed he was for sale: 'The condition was something in
the shop, someone did not come and buy it.' Eventually, a
widow called Nganley bought him, for twenty cows. She had
four daughters and no sons, and she was old, he says, maybe
even forty-five. She had over one hundred cows (a widow with
many daughters acquires many cows through their marriages)
and she told him all her cattle would one day be his (a widow
without sons finds it harder to mobilize cattle-keeping labour, or
support in old age). He hated his abductor, but Nganley's girls
were very, very, very nice, he says: 'I see them innocent, and I
shared their happiness.' Gabriel could not stand the separation
from his family, however, and at the age of twelve he decided
to make a run for it, living off raw game during a five-day walk
across the drylands between Murleland and the river, where he
was joyously reunited with his parents.

The miracle of money
South Sudan has many former abductees and their stories
are emblematic of their country's wars, displacements and dis-
junctions. Abductees often manage with remarkable generosity
sympathies that have been divided between an abducting family

and a birth family. Two decades on, Gabriel wants to write a book about his childhood story, and he reflects lucidly on the motivations of his abductor-adopters. It was mostly about money, he says.

The people who abducted him don't use money. They don't understand money, says Gabriel, they are not good at making it. 'There were no modern things in the house except saucepans. Nothing else except guns – AK47s.' Twenty years after Gabriel escaped, people in Nanaam, the remote westernmost part of Murleland, the edge of the arid belt where he stayed, still possess only the simplest commodities. In contrast, the market in Bor town (where Gabriel was working and studying) had smartphones, cosmetics and banks serving a government salariat. Maybe people would give up abduction if their life 'is changed by a miracle – the life of money is better than the life of cows', says Gabriel.

Gabriel's abductors may not have understood money, but they appeared to be learning to understand the convertibility of children – Gabriel sensed that he was 'for sale'. His abductors were Murle, but they were not representatives of a unified, corporate group. There are fewer than 200,000 Murle people in Pibor county but their traditional livelihoods are exceptionally diverse. The western Murle people who abducted Gabriel occupy an economic niche – a cattle-rich area that is still evading market penetration. Unlike most Murle people, they depend almost entirely for their diet on their cattle, even bleeding them in the dry season, to mix their blood with milk. Growing grain is difficult in the relatively arid corner of Jonglei, and most Murle people deal with that aridity, in part, by trading or exchanging grain. Eastern Murle people are cattle-less agriculturalists. Cattle people call them Ngalam or ants, because they scratch the ground for a living (Arensen 1992: 35). Intellectuals and political leaders come from different groups. Many were raised in Khartoum and are attached to its version of cosmopolitanism: some politicians speak no Murle, only Arabic. Others were educated through membership of churches, membership of the Sudan People's Liberation Army (SPLA) or at schools and universities in Nairobi and Kampala. But economic, educational and social differences are often concealed by the language of kinship or ethnicity.

Some Murle politicians and intellectuals feel too disconnected from the experiences of young Murle raiders to try to interpret them. But others try to explain things. One argued that abduction is an old phenomenon in Jonglei, the most coercive of the many ways in which all of its radically formulated pastoralist societies (and not just Murle society) would assimilate outsiders during the wars and migrations of the nineteenth and twentieth centuries. But it is changing: 'Someone does not necessarily want son or girl. He went for abduction to trade it to get cows. Just like any goods in the shop. Which did not exist before.' In Murleland, at the start of South Sudan's independence, abduction became a symptom of the chaotic encounter between historically egalitarian societies that have emerged from those long wars into the life of monetization, accumulation and commodities.

Mainstream economic theory often posits the existence of pre-monetized societies living by barter, until barter becomes too much of an encumbrance, whereupon societies (or markets) invent money as a replacement. But historical evidence suggests that people living without money live by complicated systems of reciprocity, until states impose money on them by force (Graeber 2012). Money is not so much a technical solution as a means of reframing tangled social networks with more legible hierarchies. And these hierarchies are spatial as well as social – money reconfigures the introverted economies of remote hinterlands around the interests of moneyed towns. Over the past century or two, Jonglei has witnessed that process – of war substituting money for reciprocal obligations, and of hinterlands becoming peripheries. The process was still under way in 1992, when Gabriel was abducted. In 2012, he lived off a salary, but then he and his family depended on cattle and sorghum.

Jalle [part of Bor county] was bad in 1992. People depend on cattle and sorghum. Nuer took all the cattle and killed many people. I was very miserable. A lot of people died because of hunger. My family was strong. My father was strong. We were really lucky not to lose one dead.

The Jonglei mix

The Nuer who took all the cattle in the wars of the early 1990s are the linguistic cousins of the Dinka – two ethnic groups who (like the linguistically distinct and ecologically isolated Murle group) pasture cattle on the vast flat plains that drain into the White Nile. For the rainy half of the year, the plains turn to swamp, and cattle people retreat to homesteads on low ridges, where they can get two harvests of grain from Jonglei's fertile, poorly drained soils. Cattle act as mobile insurance against climatic glitches that can parch or swamp a crop; or against soldiers that might steal it. When the rains end, young people set up cattle camps near the retreating pasture; and by the shrivelled end of the season, everyone leaves the homesteads to camp by water sources. These movements make cattle a central feature of social life. Cattle are herded by small local groups of age-mates, friends and relations who call each other by the names of their favourite oxen; cattle are the bridewealth that legalize marriage and the compensation for homicide.

'*Cherchez la vache*' was the advice of the colonial anthropologist E. E. Evans-Pritchard to students of Jonglei's societies (1940a: 16). His descriptions of the Jonglei mix of cows, precariousness and adaptability are still recognizable today. But the Jonglei mix is now more complicated – alongside the cattle-and-grain system, people get food from town markets; from humanitarian aid; from army supplies; and from looting. Each of these food systems has its own unreliability which the youngsters caught up in Jonglei's violence have to manage.

In retrospect, the 1991 'Nuer' attack that took cattle, killed people and brought Gabriel to Bor on his luckless search for food was a milestone on Jonglei's road towards the chaotic food economy of today. The attack came in 1991, at the end of the Cold War, when the communist government in Ethiopia fell, and the southern-based rebels of the SPLA split into factions after losing their bases there. The dissidents were led by Riek Machar, a commander and politician with a career of advancements, defections and reinventions that in 2013 saw him get sacked from the vice-presidency, flee to Jonglei, and start a rebellion. In 1991, he led another rebellion from Jonglei. Then, he and his commanders failed to rally the SPLA's mainstream, and instead decided to attack Bor, the Dinka home town of John Garang, the leader of the mainstream. The Khartoum government supplied them with weapons, and they mobilized ad hoc fighting groups from the Nuer cattle camps north and east of Bor, with the promise of looted cattle. The South Sudanese liberation struggle which began as a protest against a Khartoum government's policy of marginalizing its southern periphery by fostering its divisions was shifting into a South–South war commanded by elites mobilizing around ethnicity.

The food economy was reshaped, not so much towards markets, which operated sporadically in wartime, but towards cattle looting or food aid. Cattle looting had existed before, but the old booty distribution systems were designed around the social reciprocity principle – even abductees could acquire rights to spoils. But during the war, says one South Sudanese analyst, 'there was this culture of commanders taking over people's property, and nobody talks about it, and that's still happening. Cattle raiding distribution was about egalitarianism, now it's about accumulation.'

In the Nuer and Murle hinterlands, militias were armed by the Khartoum government. Militia commanders often believed that they were Southern nationalists, who rejected Khartoum's project to subordinate the south. Commanders muddled through the resulting ideological confusion by emphasizing ethnic loyalties, militarizing cattle camps, and operating new systems of accumulation, denominated in cattle. Meanwhile, Bor's population – the Dinka people living along the White Nile – were forced into dependence on Garang's mainstream SPLA, which was in turn associated with Dinka-ness. Most Bor people fled into traumatic or transforming encounters with modernity in cities and refugee camps in East Africa or resettlement programmes in Europe, America and Australia.

In 2005, at the end of the long war, Jonglei's hinterland had plenty of militias but no all-season roads. Bor, in contrast, had become a state capital. Oil revenues financed the peace. Militia commanders got generous incentives to join the government, and Bor acquired an improved road to the national capital, a bureaucracy and a barracks. But Jonglei's salaried jobs, markets and schools were from the start unevenly distributed between hinterland and capital: the state capital spent about 90 per cent of the state's annual budget. In a diverse society like Jonglei's, such regional differences amount to ethnic differences – the state capital concentrated the possibilities of modern life in areas where mostly Dinka people live. Paradoxically, the trauma of their displacement helped many of Bor's Dinka people to enrol in schools in the cities of Sudan, Kenya or the United States. After 2005, the salaries and markets of Bor brought many exiles home – and those Dinka people who had suffered the longest displacement and applied themselves most assiduously to education fitted in perfectly. '[Dinka people] have been affected harder than Nuer,' said one Bor academic, 'but there are over forty PhDs in Bor' (interview 87/2012).

The academic was speaking in 2012. In December 2013, Bor was overwhelmed by young armies from Jonglei's hinterland within days of a Juba political crisis that pitted the ambitions of the president, Salva Kiir, against those of his erstwhile deputy, Riek Machar. The young men of the hinterland were easy to mobilize. Rural youngsters had seen no opportunities for themselves in the new oil-funded urban bureaucracies and markets. They had no formal education, and they refashioned their ambitions around the new raiding economy. They needed guns to navigate the unreliabilities and inequalities of the rural food economy – but this made them a target for the SPLA's coercive disarmament campaigns. Modernity worked its way through their lives at the point of a gun, not with a PhD and a superannuated salary. When the system established by the Comprehensive Peace Agreement faced crisis, they joined defecting army soldiers in the sack of Bor, in an implausible coalition of well-fed politicians, hungry rural youth and soldiers on the run from massacres that had convulsed Juba, which apparently targeted people from the Nuer community. Contradictions spilling out from the periphery transformed South Sudan – not for the first time.

A history of abduction

Jonglei's abductions and lootings tell the story of its incorporation into a new economy and a new republic which has been shaped by war, migration and abduction. Between 1956 and 2011, Sudan was one independent country. South Sudan spent most of those years in a long war with successive Khartoum governments. Those central governments inherited social contradictions from the slave trade that shaped Sudan's colonial era, and tried to overcome them with national projects that generally used Arabic language and authoritarian versions of Islam as templates for unifying Sudan's remarkable diversity. These national projects were often intensely violent: during the last phase of the civil war, elements from Arabic-speaking pastoralist communities in northern Sudan were deployed as militias in South Sudan. Paid only in booty, the militias abducted thousands of people for forced labour and forced marriage, in a process of subordination that drew abductees into northern Sudanese Muslim culture.

By the late 1990s, the story of abduction and slavery by 'Arab' and 'Islamic' militias was firmly entrenched in SPLM strategies for mobilizing international support. Sudan's ferocious national project attracted more critics as the War Against Terror got under way: powerful international actors sought out examples of what they saw as authentically 'Arab Muslim' wickedness in Sudan, to set against the victimization of Arabs and Muslims elsewhere. One year after the September 2001 attacks on the American mainland, a rattled Sudanese government signed a bilateral treaty with the United States pledging to end abduction in South Sudan.

North–south abductions have largely ended. But the abductions that were a by-product of South Sudan's complicated proxy wars have increased since the 2005 peace agreement. Most reported abductions happen within and between the cattle-keeping groups of the hinterland. Raiders from Nuer, Murle and other ethnic groups all bore responsibility for the practice. But Murle society, not Murle or Nuer raiders, got the blame. Murle society as a whole was seen as responsible for perpetuating and updating an old system of forcible adoption. This system yields dramatic results, as one humanitarian worker explained:

> When [children] are abducted [Murle abductors] torture them. They put a sharp stick in their mouth so they don't cry, or beat them so that they will not cry. They are told, if you escape, we will kill you. Until the child is comfortable [with her new surroundings]. In terms of feeding and keeping the Murle keep the children very well. That is why the children stay with the family. Some children eventually develop positive relationships with family. Some of the children, when they are reunified [with their birth families], they want to go back to Murle. It takes some time until the child gets comfortable.

Forced adoption was part of the migrations, assimilations and slave trading that involved all of Jonglei's ethnic groups in the nineteenth century. But the humanitarian worker quoted above saw Nuer abductions of Murle children largely as a response to Murle provocation:

In Nuer the reason for abduction is a kind of revenge. Because children have been abducted for many years. People expected the government to end abduction. But it increased and got worse. The experience for [abducted] Murle children is that they are discriminated by other children. They make the abductee like a slave.

This account is at odds with other accounts of the recent and distant Nuer past. The young Nuer men who joined the attack on Bor in 1991 abducted women and children; and in subsequent internecine fighting between Nuer sections, many children were abducted. In the early twentieth century, Evans-Pritchard described Nuer systems of forcible adoption: 'A Dinka boy is brought up as a child of his captor's household ... People say ... "he has become a member of the community," and they say of the man who captured him that "he has become his father"' (Evans-Pritchard 1940a: 221f.).

National identity

If abduction is such a deep part of South Sudan's story, why are Murle people blamed for it? The answer may lie in the search for national identity in the new, liberated, independent republic of South Sudan. The SPLM (once the SPLA's political banner, now South Sudan's ruling party) rallied the people of the south in opposition to the Arab-Muslim identity that Khartoum tried to impose on the many societies of the south. But the new SPLM-led government in Juba needed to create from South Sudan's human diversity a standardized national culture, perhaps fringed here and there with 'minorities'. Murle people are particularly suitable candidates for minority status: their leaders had a long and durable alliance with Khartoum; they are isolated by language and ecology; and their hinterland economy is configured around the looting system. In this view, Nuer and Dinka politicians and commanders who had fought each other during the war reached an entente in order to share state power between themselves: many Murle people believe these politicos needed a scapegoated Murle minority to avoid addressing the history of antagonisms between themselves. They believed that their scapegoating postponed and prefigured a larger war that would turn Jonglei's people against each other.

The process of turning differences into majorities and minorities is often a bloody one. Is the new Southern nation doomed to repeat Sudan's mistakes? The talk of Murle people as diseased criminals and provocateurs was taken up by members of many communities across Jonglei. At a 2012 peace conference, one Nuer leader stood up to denounce Murle representatives: 'Murle women can't conceive. Let the government send men to impregnate them.' If the government did not deal with the problem, he said, he would even go to Khartoum to get weapons. Khartoum may indeed have played a role in the conflict, sponsoring militias in Murleland and across Jonglei as part of a proxy war with Juba: throughout 2012, each government accused the other of supplying weapons to the other's dissident armed groups. The situation there could destabilize the whole country, said one government minister: generals in Juba kept huge maps of Jonglei on their office walls.

The army (which failed to protect the people of Pibor county during the Christmas attack) began a disarmament campaign in Murleland in March 2012 which was widely criticized for its excesses – SPLA soldiers reportedly raped and tortured villagers in a sustained attack that many in Pibor county saw as both state-led and ethnically targeted (HRW 2013). Salva Kiir had promised as much to the American activist:

> If they fail to bring all the guns, we will have to use force, to disarm everyone by force. Of course, that will result in a lot of casualties. And the same thing you are asking now, you will be the same person that will come back and ask me why are you killing people. It is either I leave them with the guns and they terrorize the rest of the people, or I crush them to liberate the

other people from being always attacked by the Murle. What will you take in that case? What do you expect me to do?[2]

In 2008, when this interview was conducted, the government in Juba and its international supporters were preoccupied with managing the intricate coalition politics of the Comprehensive Peace Agreement, and coordinating a diplomatic campaign for support for Southern independence. The government had undertaken bloody disarmament campaigns, mostly targeting young, armed cattle keepers in rural Jonglei and other parts of South Sudan. The campaigns were often targeted ethnically and poorly sequenced, leaving some communities armed and others exposed, in a process which did not diminish the violence and left some people – including many Murle people – with the belief that the state and its army had deliberately attacked their community (Diana Felix da Costa, researcher, interview 2/2014). Kiir was able to evade international censure for these violent campaigns of disarmament, which were at odds with his government's commitments. Interviews with American activists were one of the ways in which his government was able to manage international pressure, and lower expectations for his liberation movement in terms of respecting human rights.

In the event, the government moved to disarm Jonglei's youth in early 2012, in the aftermath of the Christmas massacre. The disarmament began just as South Sudan and Sudan were drawn into a border war over the oil infrastructure whose revenues had paid for peace. The hot war ended quickly, but the subsequent cold peace was apparently organized around proxy wars, with Juba allegedly supporting dissidents in Sudan's restive peripheries of Darfur, South Kordofan and Blue Nile; and Khartoum allegedly supporting Jonglei's dissidents. The use of peripheries to exert military pressure on national capitals is a consequence

---

2 Interview available at www.you tube.com/watch?v=FhsQb8UR7AQ, accessed 25 May 2013.

of the spatial distribution of dissidence and subversion in South Sudan and Sudan. Both countries are deeply unequal, and that inequality is a function of place as much as it is a function of status. People far from the centres of power and money live lives surrounded by poverty and violence, while those at the centre can make do. In that sense, versions of inequality in South Sudan and Sudan reflect global inequality, which keeps wealth and peace in places like Manhattan and Kensington, and war and poverty in places like Iraq or Bangladesh.

For South Sudan's lugubrious corps of foreign analysts, the country's wars are unintelligible causes for pessimism. But their pessimism is out of tune with Jonglei's many bright, self-possessed voices. Perhaps, they say, South Sudan's leaders will come up with a route to development that will include the youth of its hinterlands. Perhaps Jonglei's unexplored oil deposits, fertile soils and wildlife herds will turn into salaried jobs for its young people. At the many peace conferences of 2012, some people indulged in racist rhetoric, but others invoked South Sudan's influential vernacular systems for reconciliation. 'Let our stolen cattle be the bridewealth of peace.'

The aims of this book

Gabriel Anyang's story raises many questions about South Sudan's national story. Why did the wars pitting South Sudan's liberation armies against successive Khartoum governments not liberate Jonglei? Can a liberation movement address inequalities during an armed struggle, or must it postpone fairness until some victorious future? Is liberation a gamble on the future, or something that people work out in their daily life? Why did the Comprehensive Peace Agreement mark a setback for some regions and communities? His story raises questions about the spatial and social unevenness of development, and the role of towns, money and states in creating and managing social inequality and uneven development.

South Sudan's answers to all these questions about the slow, violent path to liberation are often inconclusive. But it is an inviting place to ask these questions. In part, that is because South Sudanese biographies are compelling. The mix of disorienting violence and dispassionate hopefulness in Gabriel Anyang's story is not unusual. But South Sudan also invites big questions because its experience of the uneven and violent nature of development and the contradictions of national liberation are familiar from other places with protracted liberation struggles; or with oilfields and militias; or with mysterious and apparently dysfunctional social diversity. South Sudan's path to liberation and development might be exemplary rather than exceptional.

This book addresses all these questions, mostly from the vantage point of one of South Sudan's hinterlands – the flat muddy plains of Jonglei. For several decades, Jonglei has been a persistently violent place. Mutinies that started or spread there turned into civil wars which deeply wounded Jonglei's people and their neighbours. This book tries to look deeply at South Sudan's experience of uneven development, of spatial inequality, and it presents Jonglei as a case study. Jonglei's violence and marginalization might also not be exceptional – Jonglei exemplifies patterns of violence and exclusion that can be found across South Sudan and other marginal regions of the world.

How does this book address these ambitious questions? The book starts by looking at the way social relationships are described in South Sudan. Categories like race and ethnicity are important for analysis but they cannot explain violence or history. In the nineteenth century, the whole of Sudan was organized around race. In this book, race and racial oppression are references to a system for explaining and justifying dramatic new forms of inequality that emerged then. South Sudan was the first part of the African interior to be drawn into the world systems of trade and production. That system operated differently in different parts of Sudan. In the northern Nile valley, an Ottoman-Egyptian colonial state taxed people in money, more or less for the first time. From monetary taxation, they constructed a zone of wages, debt and rent. Peripheral areas – the Nuba mountains, the southern Blue Nile and eventually South Sudan too – were raided for ivory and eventually for slaves. Slave raiding expanded dramatically in the 1850s, when new international rules on free trade and finance began to be implemented in Sudan, and the state monopoly on raiding was replaced by a privatized, financialized system that drew South Sudan deeply into the booms and busts of Egypt's nineteenth century. The armies of private slavery entrepreneurs eventually overran the state, in spite of government attempts to check them by reinstating their monopolies. Enslavement was garbled into legitimacy using self-serving versions of Islamic law which argued, against the canonical texts, that South Sudanese were unbelievers who could be 'lawfully' kidnapped and enslaved. Relations between the money zone and the raiding zone were further complicated by the way that Sudanese elites sought inspiration from the Arabic culture of cities in the Hijaz and the Mediterranean, casting the difference between the people of the money zone and the raiding zone as a difference between Arabs and Africans.

This book argues for the continued relevance of South Sudan's nineteenth-century encounter with the international system for understanding how South Sudan became a periphery of Sudan, and the way that global crises throughout the twentieth century were transmitted through Sudan to South Sudan. These set the stage for subsequent uneven local development and the liberation wars that tried to counter that unevenness.

When people say that South Sudan is one of the most underdeveloped places in the world, with only a few miles of paved roads, they mean that South Sudan did not recover from its nineteenth-century experience. For most of the twentieth century, governments refused to address this underdevelopment, and managed the periphery through neglect. The efforts of a revolutionary regime in Khartoum to reverse South Sudan's de-development in the 1970s fell apart in the global economic crises of that decade, and South Sudan became a violent transmission zone for those crises.

Violence in South Sudan is ensnared in those spatial inequalities. But they cannot be understood only in terms of the actions of predatory or unresponsive external actors. South Sudan's spatial inequalities are played out in a particularly complicated social terrain. Successive states have used ethnicity to organize their relationships with rural (and subsequently urban) populations, and this has made ethnicity part of South Sudan's political order. In this book, 'ethnicity' does not mean the same as 'race' or 'tribe'. Ethnicity is a set of cultural contingencies that characterize all human groups. South Sudan brings a particularly rich set of contingencies to the human mix, and some of them are described in the next chapter. In fairly small populations, even within counties, can be found differences in ecology, language, livelihoods, cultures and political systems, all tied up in mostly unwritten histories of migration. 'Race' was a system for ranking people by making a handful of simplified, arbitrarily chosen characteristics – skin colour, say, but not height – into determinants of a social order. The 'tribe' was a way for states to improvise local political orders with recognized leaders and bounded 'ancestral' territories from ethnic or kinship structures. Race/tribe give outsiders the power to classify, in a way that ethnicity does not.

In South Sudan, governments have long used ethnicity to organize their relationships with predominantly rural populations. The government appoints 'chiefs' or neo-traditional authorities to manage the local legal system and to allocate shared natural resources – such as land and water – within kinship or ethnic groups which it defines. In a crisis, governments and rebels may use these authorities to mobilize young men to fight in ethnic militias. The notionally unitary ethnic or kinship groups led by these local neo-traditional authorities conceal social hierarchies.

The social hierarchies within ethnic or kinship groups cannot be explained through conventional class analysis, which is about the haves and the have-nots – the people who own productive resources like land, and the people who have to sell their labour to the owners. That model does not work in rural South Sudan, where the ownership of many productive resources is negotiated constantly within ethnic groups or even within families. Common ownership limits possibilities for accumulation within these ethnic groups.

Accumulation – the basis for many hierarchies – mostly happens when people access state resources, and that access happens in towns. So relationships between towns and hinterlands determine patterns of accumulation. The spatial differences between moneyed towns and cashless hinterlands have played out in social differences. But because the cashless hinterland still organizes economic life around kinship groups, these differences are often experienced as ethnic ones. South Sudan's uneven development happened because of the way that South Sudan was incorporated into and simultaneously marginalized by global empires and markets. But because development was uneven, oppression and liberation took different paths in the periphery and in the 'centre' – the part of the country most closely linked to the international system. This book presents South Sudan's history in a way that foregrounds these processes, with the aim of showing how they have slowed down liberation, and why they have pushed South Sudan towards violence.

The complicated social terrain at the periphery did not lend itself to transformation through armed struggle. Revolutionaries tried instead to capture the state. But it was a state for which society's productive resources were mostly out of reach. All twentieth-century administrations in South Sudan lived off subventions from Khartoum, drawn against export earnings or international debts. This book reviews South Sudanese budgets over more than a century to demonstrate the stark dependence of Juba governments on these external resources. It also foregrounds an important by-product of dependence: the economic autonomy of the state vis-à-vis the productive capacities of society. This dependence/ autonomy did not substantially change when the twenty-first-century commercial exploitation of South Sudan's oil reserves transformed the scale of South Sudanese budgets. The complicated social terrain, and the dependence/autonomy of the state, shaped the possibilities and limitations of liberation struggles.

This book pays a lot of attention to South Sudan's first liberation struggle. It led to the establishment of the first Southern Regional Government in 1972, after a long civil war. Previous governments were led by people from outside South Sudan and had fostered neglect or predation. The new government's business was development and representation. But the government was still not aligned to the productive capacities of society, it was still dependent on Khartoum subventions. Its political task was the allocation of these externally generated resources or rents. The dilemmas of allocation shaped political contests then and now. Once a government claiming to represent people began allocating these rents, South Sudanese from smaller groups began complaining of domination by larger groups, and the notion of 'minorities' was born. The political contest focused on post allocation – which groups benefited from the resources of the dependent/autonomous state. And groups were defined by ethnicity, the framework around which the state's relations with society were constructed.

The complexity and depth of South Sudan's oppressions made the task of theorizing social change and liberation a very hard one. Theories of development or liberation do not readily fit the south's historical experience. One of the first and most dramatically successful liberation movements in Sudan was the Mahdist movement, which revolutionized nineteenth-century Sudan, mobilizing some South Sudanese for its struggle against the nineteenth-century colonial state, and constructing its theory of liberation around the Day of Resurrection. But Mahdism perpetuated slave raiding in nineteenth-century South Sudan, and in the twentieth century allied with colonialism. Mahdism showed how religion (like song and poetry) can help conceive of liberation – but it also shows that a religious theory of liberation may have mixed results. In any case, this book focuses on secular, social and economic projects for development and liberation. Three influential projects are considered here: those proposed by Marxism, mainstream economics and dependency theory.

The version of Marxism adopted by the Sudanese Communist Party envisaged a process of development and liberation led from the centre, not the peripheries – led by the small group of waged workers in the factories and railways of the northern Nile valley. Looking back over the twentieth century, this was an idealized periodization and characterization of liberation. Sudan's revolutions generally emerged when Khartoum governments passed the costs of their periodic economic crises to Sudan's peripheries, which were violently transformed by their experience of these external crises. These areas had no wage-earning proletariat to speak of, but their resistance often encouraged the wage-earning proletariat of Khartoum on to the streets. The peripheral populations were not directly resisting exploitation by capitalists – they were resisting the way that they had been subordinated by racism and divided by ethnicity. Communists acknowledged the damage that racism had done in twentieth-century Sudan, but they fitted their ideas about racial oppression into the 'nationalities question' formulated by Soviet leaders Vladimir I. Lenin and Joseph V. Stalin as part of their efforts to transform the multinational Russian empire into a socialist union (Ahmad 2005).

Theories of development offered by mainstream economics had less explanatory power. One reason is that mainstream economics habitually measures economic activity with money, and many of its analytical tools are blunted when used to describe partially monetized economies. Another reason why mainstream theory lacks explanatory power in South Sudan is because the theory misrepresents the chaotic and violent way that money enters previously unmonetized economic systems. Instead of describing the violence, it offered a progressive, economistic theory of history that was mapped out most famously by the Scottish philosopher Adam Smith. In the 1930s, many British colonial officials in South Sudan believed that Smith's dreamy progression would determine the future. Ancient systems of barter would be replaced by the efficiency of money. Unproductive group solidarities would be replaced by rational desocialized individuals who would participate in idealized competitive markets which promote general welfare. Capital derived from exported raw material would accumulate in private hands, and be directed towards industrial develop-ment. This story never really happened anywhere. But in South Sudan, colonial officials could see it not happening, so to speak, before their own eyes. There, the state was the prime economic actor – an actor that in some regions and sectors promoted competitive markets, and in others promoted unproductive group solidarities in the form of 'tribal' government. In South Sudan, the state repressed the movement of people and goods, using pass laws and closed districts to cut South Sudan off from the export markets and grain and cotton production centres which it had set up around Khartoum. Privately accumulated capital and competitive markets played only a minor role in the colonial route to development – instead, the state decided which regions would be exploited for profit and which would be ignored, creat-ing stark regional inequalities in the process. Nonetheless, many colonial officials believed that Smith's idealized progression would come to pass in some South Sudanese future. But they did not have theoretical resources to understand their present, and were sometimes baffled by their own economic policies: in 1939, at the contradictory apogee of southern de-development policy, the governor of Equatoria argued that the colonial state's *dirigisme* was in fact 'state socialism' (Sanderson 1985: 101).

By the end of the colonial period, regional inequalities had become a pressing political problem, as South Sudan was integrated into Khartoum's political and economic systems. Policy-makers began to promote economic development in South Sudan. At the time, the emerging theoretical framework for development in mainstream economic theory was 'modernization'. Modernization theories sought to hurry Smith's idealized periodization along, using the resources of the nation-state to accumulate and productively invest capital. In the 1970s, modernizers hoped that development would unify Sudan's diverse and divided people around new, shared economic interests. These shared interests were exemplified by plans to develop agricultural projects along the north–south borderlands which for most of the previous century had marked slaving frontiers, closed districts and civil-war front lines. These national projects were financed by international credit markets, and survived until the late 1970s, when modernization ended for good in a global financial crisis which bankrupted Sudan and pitched it into a long war in its peripheries.

After modernization came and went, international financial institutions established a new theoretical mainstream. Programmatic rather than descriptive, their version of neoclassical economic theory abstracts economic life and value away from society and history, situating it in the moment where demand meets supply. Instead of a path to liberation, it offered a programme for a smaller state, increased international trade, and the financing of government operations through markets in bonds and other debt-based instruments, in preference to taxation, shifting decision-making powers away from governments to a narrower and less accountable group of financiers. Sudan's Islamist movement took power during the theoretical shift from modernization to neoclassical economics, and read it astutely. Its cadres benefited from its powerful mix of austerity, privatization and trade liberalization, and had the nerve to fight the wars that these policies aggravated.

At the outset of the twenty-first century, World Bank theorists explained the violence that accompanied their policies as products of (African) 'greed and grievance' (Collier and Hoeffler 2001).

Twentieth-century Sudan did not succeed by one of the World Bank's favoured measures: real gross domestic product remained around three hundred dollars per capita between 1960 and 2000 ('real' means that this figure is adjusted for inflation). Real per capita gross domestic product began to increase in 2000, when Sudan's path to development was transformed by new oil revenues. Sudan's Islamist experiment had isolated it from many of its traditional trade partners, and its leaders used that isolation to build relationships with China, which constructed the oil infrastructure that undergirded the 2005 peace deal, provided an export market and eventually provided influential models for South Sudan's and Sudan's political development too. But the Chinese model, like the models that preceded it, has not adequately addressed the spatial inequalities in South Sudan and Sudan, which are deeply implicated in its wars.

Neither mainstream nor conventional Marxist theories of development adequately account for these spatial inequalities. In the 1980s, the liberation movement in South Sudan encountered an explanation for the geography of underdevelopment in dependency theory, a collection of Marxian and non-Marxian critiques of capitalist development that was in vogue in Dar es Salaam University and across East Africa. Dependency theory's depiction of spatial hierarchies – of the difference between the centre and the periphery – is still a commonplace in Sudanese and South Sudanese writing. It remains attractive in a society where social hierarchies are concealed by ethnicity; and class analysis lacks relevance because private property is weakly institutionalized. Instead, dependency theory begins with more tangible spatial hierarchies. In the 1950s and 1960s, dependency theorists argued that colonialism had created a spatial hierarchy that was surviving formal decolonization, of 'peripheral' colonies and post-colonial states contributing labour and raw material for factories in the developed 'core' states. They observed that the terms of trade between periphery and core were in decline: peripheral countries were able to purchase fewer manufactured goods from core countries in exchange for a given quantity of their raw materials. Dependency theory explained why Sudan's incorporation into twentieth-century global systems of trade and finance had not led to the emergence of a local class of entrepreneurs who could accumulate and invest capital. It explained why those trade and financial systems had instead simultaneously revolutionized and de-developed South Sudan. It was better able to explain a history made up of violent reversals interspersed with violent progressions, a zigzag that created stark, racialized differences between Sudan's periphery and its centre.

South Sudanese writers argued that international spatial hierarchies were reproduced within Sudan. Poorer parts of Sudan were not able to accumulate capital, develop industries and escape economic subordination, because richer parts of Sudan needed to capture their labour and resources to export them in order to keep up with the declining terms of trade. For some dependency theorists, the potential for revolutionary change lay in the periphery, whose long crises were in fact an indicator of rapid social transformation. Dependency theory's understanding of spatial hierarchies helped South Sudan's liberators identify the revolutionary group as the peoples of the periphery. Its account of spatial difference was so convincing that it is today difficult to find a text on South Sudan which does not contain the theory's catchphrase, 'core-periphery'.

Nonetheless, dependency theory is no longer in vogue, for many reasons, many of them good. The theory was more a critique of development than a theory of change. It was fixated with the way that places like South Sudan had been subordinated to externalities – how Europe underdeveloped Africa, to quote the title of a famous text. That phrase scarcely resonates today, when a deindustrialized Europe no longer has the productive capacities to use African resources, which are now exported to East Asian production centres selling finished products to global consumers. The theory's fixation with the mighty power of the oppressor made it overlook the organic possibilities of change within African societies. In South Sudan, dependency theory helped orient the liberation struggle away from social transformation and towards state capture – society could be liberated only through the power of the state. So dependency theory may have contributed, in its way, to the violence of the liberation struggle and its aftermath, state capture being a very violent affair. The theory did not offer much in the way of policy once the state was captured, and its grand, Marxian perspective was abandoned after the end of the Cold War.

This book examines South Sudanese theories of liberation more carefully than most. They were experiments in making sense of a complicated predicament and in changing it, and both failed and successful experiments deserve attention. The failures of the liberation struggle meant that social change often happened through war – not because the liberators captured the state and made everything better. The transformations of war and violence were never described very attentively by South Sudan's liberators. But they are very evident in the remotest peripheries, where the state barely intervenes. There, local histories of war can explain how local patterns of production and local social relationships have changed. The introduction of weapons as an adjunct means of production changed social relations and is entangled in processes of monetization and of labour market formation. But the situation still resists class analysis – instead, it is necessary to use gender or generational frameworks to understand power shifts within society. The final chapters of the book try to understand the experiences of young raiders, and of childless mothers who forcibly adopt abducted children. It asks whether these raids and abductions are a form of resistance to the mighty forces surrounding them, or an equally self-defeating attempt at participation in an economy distorted by long wars.

Sources

The book is based on approximately two hundred interviews with individuals or small groups, and notes of public meetings. Most were conducted in Jonglei and other parts of South Sudan in 2012 and 2013. Twenty-three interviewees were female. About twenty interviewees, both male and female, were under twenty years of age. An even smaller number lived in villages. Most interviewees were South Sudanese males aged between thirty and sixty who spoke Arabic or English and lived in towns – many of the book's accounts of life in young, rural South Sudan are based on their descriptions, and the book tries to be transparent about some of the biases that are inherent in this method.

The book also presents a great deal of quantitative information: colonial and post-colonial censuses, budgets, surveys of population, health, education and livestock. It reviews most of the publications of international financial institutions on South Sudan and Sudan over the past sixty years – a rich historical source that has recently been archived on the worldwide web. The work of the National Bureau of Statistics (formerly the Southern Sudan Commission for Census, Statistics and Evaluation) sets high standards of clarity of expression and transparency about data limitations. There are many limitations to these kinds of surveys. Many ordinary South Sudanese respondents are as alert as any postmodern scholar to the oppressive potential of statistical information. The aims of statistical oppression change over time too – there are fewer misrepresentations of ethnicity and more misrepresentations of economic relationships in contemporary statistics. It is difficult to maintain faith in the enumerators' coverage of transhumant populations, and their ability to describe societies with cultural aversions to counting cattle or children. Much statistical information is no more than suggestive (Cordell 2010).

Hatashil Masha Kathish was the first South Sudanese to publish a book in English, in 1889. It was a memoir of his eventful life as a child in Dinka-land, a slave, a gun-carrier and a trader, and it was written after he had become a Christian missionary. It was aimed at English Sunday-school children. Fourteen thousand copies of the first edition were sold; it is seventy-nine pages long, and everyone interested in South Sudan should download it from the internet and read it. Most published or accessible twentieth-century texts on South Sudan were written by outsiders, who have produced a large corpus of texts on the country, and this corpus was reviewed extensively in preparation for writing this book. But the book has a preference for South Sudanese writing. In the last three decades of the twentieth century, books by South Sudanese people about South Sudan began to appear. Many of these texts are political memoirs or doctoral dissertations – an improbable start for a national literary canon. This book draws primarily on these South Sudanese sources, and uses texts written by outsiders to complement them, rather than the other way round. The two bodies of texts – South Sudanese and non-South Sudanese – are surprisingly disconnected, to judge from the citations in their respective bibliographies.

Organization of chapters

The book is divided into an introduction, three main parts and a conclusion. This introductory chapter sets out some of the book's themes: South Sudan's diversity, and the role of states, wars, markets and towns in creating and managing the social and spatial differences that arise out of that diversity.

Part One looks at the way that the state and society interact in South Sudan, looking back over two centuries of historical patterns that can help explain government behaviour today. It begins with Chapter 1's account of the ecological, linguistic and historical factors underlying social diversity in South Sudan. Chapter 2 discusses South Sudan's chaotic incorporation into the global system in the nineteenth century. That incorporation shaped ideas about race and ethnicity, and began a history of uneven development that was implicated in subsequent wars. Chapter 3 looks at twentieth-century implications of uneven development. South Sudan's wealth was not developed. State administrations depended on outside subventions. The economically autonomous state faced dilemmas of representation and resource distribution, and it often resolved these dilemmas by ethnic post allocations. Chapter 4 presents South Sudanese accounts of the predicament of the periphery, and the way that would-be liberators theorized social change. Chapter 5 relates how the experience of the periphery shaped the possibilities and limitations of the new Republic of South Sudan, to 2012.

Part Two looks at the violence that overwhelmed Jonglei state after the 2005 Comprehensive Peace Agreement. It begins in Chapter 6 with another life story, of a gifted graduate from Jonglei who tried to transform his remote part of the periphery by attracting state posts there. He established one of Jonglei's first ethnically based militias. Through the second half of the twentieth century, these militias became central to government and rebel military strategies. Chapter 7 looks at their role during the 1983–2005 civil war, and Chapter 8 sets out some new evidence about the way that violence played out after the 2005 peace, which never really reached Jonglei, where peripheralization and mutiny are two sides of the same coin.

Part Three looks at how Jonglei's wars and ethnic militias became central to social processes, creating new winners and many new losers. Chapter 9 looks at the way that the food economy has been reshaped by young raiders, and Chapter 10 looks at transformations to local gender orders. The book was researched and mostly written before the end of 2013, when a political crisis in Juba suddenly morphed into a civil war. The book's conclusion relates the book's main themes – Jonglei's place in the slow, patchy liberation of South Sudan – to that crisis.

PART ONE
SOCIETY AND STATE

Literature about South Sudan makes up much of the early nine-teenth-century travel writing about the African interior. Twentieth-century colonial governments were consumers of anthropology, and South Sudan's societies were represented in founding texts of that discipline. Since Sudan's independence in 1956, it has attracted the attention of notable historians and anthropologists, and in the past few decades South Sudanese writers and academics have produced detailed and extensive accounts of their country's history, society and politics. Yet this large corpus has some unexpected gaps. First, South Sudan's slave trade has no comprehensive history, although it was the basis for the construction of racism in twentieth-century Sudan. It is now unfashionable to reject 'constructivist' accounts of race and racism – the idea that race is not objective and natural, but an outcome of historical interactions, language and symbolisms – but many writers only equivocally accept constructivist accounts, inadvertently populating their histories with 'real Arabs' or 'real Africans' or even 'Arabs who are really Africans'. Secondly, the history of the state was mostly written from the vantage point of Khartoum, with little account of the state's performance in the peripheries. The occasional counter-histories written from the peripheries often presented the history of the state as a conspiracy against the periphery. Both genres were more likely to invoke than to explain the unhappy relationship between the centre and the periphery. This reflects a wider inattention to the structural factors that keep the peripheries downtrodden. Finally, there are few works on South Sudan's economic history, and fewer that relate South Sudan's economy to its unhappy entry into the world economy, or to the economics of daily life (Johnson 1997; Fearon and Laitin 2000).

This section of the book does not deal with all these gaps in the literature in a comprehensive way. It is a series of short and hopefully sharp essays that look critically through an extensive literature to find out whether that literature can explain South Sudan's jagged path to development and liberation. It sets out the nature of South Sudan's diversity (Chapter 1), the process by which South Sudan was incorporated into and marginalized by the economic processes of the nineteenth and twentieth centuries (Chapter 2), the way the state patterned its relationships with society in the twentieth century, and the way that South Sudan's would-be liberators critiqued those patterns (Chapters 3 and 4). These essays are a preface to Chapter 5, a longer chapter that explains the way that the contemporary state – the Republic of South Sudan – is relating to society in Jonglei.

1 | THE SOCIAL LANDSCAPE

The centre of this book's focus is Jonglei state, a remote and diverse periphery that is one of the ten states of the Republic of South Sudan. Jonglei state has five major ethnic and cultural communities. The term 'ethnic and cultural communities' is taken from South Sudan's Local Government Act of 2009. Its drafters, South Sudanese political leaders and lawyers, self-consciously eschewed the more enigmatic and controversial term 'tribe', a word which has no ready translation in South Sudanese languages.

Delineating differences between ethnic communities or 'tribes' is not straightforward. Ethnic communities are partially defined by their economic systems – Nuer, Dinka and Murle people are often described as 'pastoralist' to distinguish them from 'agrarian' neighbours, although within all three ethnic communities people practise both livelihoods. The particular type of transhumant agro-pastoralism that most of them practise is unusual in Africa, and is shaped by the ecology of the flood plain. They are also defined by the way that their economic systems are socially organized. Some South Sudanese groups, including some of the Anuak people, the eastern neighbours of Murle and Nuer people, have traditions of centralizing authorities, and others – such as Murle and Nuer people – traditionally organized themselves with the help of societal experts and mediators who have powers of consensus-building rather than powers of command. Subjective factors also play a role in definition – a sense of common identity or belonging that is often linked to histories of migration, language, communication and exchange that brings some groups together and pushes others apart (see Kapteijns and Spaulding

1991: 84). To make sense of a throwaway phrase like 'tribal conflict', an examination of all these constantly changing factors is needed, and this chapter tries to look at how landscapes, livelihoods, languages and migrations, and social systems make up differences between South Sudanese people.

Ecology and economy

Jonglei's landscape has already briefly been described. It is part of a vast flood plain that covers about six of South Sudan's ten states. The flood plain is bounded to the west by an ironstone plateau running up to the Congo–Nile watershed; to the south by the Equatorial hills and mountains and the arid area west of Lake Turkana; and its eastern border runs just west of the edge of the Ethiopian highlands. To the north lie the central rainlands, today the southern borderlands of Sudan, which take in the trunk of land along the White Nile that is the northernmost point in South Sudan. The flood plain, and the country, is approximately bisected by the White Nile, which flows north from the African Great Lakes: the stretch running through the flood plains is called the Bahr al-Jebel. The Bahr al-Jebel makes up Jonglei's eastern border, and the Sobat river roughly forms its northern border (SDIT 1955: 3). The other major river system in Jonglei is the Pibor river and its tributaries, lying in the drier south and east.

According to the linguist-historian Christopher Ehret, the central rainlands, which lie along the borderlands between South Sudan and Sudan, are where humanity first domesticated cattle and first cultivated crops, and first worked out a grain-and-livestock repertoire of subsistence practices. This repertoire allowed early human populations to grow and to define themselves against older systems such as hunting and gathering. After several centuries of climate change, the Sudanic system of agro-pastoralism moved into the flood plains, hitherto too wet for cattle, and there they added fishing to their subsistence system. The invention of iron technology in Africa came several millennia later: communities

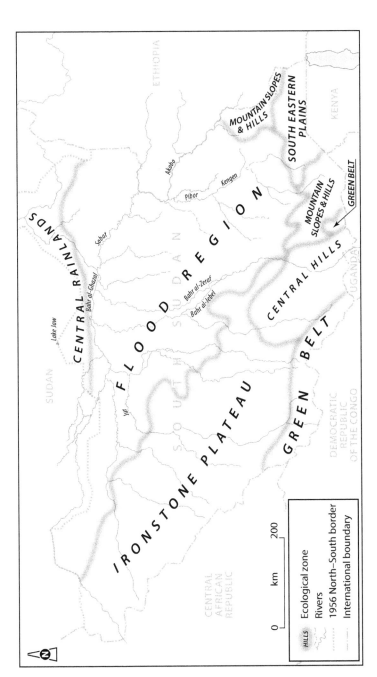

1.1 South Sudan's main ecological zones (*source:* Craig 1991: 281)

with iron-working skills lived on the ironstone plateau, leading to exchange between them and the communities of the flood plains. Although many communities in the ironstone plateau and the Equatorial hills have historical memories of cattle-keeping, most of them now have agrarian livelihoods. Ecological and economic differences shaped cultures and notions of ethnicity: people in the ironstone plateau today still use hoes and gifts of labour for bridewealth, while those in the flood plains use cattle (Ehret 1982; Lienhardt 1961: 1; Santandrea 1980; Ochalla-Ayayo 1980: 92; Andretta 1985; Deng 2010; Ehret 2002: 65–72).

But these striking differences in livelihoods and cultures are sometimes misleading for would-be classifiers of ethnic groups: no ethnic community follows a single pattern of livelihood. Nuer and Dinka ethnic communities incorporated individuals and groups with different economic specialisms: fishing, cattle-keeping, agriculture, iron-working and spiritual or technical experts. Murle people have a particular wide range of specialisms. Murle-speakers in the Boma plateau in south-eastern Jonglei practise agrarian livelihoods. In contrast, Murle people living in the plains have a largely pastoral economy and produce and consume less grain than do the groups living along the Sobat and Bahr al-Jebel. Murle pastoralists near Nanaam, the westernmost river of Murle-land, are the most cattle-dependent group in South Sudan, living off blood and milk with very little in the way of grain (SSCCSE 2006: 62, 97). These different food economies are partly attributable to ecological differences. The Murle area of the plains is drier than the rest of the flood plains, and it has some similarities with the arid plains of south-eastern Equatoria. Outside Boma, grain is harder to grow.

According to Jonathan Arensen, who conducted research there in the 1970s, Murle people in the farthest west are purely pastoral, practising no agriculture at all (1992: 30). When Elizabeth Andretta studied ethnic and gender identities in agrarian and pastoralist areas of Pibor county in the 1980s she concluded emphatically that different groups of Murle 'consider themselves as sharing one over-arching ethnic identity' (1989: 17). The role of Murle raiders in the crisis in Jonglei has led to forcible disarmament campaigns which appear to target Murle people indiscriminately (HRW 2013). This threat of indiscriminate attack leads some in and outside the community to emphasize the differences between Murle people of the plains, the group from which most raiders appear to originate, and the agrarian Murle people of the hills (the two groups are sometimes respectively called Lotilla, after one of the tributaries of the Pibor river, and Ngalam, or ant, because of the hard work needed for agriculture). This controversial attempt to turn livelihood differences into cultural ones is linked to a political project to create a separate county in the Boma plateau.

Landscapes and transport

Landscapes and rivers also shaped histories of transportation and urbanization. Until the mid-nineteenth century, most of South Sudan was cut off from the Mediterranean world by the Sudd, an unnavigable swamp that military expeditions from the ancient Mediterranean tried and failed to penetrate (Seneca 1972: VI.8.3–4). In 1839, a Turkish frigate captain named Selim, in the service of the viceroy of Egypt, made a passage through the plant-entangled waters up as far as the unnavigable rapids that lie to the south of Juba, the present-day capital. His journey was a prelude to the nineteenth-century slave trade that transformed South Sudan. Thereafter, the White Nile became the communications artery between South Sudan and the cities and markets of Sudan and the Mediterranean. Once the colonialists and slavers had made their way through the Sudd they moved west towards the more accessible ironstone plateau. Its laterite soils can harden into all-weather roads, and these roads shaped patterns of settlement and communication. The road that links Juba with the major towns of Rumbek, Tonj and Wau runs along the edge of the ironstone plateau, just as it meets the flood plain (Gray 1961: 60). The road connected forts established by slavery entrepreneurs along the edge of the plateau, and these forts became South Sudan's first towns, 'nodes' of state power that broadcast state authority over the surrounding countryside (Leonardi 2013). In 1955, after more than a century of colonial domination, less than 2 per cent of South Sudan's population lived in towns (Henin 1958: 56). But communities nearer the towns learned how to understand and negotiate with slavers and state authorities more quickly than hinterland communities. Apart from a few river ports, the flood plains remained inaccessible for much of the year. The first all-season road in the flood plain was built only in the late twentieth century, and serves oilfields rather than populations.

A recurring theme of this book is the unevenness of development in South Sudan and Sudan. The country's incorporation into global empires and markets created not only stark social hierarchies, but stark spatial ones. Oppression and liberation took different paths in different peripheral areas, and different paths again at the 'centre' – the parts of the country most closely linked to the international system. And because ethnic groups are scattered in concentrations across this uneven geography of development, ethnic groups experience development and under-development unevenly. Before the arrival of the state, people may have based decisions about settlement on access to pasture or water, among other factors. People ended up in hinterlands because of force of circumstance or because of ecological conditions. Their hinterland settlements were not necessarily more or less 'remote' than other settlements. But the reach of the state, headquartered at Khartoum, was determined by transport requirements, such as steam-navigable rivers, or quick-draining soils on which roads could be built. The state's arrival made areas far from the transport infrastructure into remote, peripheral places and burdened their societies with new contradictions.

Language and migration

South Sudan's different ecologies and economic systems shape cultures and notions of ethnicity. Language can serve as a means of understanding the distinctions between different ethnicities and the cultural and material complexes underlying them. South Sudanese in the flood plains and Equatorian hills speak Sudanic languages, a subset of the Nilo-Saharan language family, which historians believe was the language spoken by influential groups of the middle reaches of the Nile who initiated the agro-pastoralist transformation in Africa over ten thousand years ago, and whose descendants spread across East Africa (Ehret 2002). Some South Sudanese in Western Equatoria and Western Bahr al-Ghazal speak languages that are linked to the Niger-Congo language family that is most associated with West and Central Africa. One important sub-family of Sudanic languages is the West Nilotic group, which includes several Dinka and Luo languages and Nuer. Speakers of these languages make up over half the population of South Sudan, and much more than half of the population of Jonglei.

Language studies are politically important, because of the role that language plays in creating cultural identity – a key subjective component of the definition of ethnic communities. The biggest language survey in South Sudan took place in 1955, as part of the Sudan census that was published the following year. 'What language do you speak in the home?' it asked. It used a list of thirty-one Sudanese language groups, of which fifteen language groups were associated with South Sudan. It listed languages by province (South Sudan was divided into three at the time). The census data is still useful as a rough indication of speaker numbers and, by extension, the size of the different ethno-linguistic groups within the three Southern provinces, as defined by colonial linguists and anthropologists. So, for example, about half the 1955 population of South Sudan spoke Dinka and Nuer. Census officials created language groups by aggregating languages which they believed to be related: for example, Northern Luo (also spelled Lwo, Lwoo) includes the related Shilluk language of Upper Nile, Jur-Luo of Bahr al-Ghazal and Acholi in Equatoria, among others. But they did not aggregate other related languages, such as Bari and Latuka (PCO 1958: vol. 9, 7–15). Table 1.1 gives the 1955/56 census results for the nine largest language groups, amounting to 94 per cent of the total population enumerated.

TABLE 1.1 Responses to the 1955/56 census question 'What language do you speak at home?' for the nine largest languages in the Southern provinces of Sudan

	Bahr al-Ghazal	Equatoria	Upper Nile	TOTAL
Dinka	865,762	2,674	225,940	1,094,376
Nuer	14	2	463,867	463,883
Teso[1]		175,388	43,754	219,142
Zande	3,679	214,780	149	218,608
Northern Lwo[2]	45,872	19,536	122,110	187,518
Bari	712	165,824	62	166,598
Latuka		116,706	2	116,708
Moru-Madi	343	92,537	740	93,620
Ndogo-Sere	28,898	22,475	3	51,376

Notes: 1. Teso included Toposa, Didinga and Murle, now widely viewed as belonging to different sub-families; 2. Mostly Shilluk speakers in Upper Nile and Jur Luo speakers in Bahr al-Ghazal
Source: PCO (1958: vol. 9, 7–15)

In 2003, the influential publication *Ethnologue* listed fifty-three South Sudanese languages, and the government subsequently proposed a figure of sixty-three languages (Marshall 2006). Many of these languages had only a few hundred speakers. *Ethnologue* estimated speaker numbers from language surveys conducted in the previous three decades. Dinka languages made up the largest group, with an estimated 2,358,972 speakers, or about 32 per cent of the estimated population. Nuer speakers (1,335,125) came second. Teso speakers were estimated at 100,000 (reflecting changed language classifications) and Zande speakers were estimated at 350,000 (ibid.).

Conceptions of ethnicity are deeply rooted in language, and this means that the processes of aggregation and disaggregation of language groups made by demographers are as influential as they are problematic. Many colonial linguists accepted racial theories about language, believing, for example, that languages with polysyllabic words or gender exhibited a complexity that could have been brought to Africa only by ancient migrations of pale-skinned Middle Easterners (Seligman and Seligman 1932). Their classifications shaped the 1955/56 census, and these classifications are important in shaping perceptions of ethnic groups. The 1955/56 census gives a picture of a Dinka majority in South Sudan. *Ethnologue* linguists divide Dinka up into five languages – just as Luo languages are divided up – giving a more plural picture of the country. But some Dinka speakers argue that a standardized version of Dinka has emerged from decades of migrations and displacements.

Migrations as connections

Language similarities are evidence of migration, extended contact and mixing between language groups (Nyombe 2007: 39ff.). Historical linguistics and origin-stories can shed light on these processes. The flood plains are now associated with Dinka and Nuer groups but Luo origin-stories begin in the flood plains, near present-day Rumbek, now an area associated with Dinka and Atuot people. Place names and Dinka and Atuot section (or clan) names there still echo the Luo past. Between the fourteenth and sixteenth centuries, Dinka people expanded into these Luo areas around Rumbek, and Luo people began a movement that took their language to present-day Ethiopia, Kenya, Tanzania and Congo. The largest Luo-speaking group in South Sudan is the Shilluk group, who live in the northern Upper Nile. Nyikang, the Shilluk migration leader and culture hero, is credited with the establishment of a stratified political order centred on a king inheriting his powers (Crazzolara 1950).

Migrations also shaped relationships between Dinka and Nuer people, and between them and the Murle people. In the early nineteenth century, Nuer groups whose origin-stories begin on the west bank of the Nile began migrating to the east. The migrations began with people from the Jikainy Nuer territorial grouping. Jikainy origin-stories link the grouping to an Anuak prince named Kiir from the eastern flood plains whose mother set him floating down the Sobat river, and who was adopted and then rejected by Dinka people, and ended up living among strangers on the west bank of the White Nile. Kiir's four sons founded the four main Jikainy sections (Jal 1987: 15–20). The Jikainy homeland lies in the triangle of land south-west of the junction of Bahr el-Jebel and Bahr el-Ghazal (see Figure 1.2). Neighbouring Nuer and Dinka groups prevented their move from this flood-prone land into adjacent areas. So in the 1820s, some Jikainy groups began raiding Dinka villages on the east bank of the Nile. After this initial violence, they began to negotiate places of settlement with the east bank population, and these settlements expanded by attracting new immigrants from western Nuer lands and by assimilating Dinka populations in the area. Some assimilated Dinka people were captives; some were defeated and impoverished by Nuer raids; others may have sought military support during the turbulence of the nineteenth-century slave trade; and others may have been attracted by the radically formulated egalitarianism of Nuer society. As these Nuer frontier settlements swelled, some groups migrated farther east, assimilating and displacing more Dinka people in the process. Up to 80 per cent of Jikainy Nuer society in the areas bordering Ethiopia may be of Dinka origin (Johnson 1994: 54ff.).

Both Nuer and Dinka groups border Pibor county, the area of south-east Jonglei where Murle-speakers predominate. Murle is a Surmic language, and most Surmic language-speakers live

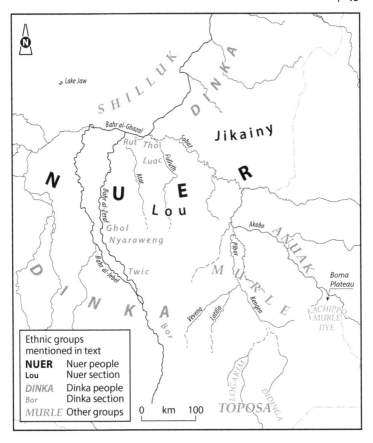

1.2 Ethnic groups of the Great Upper Nile (*source*: Southall 1975: 465)

in the south-west corner of Ethiopia that borders Jonglei, at the foot of the Ethiopian highlands, where the Omo river flows into Lake Turkana. Surmic language-speakers probably first came to present-day South Sudan in the first millennium BCE (Ehret 1982: 23). The lower Omo valley, surrounded by the ecologically and culturally distinct Sudanese flood plains, Ethiopian mountains and Kenyan steppe, was little known to outsiders before the late nineteenth century, when it was incorporated into the expanding

Ethiopian empire (Tornay 1980). Today, it is being transformed by land-leases to foreign companies, part of an Ethiopian experiment to address the country's history of food insecurity through commercialized agriculture, which may force people speaking languages similar to Murle to move (David Turton, researcher, interview 7/2013; HRW 2012a).

Murle people and speakers of the other Surmic languages in South Sudan (Didinga, Longarim/Boya, Tenet and Kachipo) give the same story of their origins: an argument about a hunter's stew. In the story, Murle people lived with people who spoke the same language. One day, youths and men out hunting split up into two groups, because it was the dry season and game was hard to find. One group caught an oribi (antelope) and made it into a soup. The other group, which caught nothing, demanded some soup, and were refused. The two groups parted ways (Arensen 1992: 25). These memories of hunger, anger and separation are used to explain the formation and fragmentation of these groups. Sometimes, the memories are forgotten: in the 1980s, Arensen found old ladies who were speakers of the East Nilotic language Toposa who could communicate in unrelated, Surmic, Murle, without knowing the name of the language. He believed that they probably belonged to a group with Murle origins who had attached themselves to a different group, perhaps in response to an ecological crisis or opportunity that may one day be remembered as another argument over soup (ibid.: 35).

Exogamy and multilingualism

Many Luo, Dinka, Nuer and Murle migrations happened before the colonial period. In the twentieth century, colonialists accentuated the process of ethnic group formation, sometimes inventing ethnic borders and leaderships. Some smaller groups in western Bahr al-Ghazal were forcibly moved into ethnic territories specially created for them (Thomas 2010). Even language policy was intended to intensify differences between people, to classify South Sudanese people into 'self-contained racial and tribal units', as one influential policy document from 1930, the Southern Policy memorandum, put it (Nyombe 1997). A pass system prevented people from moving around, and groups of territorially contiguous language-speakers, such as Nuer and Dinka people, were easier to aggregate. Scattered groups, such as the Luo, were not aggregated – Shilluk and Jur-Luo people are not considered to be part of a single unit, while Dongjol and Rek, two Dinka sections neighbouring Shilluk and Jur-Luo, are turned into a tangible, unified Dinka group.

The 1956 census question 'What language do you speak in the home?' concealed multilingualism, and emphasized disconnections between groups that had been reformulated as 'self-contained' or 'tribal' (Thelwell 1978: 4, 11). South Sudanese multilingualism is unstudied but widespread, and it is an indicator of interconnections between groups, as the example of the elderly Murle-speaking Toposa ladies shows. In South Sudan, many migrations are not large group movements led by cultural heroes, but personal and female. Most South Sudanese societies practise exogamy – they marry outside their social group. Often, this leads to people marrying across ethnic divides, and these outside brides can connect different social groups, and bring a sense of extroversion and fluidity to the group they join. They also learn new languages and often raise multilingual children. Sometimes, people become multilingual for other reasons – Gabriel Anyang, encountered in the Introduction, still understands Murle because of his abduction.

Arabic and urban migration

The proportion of South Sudanese living in cities has probably increased about tenfold since the end of the colonial period – the 2008 census, undertaken before many displaced South Sudanese people had returned from Sudan and countries of refuge, found that 17 per cent of the population was urban (SSCCSE 2010: 9). South Sudan also had one of the highest populations of war-displaced people in the world, and much of its urbanization is traumatically related to twentieth-century wars. But in many places, that trauma has been mixed with curiosity, adventurousness, economic pressures and aspirations, and urbanization rates have maintained their buoyancy even when violence peters out.

Urbanization has also spread the Arabic language, which came to the south in the days of the slave trade and spread rapidly: the language survived a period of repression under the 1930–46 Southern Policy, which closed the south to northern influence. Juba or Southern Arabic today is a lingua franca; the primary language of some urbanized groups; and a preferred language even among people fluent in English (Mahmud 1983; Abdelhay 2007: 54). Mapping the distribution of Southern Arabic and English helps to identify communities not primarily defined by ethnicity: urban groupings of salaried families, or sex workers, or market traders, or national footballers, or members of new urban-based Christian movements, such as Pentecostalist churches, whose preachers flit expressively from East African English to Juba Arabic – churches established in the colonial period are more likely to use South Sudanese languages (McMichael 2010; Groenendijk and Veldwijk 2011). In the late colonial period, writers talked about 'detribalization' as a corollary of political consciousness in Equatorian towns (Badal 1976), and 'detribalized' groups spoke Arabic. Many of these groups were demobilized soldiers, and Arabic remains a military language. From its foundation, the SPLA used Arabic as a language of command, and even a language of song, as it sought to create an army that unified different ethnic communities. The 2006 Juba Declaration incorporated many South Sudanese militias formerly allied to the Khartoum government into the SPLA. Personnel from these militias – many of them Nuer-speakers – were often mixed into existing SPLA units rather maintaining their existing structures. SPLA units were seldom monolingual as a result, and Arabic was often used for communication. The post-Juba Declaration SPLA was an attempt to build a unified national identity around the army, and Arabic was often the language in which that national identity was discussed. When in late 2013 the SPLA in Juba collapsed into ethnically targeted internal massacres, some soldiers used Dinka language tests to identify and murder Nuer colleagues (UNMISS 2014: 11).

States and stateless societies

All South Sudanese ethnic communities have been deeply exposed to state power for over a century. Some had an earlier experience of state power. Pre-colonial states did not survive colonialism but they have a minor afterlife in the Local Government Act (2009, Section 113):

Types of Traditional Authority

(1) There shall be two types of Traditional Authority in Southern Sudan:–

(a) Kingdoms with centralised monarchical systems of rule, whose institutions shall perform local government functions while maintaining their status as the institutions of the kingdoms concerned, in given States of Southern Sudan covering the territorial areas of one or more counties …

(b) Chiefdoms with decentralised system of rule, which shall perform traditional and local government functions covering the territorial area of counties where the traditional authorities are organised on the basis of lineages and clans

In decentralized systems in the flood plains, leadership was distributed among mediators and experts rather than authorities with powers of enforcement. Social coherence was promoted by age-sets or age-grades, which brought together males (and to a lesser extent females) from a spread of local communities, and gave them a sense of being part of a wider social group. These decentralized systems were able to organize pastoralist

transhumance and longer, more permanent migrations. Sometimes, these systems outperformed more stratified systems around
them, organizing more effective responses to ecological crises and
mobilizing bigger military forces than could neighbouring states
(Johnson 1988: 64). In other cases, decentralization was a means
of evading state power. Western Bahr al-Ghazal, for example,
was a refuge for fugitives and maroons from the harsh labour
systems of the pre-colonial sultanate of Darfur and from the
Central African wars that came at the start of colonialism. They
improvised decentralized political systems and forest livelihoods
to escape the state (O'Fahey 1982; Kapteijns and Spaulding
1991; Thomas 2010).

Stratified, centralized systems also emerged in South Sudan.
Some of the Luo migrants who moved north from Rumbek
eventually reached the fertile banks of the White Nile, north of the
Sudd. There, the migrants were gradually unified under a Shilluk
kingship which established a capital in Fashoda at the end of the
seventeenth century. From then, kings controlled the populous
Shilluk heartlands along the upper reaches of the White Nile, and
controlled trade with the Sinnar sultanate, a state established in
the sixteenth century with its capital on the Blue Nile, in present-
day Sudan. Shilluk canoe raiders dominated the White Nile as
far north as the 12th parallel. Raiding groups exacted tribute on
pastoralists, agrarian villages and merchants in the borderlands
(Schweinfurth 1874: 85; Mercer 1971; Spaulding 1985: 284; Akol
2007: 2). In the eighteenth century, a collection of Zande states
emerged on the Nile–Congo watershed, in the far south-west of
South Sudan. The ruling elite of the Zande states unified groups
of shifting cultivators by a complex and persuasive reworking
of systems of agricultural production and social reproduction.
Sometimes both centralized and decentralized structures coexist
in a single ethnic community. This is the case with Anuak people,
who are organized into people of kings, and people of chiefs, the
former being descendants of a royal culture hero and the latter

assimilated or captured peoples. Different Anuak villages follow kings or chiefs accordingly (Jal 1987: 118–19).

These different political traditions have a modern relevance. First, states and other powerful actors sometimes used traditional authorities – kings, chiefs, spiritual leaders and consensus-builders – to collect taxes, recruit labour or discipline local populations. Sometimes traditional authorities rejected this work, and the state bargained for or imposed chiefly taxmen and judges on local communities who exercised a different, neo-traditional administrative authority from that of the spiritual and moral leaders of the community. The use of either traditional or neo-traditional leaders meant that the state and other powerful actors organized their relationship with the local population through ethnicity (Leonardi 2013). Secondly, different political traditions influenced colonialist perceptions about the likelihood of resistance to the interventions of the colonial state. People from decentralized systems, particularly those from pastoralist groups, were seen as unruly and impoverished people, with kinship systems unintelligible to all but a contrary assortment of anthropologists. Colonialists believed that people from these decentralized systems were predisposed to reject the disciplines of the state, the law and the market (even though Sudanese and South Sudanese pastoralist groups generated leaderships who were neither poor nor marginal; who had state ambitions; who aspired to, rather than evaded, state power). People subordinated to kings, however, were seen as more tractable. The Zande ruling elite assimilated other groups by bringing young men to serve as agricultural labourers at royal courts and controlling their marriages by controlling bridewealth, which was based on iron spears accumulated and controlled by kings and patriarchs. Colonialists selected Zande areas for South Sudan's only colonial development scheme, a cotton complex established after the Second World War, in part because they believed that this history of subordination would make it easier to mobilize plantation and factory labour (Evans-Pritchard 1963; Reining 1966: 53;

Lloyd 1978: 245–95). Colonialist understandings of pre-colonial political history deepened over time. Their beliefs about histories of subordination affected their decisions about the geographical spread of colonial development and contributed to a history of differential access to state power and resources that is still evident today. This differential access was also a function of geography and of the possibilities of road building and communication, but because ethnic communities are often concentrated in particular locales, this differential access sharpened ethnic difference. For example, shortly after Sudan's independence, in 1960, there were stark variations in boy enrolment ratios in the three colonial provinces: 46 per cent for Equatoria, 16 per cent for Bahr al-Ghazal and 11 per cent for Upper Nile (IBRD 1973: Table C-3). Such differences created political antagonisms between 'educated' Equatorians and 'uneducated' people of the flood plains. These differences were sometimes given an ethnic colouring.

Representing and misrepresenting diversity

South Sudan's diversity, like diversity anywhere, has its roots in ecology, livelihoods, language, migration and political histories, all of which are fluid and historically contingent. This chapter has reviewed this fluidity and contingency somewhat laboriously, because it is sometimes forgotten, both by outside observers, like the journalists covering recent attacks on Murle towns, and by local people, making hate-filled calls for the forcible impregnation of women from enemy groups.

Representations of South Sudan's diversity are implied in discussion of how South Sudanese society works. Until the late nineteenth century, most South Sudanese people lived remote from states or markets, or even consciously evaded them. People living within state and market systems represented their South Sudanese contemporaries as part of a primordial past. Primordialism (in one influential formulation) is the belief that 'congruities of blood, speech, custom' are ancient and inescapable (Geertz 1973: 259).

It was politically useful for the colonialists who once tried to immobilize and isolate South Sudan's fast-changing, open societies.

Primordialism today has few outspoken theoretical supporters but nonetheless seems to emerge in crises. For many journalists, aid workers and diplomats working in Africa, primordialism offers a set of radical simplifications that allow them to overlook social and historical complexities to see a big, rugged, instinctual picture. It can also work as a resource for different South Sudanese communities. In a polarized and violent situation, primordialism can help people map and navigate social difference, and provides a means for people fearing encroachment from other ethnic communities to demarcate identities and interests. In the 1990s, Dinka and Nuer identities were caught up in the war between the SPLM and the Khartoum government, and emphasized the 'overwhelming importance of lineage' during periods of defeat (Jok 2005: 160).

Some of the Nuer people angered by abductions quoted in the introduction used the language of blood and speech and custom in this way. This version of primordialism allows people living in times of violent social change to resist threats to their identity. But not all Nuer discourse is exclusive. Dereje Feyissa recently studied Nuer and Anywaa (or Anuak) views of identity in the borderlands between Ethiopia and South Sudan. He argues that many Ethiopian Nuer people have 'an inclusive identity discourse that places a high premium on ethnic conversion' (Feyissa 2011: 17). Malleable Nuer identities allow for the assimilation of Anywaa/Anuak and other groups who are losing out to encroachments from the state and migrants from other parts of Ethiopia. For Anywaa/Anuak at risk of assimilation, primordialist views of identity offer a kind of cultural defence (ibid.: 15ff.).

Despite its political utility, primordialist thinking requires a disavowal of complexity; it looks backward, it erects defensive boundaries, and makes it difficult to map out possibilities for social change. The evidence reviewed here suggests that ethnic communities are centres of rapid adaptation and multiple interconnections.

So why should primordialist thinking emerge at South Sudan's republican dawn? It may help people to explain and survive the violent and uneven nature of social and economic change. It may help some people to build political constituencies that can make claims on the new republic, and channel resources along ethnic lines (rather than, say, gender or generational or regional or other lines that might help structure the state's relationships with society). It may help other people to build constituencies that can evade the new republic. Finally, primordialist accounts of ethnicity may reflect popular conceptions of the liberation struggle. For South Sudan's leaders and their interlocutors, the liberation struggle was about making the future a fairer place, but many ordinary people were caught up in violence because they believed they were defending their traditional ways of life or avenging their past victimization. The armed struggle has transformed traditional ways of life altogether, and primordialism may be a defensive response.

Faced with these memories of struggle and attempts at constituency-building, the new republic sometimes acts in ways that emphasize ethnic differences between people. But many in the state recognize the risks of this. During the debate on the interim constitution of the Government of Southern Sudan in 2005, a draft annexe was produced that listed sixty-three indigenous communities of the South (text in Marshall 2006: 115). Indigeneity needed legal definition at the time, because it was to be a condition for eligibility in the 2011 referendum on independence, whose successful conclusion was the government's central preoccupation. The annexe presented Dinka as a single community, listed alongside communities too small to make the Ministry of Education's 2006 language list above, such as the Aja community (the Aja language has an estimated two hundred speakers). The annexe was not included in the constitution in the end, perhaps a recognition of the near-impossibility of meaning-fully dividing South Sudan into ethnic communities.

2 | SOUTH SUDAN'S ENCOUNTER WITH MODERNITY

A happy day like this should not dwell on bad memories, but it is important to recognize that for many generations this land has seen untold suffering and death. We have been bombed, maimed, enslaved and treated worse than a refugee in our own country. (Speech of President Salva Kiir on Independence Day, Juba, 9 July 2011)

The Republic of South Sudan is like a white paper – *tabula rasa*! (Speech of President Salva Kiir on Martyrs' Day, Juba, 30 July 2011)

A bloodstained chronicle or a blank page? President Kiir's speeches in the aftermath of South Sudan's independence presented two versions of the history of the state that he had just inherited, which do not appear immediately reconcilable. The 'predatory state' school centres South Sudan's political history in Khartoum and describes its extractive relationship with the peripheries of nineteenth- and twentieth-century Sudan (Garang de Mabior 1994). The *tabula rasa* view is sometimes promoted by development institutions advising and investing in South Sudan:

As a new nation without a history of formal institutions, rules or administration accepted as legitimate by society, South Sudan must build its institutions from scratch. Core administrative structures and mechanisms of political representation are only beginning to emerge ... (World Bank 2013)

Foreign experts who are also believers in their own advice

find the prospect of this clean slate understandably attractive. The notion that South Sudan has no legitimate institutions, or no institutions at all, sometimes finds an echo in the theories of colonial anthropologists, who acknowledged that they were slow to examine the government superstructure, and downplayed political history (Reining 1966; Lienhardt 1982: 22). Colonial anthropologists were influenced by functionalism, a school emphasizing social equilibrium and consensus, which tended to abstract social structures away from time and change. Evans-Pritchard (1973) acknowledged some of the weaknesses of the theory, which shaped his own work. He wrote his famous works on Nuer society as a colonial official, at the end of an exceptionally brutal campaign of pacification, and his most influential Nuer studies skirt historical questions because of censorship or self-censorship. These anthropological writings nonetheless influentially shaped scholarly and official versions of the South Sudanese *tabula rasa* (Hutchinson 1996: 21ff.).

These two versions of history are both useful starting points for the national historical narrative that the president of the new Republic of South Sudan needed to present. In the territory of present-day South Sudan, states and stateless societies coexisted and sometimes competed for several centuries before the coming of an independent, South Sudanese state. The colonial regimes headquartered in Khartoum that gave that territory its present boundaries, and the Sudanese regimes that succeeded them, all used extreme violence in creating 'Southern Sudan', which became South Sudan in 2011. But violence did not happen in a uniform way: it played out unevenly across South Sudan's vast territory, and changed different ecological and social systems at different tempos. Development was enmeshed in the violence. It did not happen uniformly or predictably, and it frequently reversed idealized periodizations of economic progress that see the introduction of private property, markets and money as a precursor to economic efficiency and social stability.

The cause of the violence – cultural irreconcilabilities or the violence of development?

This history of state violence and underdevelopment is central to South Sudan's liberation story. Many South Sudanese historians attribute the violence, at least implicitly, to antagonisms between Arab and African culture, or between Muslims and non-Muslims (Kathish 1901; Oduho and Deng 1963; Wai 1981; Mawut 1995; Deng 1995; Jok 2001; Nyaba 2005; Wawa 2008). Another view, which was once more influential than it is today, sees the violence perpetrated by the state centred at Khartoum against its vast southern periphery as an outcome of the uneven nature of capitalist development, which throws some societies backwards as it pushes others forward (Garang 1971; Amin 1972; Garang de Mabior 1994; Tully 1988; El-Battahani 2009). This chapter examines both those claims. The two dominant accounts of the causes of South Sudan's violence affect the diagnoses and prognoses of South Sudan's liberation movements and its national project. Was it caused by cultural differences, which might be resolved by the creation of a less conflicted or more homogeneous national identity? That was the view that carried many South Sudanese twenty-first-century nationalists successfully through a referendum on independence. Or were these cultural differences entangled in or created by an uneven process of development which cultural policy alone cannot mitigate? That was the view of South Sudanese revolutionaries in the 1980s, when, towards the end of the Cold War, they began their long armed struggle.

In South Sudan's few short years of existence, the coherence of the culture-first view has faced awkward challenges. The legacies of its long wars did not vanish into a nationalist dawn. Violence intensified in Jonglei and in some other parts of South Sudan, and its frequent mutinies have amplified local social contradictions and even the political contradictions of the national capital. This chapter and the entire book take the second view as a starting point. A violent and uneven process of development created many of these contradictions, and culture and society have become entangled in that violent process.

An understanding of these violent processes of development requires historical analysis, and a reconsideration of the many historical narratives that start with South Sudan's unenviable experience of racial and cultural oppression. This chapter looks mostly at the history of South Sudan during a long nineteenth century, which began as the effects of the Industrial and French Revolutions rippled over the African continent. By the middle of the nineteenth century, South Sudan was pitched into the boom-and-bust story of the Egyptian and world economy. New ways of classifying people into 'races' and 'tribes' emerged, and these classifications helped to buttress the institution of slavery, which reached deep into social life. From the middle of the nineteenth century, Sudan's foreign rulers used anti-slavery rhetoric as a central part of their claims of legitimacy. But successive regimes – the Ottoman-Egyptian Turkiya, the Sudanese Mahdiya, and the British-led Anglo-Egyptian Sudan – maintained slavery until the 1920s and beyond. This chapter sets out to show that slavery was one of several means by which South Sudan was simultaneously incorporated into and marginalized by the international system – these simultaneous processes are still operating today, and they lie at the heart of the violence in South Sudan's hinterlands.

The construction of racial oppression

Many South Sudanese societies functioned without a state and without money, depending instead on a complex system of social obligation. South Sudanese pre-colonial states also functioned without money. The non-monetized economies of the Shilluk kings of the White Nile and Zande kings of the Nile–Congo watershed maintained their capacity to capture slaves, organize labour, and trade with other states until the late nineteenth century.

These different societies sometimes engaged in exchange of goods particularly those with luxury, ritual or strategic importance.

But most exchange was organized around marriage, not markets – a kind of exchange that creates elaborate, open-ended reciprocities between social groups and generations rather than reducing relationships to credit and debt or profit and loss. Bridewealth was the most significant expression of that system. Bridewealth reflected social values (cattle; agricultural tools or labour; or weapons in times of violence) and it ensured that wealth circulated between parents, children and in-laws at marriage rather than passing from one generation to the other at death. South Sudanese states could function without money by intervening in labour and bridewealth systems (Evans-Pritchard 1963; Reining 1966: 53; Lloyd 1978: 245–95; Spaulding 1985: 105; Thomas 2010: 49).

In the first half of the nineteenth century, South Sudan's diverse societies were drawn into the money system, into vast empires with their global systems of trade and finance. The autonomous Ottoman province of Egypt conquered the Sinnar sultanate in 1820 and set up an administration called the Turkiya, which aimed to create a colonial economy based on the export of slaves and commodities. Partly for reasons of Islamic legal propriety, they were required to capture slaves exclusively from the non-Muslim societies of the Sudanese periphery. They began in present-day South Kordofan and Blue Nile, and then moved to South Sudan when the river route there was opened. In the slaving heyday, even Christian slave-owners flew banners with Qur'anic exhortations to jihad or holy war: the law of jihad provided an Islamic-law basis for enslavement of people from the south, albeit one which many contemporary Muslim observers identified as bogus (Schweinfurth 1874: vol. 1, 138; Hill 1959: 38, 76; Spaulding 1982; Clarence-Smith 2008).

The Turkiya gradually extended its control to cover a territory roughly approximate to that of twentieth-century Sudan. It created a monetized, indebted, juridically Muslim north that was structured around slave labour and a culturally plural south whose administration was structured around slave capture. Subsequent regimes maintained these separate administrative arrangements for north and south, and the religiously coloured notions of race that justified it. The Turkiya's racial system became the template for the gigantic, bifurcated Sudan that fell apart in 2011.

Slavery emphatically ranked South Sudanese at the bottom of a new political order. At the same time, outsiders began to order South Sudanese societies into tribes. In part, this was a response to the growth of trade. After 1848, the ivory trade was privatized. Expeditions were run on private credit and, in order to meet interest costs, merchants turned to raiding for cattle to barter for ivory, and eventually to slave raiding and trading. At this juncture, Khartoum entrepreneurs found a route through the flood plains to the ironstone plateau. There, all-season roads and forts could be built. The forts were small towns, surrounded by miles of cultivated fields: farmers and soldiers were often drawn from the population of the vicinity, which were organized by 'native overseers', some of them with an armed retinue (Schweinfurth 1874: vol. 1, 220).

Cherry Leonardi's work on the development of chiefship in South Sudan traces how people's customs and notions of authority were transformed by the relationships that these intermediaries set up with successive invaders. The slavers' forts were slowly con-stituted as nodes of state power that gradually extended authority into ungoverned hinterlands (Leonardi 2013: 18). The system of forts set up under the Turkiya thus established a state system that emphasized the spatial unevenness of development – more development at the nodes and less in the hinterland – that is starkly evident in South Sudan of today. This spatial unevenness had a social dimension: communities who lived near these little towns were more likely to understand the possibilities offered by trade and government, and could use intermediaries or chiefs to engage in often risky negotiations to regularize arrangements with merchant or state authorities in towns. And although different groups sometimes mobilized jointly to resist foreign aggression, there were many cases when slavers and government agents intensified differences between different groups by deploying more compliant communities against remoter resisting communities, in order to capture slaves or cattle or dramatize the government's power (Mawut 1995: 28–9).

The Turkiya period saw the beginnings of the transformation of these social groups into 'tribes' – an enigmatic, controversial and politically useful term that no one has ever been able to provide a satisfactory definition for. The 'overseers' or chiefly intermediaries appointed to negotiate with the authorities of the Turkiya informally represented pre-existing, named social structures with recognizable but porous boundaries, which were based on shared ethnicity, language and kinship. Some of these social structures had a unified central authority, but most recognized different kinds of usefulness and prestige – people with technical skills, rhetorical skills, charisma – and distributed authority among them. 'Overseers' or chiefly intermediaries made these complex systems of representation and authority more intelligible to outsiders. By fitting the groups they represented into a single template – a 'tribe' structured around kinship under a single chief in ancestral lands – they found a simple way of classifying and comparing different groups in the outsiders' gaze: compliant, threatening, taxpaying or tax-rejecting, backward or ambitious. These characteristics were often seen as inherent in particular groups, although they often reflected instead responses to a system of uneven development that concentrated gains and losses in different areas inhabited by different groups.

South Sudanese historians often use this history of religiously coloured racial oppression as a starting point for analysis, stressing the complicity of Sudanese from the Muslim, Arabic-speaking northern Nile valley in the slave trade; and the role of slavery in the construction of racism in twentieth-century Sudan. The association of slavery with the state version of Islamic culture and religion which the Turkiya brought to northern Sudan was a persuasive South Sudanese argument for self-determination – it is still politically relevant today. But centring the discussion on the cultural and religious trappings of the slave trade, South Sudanese and other historians have sometimes obscured the story of the development and underdevelopment of the Southern provinces of Sudan, which made their first appearances in the historical record during the Turkiya.

The construction of underdevelopment

This story of development and underdevelopment – the way in which global forces began to exercise decisive influence over the people of the territory of present-day South Sudan – is no less politically urgent than the legacy of slavery. The Turkiya began its penetration of the Upper Nile within a few years of the fall of the Sinnar sultanate, and by 1841 its sailing boats had penetrated the Sudd and landed at Gondokoro, near present-day Juba. This 'lunge' into the African interior happened at a time when colonial contact was largely restricted to coastal enclaves (Gray 1961: 1). Botanists, mineralogists and social scientists published lengthy descriptions of the Turkiya's new southern territories; state monopolists and private entrepreneurs took South Sudan's commodities to world markets; and in spite of the piti-less adversity they faced, the labour of enslaved South Sudanese workers and soldiers permanently transformed the production and destruction systems of powerful states in north-east Africa, and set the stage for the colonial penetration of central Africa (Mawut 1995; Cordell 1985).

This is a paradox. How did South Sudan's head start in the African encounter with the global system yield today's hyper-underdevelopment? Why was it necessary, sixty years after the end of direct foreign rule in Africa, to set up a new state in South Sudan to deal with this underdevelopment? Was it an outcome of the state's predation and use of racial oppression; or of the state's institutional absence? Or was an outcome predictable from the nature of externally initiated, colonial development? Responses to these questions shaped twentieth-century liberation movements and set out many of the possibilities and limitations of the new Republic of South Sudan. Global forces reshape places where economic processes are violently entangled with religion and ethnicity. But their influence is not unilinear or predictable. Most of this book tries to look at both global and local forces shaping South Sudan today, during a new clutch of violent entanglements. Its past experience can offer some guidance.

The Turkiya's establishment in Sudan came near the start of a tumultuous century which turned Egypt from an autonomous province of the Ottoman empire into a British-occupied debt farm, and Egypt's booms and busts were played out in its Sudan colony. In the late eighteenth century improved European production processes for cloth and other goods generated surpluses which led European countries to seek out new markets. In the eastern Mediterranean, Britain and France fought for control of Egypt's markets. Mehmed Ali, the ruler of Egypt, set up a state monopoly of land and agricultural production and a new conscript army to forestall British economic and military penetration. Imports from Britain were increasing rapidly and slaves from South Sudan were expected to provide the labour for this transformation. Egypt hoped to resist more powerful countries by imitating their economic strength and diversity, but its strategy paradoxically made Egypt more dependent on European technology, trade and finance. By 1840, free trade agreements with Britain opened Egypt to foreign manufactures, ending its industrialization drive. By 1860, Egypt was borrowing European capital to finance its development, and by the end of the century Egypt was a primary commodity exporter that earned nearly all of its foreign income from cotton and spent about half its total revenues on debt servicing (Owen 1981: 57, 85; Pamuk 1987: 20; Zeleza 1993: 349; Mitchell 2002: 59, 180).

Economic tumults in Egypt set the pace of violence in South

Sudan. In the decades before the 1820 conquest of the Sinnar sultanate, increased trade and freer movement of goods in Egyptian cities empowered merchants operating between Egypt and Sinnar, and eventually those merchants broke the system of royally administered trade that emphasized the sultan's power by making him the main or only merchant, customer and consumer of slaves, weapons and luxury goods. People with money could acquire slaves and other luxuries, and the first decades of the nineteenth century witnessed an 'unprecedented expansion' in the slave population of Sinnar (Amin 1972; Kapteijns and Spaulding 1982; Spaulding 1982, 1985).

Merchants exposed Sinnar to global forces and as a result the sultanate fell with much less resistance than the more isolated Shilluk kingdom farther up the Nile, which maintained its independence for another forty years. In keeping with its early nineteenth-century policy of state monopoly, Egypt replaced Sinnar's merchant slavers with state slave-raiding expeditions. Until the 1840s, slave raiding in South Sudan was limited and partly negotiated through the Shilluk kingdom and a few merchants who had moved there from Sinnar. The Shilluk king maintained his own royal monopoly, but because trade there was much more modest than in Sinnar, merchants there had less power and the Shilluk king was able to maintain the old Sudanic system of royally administered trade. Merchant refugees expanded the royally controlled ivory market and, with the help of Shilluk raiders, kidnapped slaves from Dinka areas (Mercer 1971).

The Shilluk kingdom was still nominally independent in 1841 and was able to provide merchant refugees from the state monopolies in Khartoum with an independent raiding base. From 1841, the White Nile opened to government river craft as far as present-day Juba. Shilluk control of the river ended, and another kind of trade developed. Not a dramatic increase in slave-taking from South Sudan, but 'legitimate commerce' – an attempt to set up a state monopoly supplying a luxury commodity whose

price for European consumers was rocketing – ivory. Slave raiding in the territory of present-day South Sudan was limited in
the 1840s: most slaves were kidnapped from the Blue Nile hills,
the Nuba mountains of Kordofan and the Shilluk hinterlands.
White Nile boats might carry six or seven slaves, but the opening of the White Nile had little impact on the volume of slave
traffic in the north. A decade later, a slaver's fort in present-day
Rumbek was decorated with the decapitated heads of his victims
and whole swathes of territory from the east bank of the White
Nile to the Nile–Congo watershed had been transformed by the
slave trade. Egypt's legal measures to prohibit the slave trade in
1856 ironically served as a marker of an infamous and dramatic
expansion of the slave trade directed by European cosmopolitans
and Egyptian drifters. At the time, many European proponents
of private-sector-led development and human rights believed
that 'legitimate commerce' could root out the slave trade. Yet in
1850s South Sudan, the opposite occurred – it was not to be the
first of South Sudan's upendings of idealized periodizations of
historical development. Part of the reason lies in the trajectory
of globalization in north-east Africa at the time, and part lies in
the socio-economic system of the societies of South Sudan (Gray
1961: 28–30, 47; Bjørkelo 1989: 78).

To begin with the trajectory of globalization: Egypt's ambitious
ruler Mehmed Ali had invaded Sudan in 1820 as part of a wider
strategy to forestall the encroachment of European commerce and
challenge the authority of his nominal sovereign, the Ottoman
sultan, in the bargain. He was not able to use Sudanese labour for
this task – nearly all the Sudanese slaves he brought to Egypt died.
Instead, he refashioned Egyptian peasant society to make it supply
labour for his army and cotton farms, and started two decades of
war and occupation in Syria and Arabia that alarmed European
powers vying for commercial control of the region. Europeans
believed that profits from his monopoly system had allowed him to
build his enormous military machine, which was challenging their

ability to reshape Middle Eastern markets. In 1841, as Turkiya boats landed at Gondokoro, a British-led diplomatic consortium allied with the Ottoman sultan to demobilize Mehmed Ali's army, and used free trade agreements and fluctuations in the cotton price to break his monopolies. The sultan decreed that Mehmed Ali's descendants would inherit Egypt and Sudan in perpetuity, as a kind of consolation prize (Owen 1981; Fahmy 1998, 2002).

Pre-colonial socio-economic systems in the territory of present-day South Sudan could not be transformed as quickly as those in Sinnar because they were not monetized. Unable to manipulate South Sudan's society and economy by money, the state had to use violence instead – 'legitimate commerce' gave way to the slave trade. In northern Sudan, Turkiya policy replaced communal systems of land tenure with a market in land, which was alienated from traditional owners through a monetized tax system that indebted ordinary farmers. Turkiya legal institutions, using a metropolitan version of Islamic law, framed many of these changes: Islamic commercial and inheritance law helped to fractionalize land, and a harsh interpretation of the laws of slavery justified the expanded system of slave capture that facilitated the introduction of slave agriculture. An important condition for these changes was land scarcity – along the narrow strip of cultivable land along the northern Nile valley, demand for land was high and it was relatively easy to turn land into private property. But it was not possible to monetize the economies of the vast underpopulated lands of South Sudan, where governments could not alienate land from people, because of the resilience of customary land rights and because authorities believed that land was too abundant for cadastration. Writing a century later, a World Bank mission pointed out the problem: 'Registration of land titles does not exist and would also be useless as a security for farm credit as there is plenty of unoccupied land to which evicted farmers could move' (IBRD 1973: 24).

The inability to monetize the economy meant that trade was

initially conducted as a good-natured exchange – small stocks of ivory in the Bari areas around Gondokoro were bartered for beads (Nyombe 2007). But state agents were not able to buy ivory, and the state monopoly in ivory was relatively unsuccessful. An increase in the volume of trade came only when the ivory trade was privatized – and privatization came about as a result of Egypt's free trade agreements, which by the 1850s led the Turkiya to abolish its Sudan monopolies. The ivory trade was financialized too: Khartoum financiers capitalized southern expeditions at up to 100 per cent rates of interest. The friendly exchanges that marked the first contact could not be the basis for these kinds of returns, and traders were compelled to barter ivory for cattle. With no money in circulation, cattle could be had only by force. Traders set up forts and militias, and worked up local animosities to seize cattle to barter for ivory and provision forts. They also took slaves with which to pay soldiers (Gray 1961: 23–51; Beachey 1967: 279). The Shilluk kingdom fell to the merchant refugees it had welcomed: by the 1850s, these merchants had enough influence to challenge the royal monopoly. A new king who acceded in 1860 challenged the ivory merchants and was deposed, and his successor's power shrivelled into the mysterious 'sacral kingship' of anthropological controversy (Mercer 1971; Kapteijns and Spaulding 1982: 43–4; Spaulding 1985: 284; Graeber 2011).

The first Khartoum financiers were mostly European, and Egyptian soldiers demobilized from Mehmed Ali's army in 1841 made up many of the expeditions. But as trade shifted from ivory to slaves, personnel changed. Slaves transformed agricultural production in northern Sudan, where up to one third of the population may have been enslaved. Men from the northern Nile valley who had lost their lands to taxmen or usurers could no longer find work as agricultural labourers, and they joined the booming, interlinked slave and ivory trade in the south (Spaulding 1982). They created new, Sudanese, networks for credit and trade, outdoing those of the European financiers (Bjørkelo 1989: 122).

Anti-slavery activism – backed by European consuls and Islamic reformists – impelled the government towards abolition, but financial and trade policies – largely determined by European powers – had intensified the slave trade until it was beyond the powers of the state to control. These contradictions eventually overwhelmed the Turkiya. Until the 1860s, South Sudan had no government administration – it was ruled by state expedition and then by the forts of the Khartoum privateers. Anti-slavery activism provided the momentum to establish state structures. In 1865, the Turkiya established its first administrative districts. In 1874, the Egyptian khedive (viceroy) re-established a state monopoly in Equatoria and appointed European governors to deepen government penetration of the south through roads and posts (Birkbeck Hill 1885: xxxi, 6). Egypt's own monopolies had not been able to withstand the power of international trade and investment, which refashioned Egypt into a deeply indebted cotton farm, a bond-holders' paradise in Zeleza's resonant phrase.

In Egypt, international indebtedness led the government to increase taxation. In the third quarter of the century, increased taxes pushed small farmers into debt and off their lands, bringing about dramatic social changes (Toledano 1998: 272). The same international forces were operating in Egypt's Equatorian periphery too – but with different results. In South Sudan, Egypt's monopolies had been sacrificed to free trade treaties with Britain. Khartoum financiers and private merchants had created a chaotic slave trade. In 1863, a correspondent for the London *Times* explained excitedly that average annual profits of 200 per cent could be had: 'I may mention that the current rate of interest upon two trustworthy signatures at Khartoum is 10 per cent a month, and that nevertheless the gains are so large that the traders can afford to pay it, and realise a handsome profit besides' (29 May 1863, quoted in Stiansen 1993: 323).

The miracle of compound interest lay at the heart of the slave trade. It was the only business model that could provide the enormous returns that the creditors demanded. Ivory could not: the number of boat expeditions going south increased by a factor of nine between 1850 and 1863, but ivory trade volumes increased only by 42 per cent in the same period (Stiansen 1993: 196). But the slave trade required considerable aggression. Traders set up forts and armies across South Sudan, vividly demonstrating the way in which the commercial conventions signed between the British and the Ottomans had emasculated state power. After 1865, the Turkiya government began asserting its control over South Sudan, defeating the slavers' armies. But in the process, the armies or their defeated remnants spilled over into Darfur and Central Africa. They began several decades of devastating violence that brought down the independent sultanate of Darfur and then the Turkiya government in Khartoum and transformed the Central African interior on the eve of the colonial assault (Cordell 1985).

The new periphery defeats the centre

Attempts by African governments to resist the rapid transformations of the nineteenth century, and to accommodate the 'human rights' concerns of the anti-slavery movement, only exacerbated their dependency on pitiless external forces. Sudanese farmers who had turned themselves into slave traders in the face of these forces now found themselves fleeing from Gordon's campaigns in Bahr al-Ghazal. The slave armies they had established were multiply coercive structures that nevertheless gave some limited opportunities to South Sudanese to advance in the stark military (and marital) hierarchies that slavery had brought to the south. As Egypt moved to assert its power over the people whose lives had been turned upside down by the tumults it had brought to Sudan, a force arose that could mobilize Sudanese aspirations and disappointments. Muhammad Ahmad al-Mahdi, a Sudanese millenarian preacher, rallied Sudan's peripheries into an army that conquered the modern, European-officered army at Khartoum.

In a letter to his Turkiya adversaries, the Mahdi emphatically reminded them of the reversals of fortune: 'You say that Our only followers are ignorant Baqqara and the idolaters [al-Majūs, the non-Muslims of the south]. Know then that the followers of the apostles before us and of our Prophet Muhammad were the weak and the ignorant and the nomads, who worshipped rocks and trees' (quoted in Holt 1977: 50).

In 1885, the Mahdi took Khartoum – the only Sudanese in history to lead a successful revolt from Sudan's violent periphery. His Sudan was a creation of the Turkiya colonial venture, which had aligned the fate of the periphery to powerful economic interests in Khartoum. The Mahdist state kept many Turkiya structures, but its wars with Egypt and other neighbours cut off external trade. The state monopolized trade in the south. Slave-raiding expeditions were organized and equipped by the government treasury, not by Khartoum financiers. Expeditions were kept smaller in size: large slave-raiding armies were too much of a threat to state security. Mahdist expeditions to the southern provinces established only intermittent control there (Ohrwalder 1892: 214, 384; Nugud 2003; Al-Gaddal 1986; Johnson 1993).

The Mahdi's rise came as the Egyptian state was taken over by its creditors (after the failure of a revolution aimed at recovering sovereignty) and occupied by Britain. In the international law of the day, Egypt had 'title' to South Sudan, and a British-led Anglo-Egyptian army 'reconquered' Sudan on behalf of Egypt in 1896–98. Abolition of slavery was a declared aim of the reconquest. But the government's first priority was to restore agricultural production in the Nile valley. The Mahdist state forcibly displaced large constituencies of people from Darfur to its rapidly growing capital of Omdurman, and awarded land to the displaced. Slavery remained the basis of agricultural production but the wars and displacements of the period meant that the fast-growing capital could not be fed. The policies of war and displacement were aggravated by climate change, and in the late 1880s food insecurity turned into a series of memorable famines. Grain had to be imported from the peripheries, including from Shilluk farmers in present-day South Sudan (Ohrwalder 1892: 285; Davis 2002: 133ff.).

The Mahdist period disrupted the course of nineteenth-century history, briefly reversing the course of colonialism. But it kept many of the important structures and patterns of the Turkiya intact, particularly its military and fiscal bureaucracies and its use of slave workers from the periphery for food production at the centre. In doing so, it maintained the dominance of the northern Nile valley. The Anglo-Egyptian regime that defeated and succeeded the Mahdist state also maintained those structures and patterns. British administrators surreptitiously re-established the system of agricultural slave production, and with it the institution of slavery and the slave trade to recover food security. They used slave cultivators at the base of a system of grain production, distribution and sale that was centred on the infrastructure and markets of the northern Nile valley, and was oriented towards export and, after 1914, towards military supply (Johnson 1988; Sikainga 1996: 29ff.; Nugud 2003; Serels 2012: 243ff.).

The preceding overview has argued that from the mid-nineteenth century, South Sudan's history was shaped by powerful international forces backed by state power. Many of the structures and patterns of the Turkiya state were inherited by subsequent states, and South Sudan's long nineteenth century lasted into the first decades of the twentieth. South Sudan was simultaneously incorporated and marginalized. It is not possible to understand what happened purely from a metropolitan perspective – an understanding of local change is necessary too. The last part of this chapter looks at the long nineteenth century from the viewpoint of Jonglei, starting with its neglected south-eastern corner.

Jonglei's long nineteenth century

Some of the social divisions of nineteenth-century South Sudan pre-dated colonialism; some were deliberately sown by foreigners seeking slaves or food or ivory. Other social divisions – such as the social difference between the hinterlands of the flood plains and the more developed plateaus and hills of the south and west – emerged from the geography of uneven development. The remoteness of the eastern flood plains, and their proximity to Ethiopia's little-known frontier, gave many of its communities a different experience of wars, states and markets than that of the rest of the flood plains and the rest of South Sudan. Most nineteenth-century documentary sources view South Sudan from the Nile steamer, the slavers' fort, the government post, and their new histories of money and armies and slavery. That new history took place mostly in Bahr al-Ghazal and Equatoria – the areas of South Sudan that could sustain all-weather roads, or that were accessible by steamer. Khartoum slavers spent less than a decade in the eastern plains.

Part of the ideology of slavery was to depict societies outside the slavery system as inherently violent: for example, the Nuer migrations that brought the Nuer social system from present-day Unity state to present-day Jonglei and Upper Nile from the first decades of the nineteenth century were for many years represented as a violent conquest by enormous columns of Nuer soldiers (Kelly 1985). Subsequent research suggests that Nuer migrations were more of a frontier story of coercion, negotiation, assimilation and wayfaring pioneered by small groups (Jal 1987; Johnson 1994; Hutchinson 1996).

Murle people are another group of nineteenth-century migrants who have received much less scholarly attention. B. A. Lewis (1972: 22) describes the arrival of Murle people in the Pibor area in the mid-nineteenth century as a 'conquest' that saw off Dinka people in the west of present-day Pibor county and Anuak people to the north east, and stalled the expansion of Nuer people, who were beginning to arrive in the area to the north of Pibor. In the first decade of the twentieth century, British officials described 'annual' Murle raids targeting the easternmost Dinka settlement. But before 1908, they could not mobilize Dinka porters for punitive patrols, nor mobilize funds from Khartoum to cover the cost of them. Between 1909 and 1910, four raids were attributed to Murle attackers, an increase in frequency, and in 1912 money for a punitive patrol was made available, and Dinka irregulars were prepared to join (ibid.: 8; Mawut 1995: 72, 91). At the time, Bor people paid tax, while Murle and Nuer people did not. Both Murle and Nuer groups raided Dinka areas, and British punitive patrols on non-taxpaying groups, using Dinka irregulars, were sometimes cast as 'protection' of taxpayers from raids (Mawut 1995: 73f.).

Murle society has an assimilatory outlook, turning strangers into brothers and heirs. In the 1930s, for example, one of the Murle drum chiefs (a senior spiritual leader) was from a small Ethiopian group called Majangir (also Masango), speakers of a language related to Murle. He had been taken captive by Anuak raiders and sold for an ivory tusk to a Murle leader, who adopted him and whose spiritual role he inherited (Lewis 1972: 57). These kinds of interactions are part of the histories of every group in Upper Nile. Relationships between the peoples of Jonglei were characterized by cooperation as well as conflict. One politician and historian, from Anyidi (an area of Bor where some Murle have been assimilated into Dinka society), gave the following account of the twelve decades of Murle presence in Jonglei:

My grandfather of the fifth generation [great-great-great grandfather] was killed by Murle. That was the first attack remembered by Anyidi. It might have been about 1830. But when slavery forces were attacking in Bor [in the second half of the nineteenth century], my people in Anyidi were overrun by slavery forces, they retreated back to Murle and spent twenty-five years there and then came back and then there was fighting between Murle and Bor ... Drought came [to Pibor at the beginning of the twentieth century] and the Murle leader sent his sons to Anyidi to ask for water and the leaders at the time said – we can't let these people starve because of lack of water. They were allowed and came, they stayed in the 1960s, in harmony, although there was cattle theft between them. (Interview 43/2012)

These events are part of Murle tradition too: describing these events from Murle sources, Arensen says that a Dinka chief named Yot fled to Murle areas for safety and stayed for about eight years, whereupon the chief sent messages to his own people exhorting them to come and raid. Dinka raids killed many Murle people and cattle, and then Murle raids began in response to them (Collins 1960: 37; Arensen 1992: 31). Johnson (1981: 523) also finds evidence that Murle raiders were responding to provocations. Relations were not always and only antagonistic, however. Murle people and their neighbours learned each other's languages. There are still bilingual speakers of Murle and Dinka in Anyidi, a predominantly Dinka settlement on the road to Pibor. Evidence for Murle multilingualism comes in the earliest sources: D. C. E. ff. Comyn made early official contact with Murle people, while taking a gunboat up the Pibor river in 1904. Murle people feared he was an Ethiopian slave raider (Comyn 1911: 97). He wrote in intelligence reports that 'A few [Murle] men know the Nuer and Dinka and Anuak dialects' (quoted in Lewis 1972: 6).

Murle people engaged with Nuer culture too. The Nuer fertility cult of Nyandit became a part of Murle society (Arensen 1992: 238). Nuer prophets were key interpreters of the dramatic events of the nineteenth century, and Murle people engaged with them too. A Nuer elder in Akobo, north-east Jonglei, described Murle relationships with the Nuer prophet Ngundeng Bong (fl. 1870–

1906) to the Japanese anthropologist Eri Hashimoto. Ngundeng led Lou Nuer people in peaceful and armed resistance against external attack and inspired other Nuer prophets to organize against nineteenth-century slave raiders from neighbouring groups (Johnson 1994: 85, 139). Colonial arrivals in the Horn of Africa brought with them epidemics and epizootics that devastated the whole east and south of the continent – the rinderpest that devastated east and southern Africa in the 1880s and 1890s is remembered in Murle tradition as a monster the size of a small mountain that stalked and swallowed cattle (Rowe and Hødnebø 1994: 158). Ngundeng organized the Lou Nuer response: part of his organizational repertoire was the construction of a mound-shaped shrine (Johnson 1994: 87–90). The Nuer elder recalled Murle participation in the decoration of the mound:

> One day, Ngundeng was standing on the top of the mound
> … Ngundeng placed pieces of ivory around the bottom of the
> mound and said, 'You, bring the pieces of ivory up to the top
> of the mound'. Many of the Nuer were afraid, but some Murle
> climbed up to the mound and put two pieces of ivory on the
> top. Ngundeng said, 'You, Nuer! All of you refused to bring
> the ivory. I will curse you … All Nuer in Southern Sudan
> will get food from the Murle'. (An elderly man from Akobo,
> quoted in Hashimoto 2013: 41)

Colonial writers presented the area of the eastern flood plains bounded by the Bahr al-Jebel and Sobat rivers and the Ethiopian border – present-day Jonglei – as intractably violent. Douglas H. Johnson's work on the evolution of martial stereotypes in the eastern plains of the Nile reviews historical and anthropological sources. Slavers and officials seldom ventured far from the east bank of the river, apart from a brief period in the late 1860s and early 1870s when they set up forts and raided for slaves in the eastern plains. During their relatively brief presence, the slavers followed patterns of violence familiar from elsewhere, recruiting

2.1 John Petherick's sketch of a Murle or 'Djibba' warrior (*source*: Petherick and Petherick 1869: vol. 2, 6)

Note: Djibba is the Anuak word for Murle; many early sources use this Anuak word or the Dinka word Beir to describe them.

both Dinka and Nuer intermediaries to raid for slaves from other Dinka and Nuer sections. When the slavers left, the slavers' intermediaries were defeated by raided groups, organized in some cases by local spiritual leaders. The first British attempts at tax collection used these misrepresentations as a starting point. Dinka individuals who had formerly allied themselves to slavers were used in violent campaigns to pacify and tax Nuer communities that had once defeated them. Colonial anthropologists theorized the violence as structural to Nuer and Dinka relations, all of which further entrenched the colonial stereotype of the truculent, unruly or 'Fighting Nuer' (Johnson 1981, 1994).

Nuer people were not the only ones to make an appearance in the annals of ethnic ferocity. In 1869, John Petherick, the British consul in Khartoum, published a sketch of a Murle warrior that he had drawn more than a decade earlier during his travels on the White Nile (Petherick and Petherick 1869: vol. 2, 6). Like the 'Fighting Nuer', Murle people made their first literary appearance depicted in the person of a young, male warrior.

The geography of uneven development

Martial stereotypes intensified the violence of the long pacification campaigns that British officials organized in the eastern flood
plains. These areas were the last part of Africa to be pacified
by colonial military action: Murle areas were not pacified until
1912; and in Nuer areas pacification lasted until the 1930s. This
history of violence had its origins in hostile colonial understandings about the population, a factor that contributed to the slow
progress towards development in the eastern plains. As elsewhere
in South Sudan, violence, development and underdevelopment
were a consequence of the encounter with the international system. In the nineteenth century, the eastern flood plains became
a periphery of the Khartoum system of financialized, Islamized
slave raiding – the slavers spilled into the east only because a
temporary blockage in the main, western Bahr al-Jebel route
through the Sudd in the 1860s forced them to seek a river passage through the eastern, Bahr al-Zeraf route. In this period,
the territory of present-day Jonglei was becoming a periphery
of the Ethiopian empire too, which unleashed historical forces
that were equally mighty and globally networked in an area that
had hitherto been an unexplored hinterland. Colonial pressures
on Ethiopia pushed it reluctantly towards incorporation in the
global market economy, and the Ethiopian empire expanded into
the south-western lowlands of Ethiopia in the late nineteenth
century. These areas are home to peoples mostly speaking a
collection of Nilo-Saharan languages historically linked to the
greater Nile valley (Tornay 1980). Murle tradition recalls several
slave raids from Ethiopia, and these were linked to a trade in
ivory, firearms and alcohol that was developing along the border
in the last decades of the nineteenth century (Comyn 1911: 101;
Lewis 1972: 3; Zewde 1987; Mawut 1995). In an area that was
largely excluded from colonial development, weaponry became
an alternative vector of modernization.

The presence of the Ethiopian frontier, and its importance

in the international system, made it the most urgent priority for British officials arriving in the eastern flood plains as the twentieth century began. For the first decade or two of their occupation, they postponed 'pacification' campaigns for lack of resources. Instead, they attended to the control of trade and borders – early in the twentieth century, about 70 per cent of Ethiopia's trade with Sudan went down the Sobat river (Zewde 1987: 77). They closed the district to traders and established an ivory and rubber monopoly – evidence of the state's inability to control commercial forces. British officials even imported cattle to exchange for ivory, in order to compete with the Ethiopian traders. In 1908, the British imposed restrictions on the liquor trade in response to an epidemic of drunkenness (Mawut 1995: 86–91). These government controls on an apparently buoyant market are an indication of the rapid pace of change in Jonglei that began at least thirty years before colonial anthropologists wrote their account of social and economic life shaped by the 'illusions' and 'cycles' of 'structural time' and 'oecological time' (Evans-Pritchard 1940a: 95).

The nineteenth- and twentieth-century trade in firearms (and the allied trades in ivory and slaves) in the eastern flood plains suggest that those areas had already begun on the jagged path to modern development. The arms trade reshaped relationships between and within different groups in the Sobat corridor that connected the eastern flood plains with Ethiopia: Anuak leaders were the first to obtain firearms and they used their access to them to deepen their control of their relatively decentralized society, and build military formations that could resist encroachment from expansionist Nuer groups. Their firepower, and their position on a sensitive border, meant that the British initially sought to conciliate them rather than pacifying them (Evans-Pritchard 1940b; Zewde 1987; Mawut 1995). The government was hesitant about the costs of pacification, particularly during the First World War. But when weapons spread to other groups, raiding intensified. In 1918, the government suspected that armed men from the Gaajak Nuer (a Jikainy Nuer group living to the north of the Sobat river near the border) abducted 240 women and children from the Burun people living in Blue Nile province, to trade as slaves in Ethiopia (Mawut 1995: 97). These figures were very much at the higher end of losses and casualties in the raiding of the time. If reports from the British intelligence services are to be believed, the largest raids in the first decades of the twentieth century would result in thirty or forty fatalities.

Raided groups, particularly those paying taxes, looked to the British military for protection. But financial constraints led to repeated postponement of punitive patrols. The government hoped to use their patrols to capture conscripts and expand their army, in a practice that echoed the slave raids of previous decades. But they were not successful in looting the hinterlands for men, and they often used irregular militias drawn from tax-paying groups in their campaigns to punish non-taxpaying groups (taxes were paid by ethnic groups, not individuals). The government became a protagonist in ethnic conflicts that were being aggravated by the spread of firearms (Mawut 1995: 67, 91, 160). After the First World War ended, the British decided to deploy warplanes as part of its pacification strategy (Hutchinson 1996: 111).

The use of air power to pacify colonial subjects was a 1912 innovation from Italian Tripolitania, and the British took it up in India in 1915 (Lindqvist 2002: 102). Air power was seen as a technical solution to the problem of governing vast and remote areas: the air force advertised its squadrons to Sudan's colonial government as cheaper than a British infantry battalion: 'the best possible means ... for the effective, economic and humane control of undeveloped countries' (Trenchard 1929). By 1930, Nuer people had abandoned armed resistance. The government for its part stopped its earlier practice of using military patrols for forced conscription. It was part of a wider set of military reorganizations aimed at forestalling Egyptian influence and nationalist organization in Sudan's army, an institution with deep roots in the slavery systems that brought captives from the hinterlands into the centre of the state, transforming both captives and the state in the process. Johnson argues that the forced conscription patrols were a continuation of the nineteenth-century system of a slave army captured from the hinterlands. This system required periodic violence, and was at odds with the government's stated intention of setting up peaceful administration (Johnson 1989: 81). Instead, the government began recruiting from agrarian ethnic groups that lived in Equatoria, an ecological and social terrain where government power penetrated more deeply – in 1955, only about one hundred of its 1,770 officers and men were non-Equatorian. Eventually, these changes to military recruitment were linked to an experiment in indirect rule, which reorganized the people of South Sudan around government-appointed chiefs/tax-collectors, and limited interactions between different ethnic communities. Territorial units, like the Equatorian Corps, were one way of keeping different ethnic communities apart. Raiding, which the government viewed as a serious problem, was reduced.

Nonetheless, the early colonial military repertoire of ethnic militia and warplane remained key elements of the governance of the periphery for the rest of the twentieth century and after. And the firearms from early twentieth-century Ethiopian arms dealers were probably among those used in one of the first battles of the first Sudanese civil war, which began around Sudan's independence in 1956. In 1963, an Anuak prince gave a defecting Anuak schoolboy who was also the coordinator of the armed rebel Anya-nya movement thirty guns from a secret stock of weapons in Pochalla, right on the Ethiopian border. He used the weapons to attack a police post and start a rebellion (Pochalla politician, interview 39/2012; Poggo 2009: 70).

Conclusion

Twentieth-century Sudan was a creation of the nineteenth-century Turkiya system, which structured the country around slavery, with a slave catchment zone in its southern administrative zone, a slave cultivation system in the northern zone, and slave armies in both. The most developed part of the northern zone, running from the Red Sea coast through the northern Nile valley to the cities of the Kordofan rainlands, was transformed by slave cultivation, but also by the spread of money taxes, debt and rent. People who lived in this new financial world felt different from those who lived outside it – slave populations and the people of the southern periphery that had been plunged into violence. They also *were* different in an important respect: members of subordinated southern groups had a status lower than that of members of the dominant group (Ignatiev 1995: 1). This system of racial oppression shaped resistance in South Sudan throughout the twentieth century. South Sudanese historians who explain the history of the state in terms of its predations, and who link those predations to irreconcilable differences between South Sudanese culture and the Arab and Muslim culture and religion of the heartlands of the Sudanese state, accurately reflect the importance of racial oppression that the Turkiya initiated. At the same time, cultural differences were fostered by a system that produced uneven development: the Turkiya depredations could not have occurred without beliefs in racial or tribal difference.

The globalization of production, trade and debt in the nineteenth century had different consequences in different parts of the world: England, Egypt and Sudan all followed different lines of development. In what were then Sudan's southern provinces, these processes transmitted their influence with incomprehensible violence that zigged and zagged across the idealized, unilinear progressions envisioned by many theories of development. This unevenness, still evident today, exists within South Sudan as well as internationally. In 1983, 100 years later, SPLA revolutionary theorists used uneven development as a starting point for their critique of South Sudan's crisis. Their critique is still being used by revolutionaries in Sudan's diverse, impoverished and

resource-rich peripheries today. Then as now, the intractability
of spatial inequality is sometimes attributed to the malice of
Khartoum's elites. Hatashil Masha Katish was taken in slavery
from the Dinka areas of the flood plains, from present-day Lakes
state, and became the gun-carrier for a slaver. He described the
crisis in South Sudan as follows:

> I have followed my Arab Masters through vast tracts of
> country that had once been filled with a happy and contented
> people. We could see where their homes had been; we could
> see what had been grown in their fields, but they themselves
> were gone ... Arabs had travelled this ground before, and the
> people had been slain or enslaved by them. THEY had burnt
> the huts. THEY had desolated the fields. Like the locusts
> mentioned by the Prophet Joel, they had found the land before
> them like an Eden for fertility, they had left behind them a
> desolate wilderness. Oh! the skulls left in their track! (Kathish
> 1901: 29)

Kathish's lamentations, one of the very few examples of South
Sudanese slave writing, have the authority of the eyewitness. But
the devastating historical processes he describes are still being
played out today, and to make sense of the violence, Kathish's
evidence needs to be sifted into evidence from elsewhere. Although
nearly every South Sudanese social group experienced these global
processes violently, the pace and timing of the violence varied
dramatically from one place to another – as did the depth of commercial penetration and understanding of market ways. Jonglei,
the viewpoint for this book's account of South Sudan, was one
of the last areas to be penetrated. Violence lasted longer there,
and lasts longest in the remotest areas. Market penetration is
the slowest – in 2010, Jonglei had ten small cattle markets for
an enormous cattle population on which most of its population
depends (MARF/SNV 2010: 102). Global development is uneven
– it creates boom towns and ghost towns; rich cosmopolitan

centres and poor, violent peripheries. Jonglei's remoteness made it one of the most peripheral places in South Sudan and in the global system, and for this reason, it forms the main case study in this book's account of South Sudan's underdevelopment and liberation.

3 | DEVELOPMENT AND REPRESENTATION

Development and pessimism

Usually, when the United Nations sets up a peacekeeping mission, it needs to cajole member states into providing troops. But when in 2004 the UN set up its first peacekeeping mission to support the implementation of the 2005 Comprehensive Peace Agreement, something strange happened: UN officials said that their request for troop contributions was oversubscribed. South Sudan's vast untapped resources were no doubt a reason for the enthusiasms of defence ministries from Tokyo to Brasilia.

Historically, South Sudan benefited little from its vast resources. In the mid-nineteenth century, Khartoum financiers made big profits from ivory and slave trading. In the 1870s, governors of the Turkiya's newly created southern provinces sent relatively modest surpluses to bankrupted Cairo. But from the 1880s to 2005, no South Sudanese administration had any surplus whatsoever. The southern provinces were entirely dependent on meagre subventions from Khartoum. That all changed after 2005. Southern Sudan, the political entity established by the 2005 Comprehensive Peace Agreement, had a massive surplus from a huge gross domestic product that was based heavily on its oil industry. In 2008, the World Bank made its first GDP estimate for South Sudan. At over $15 billion, it was larger than Uganda's.[1] But a very large proportion of South Sudan's GDP left the country. In 2010 gross national income (income received by inhabitants) was 64 per cent of GDP (the value of goods

---

1 Figures from databank.worldbank.org/data/views/reports/tableview.aspx, accessed 20 February 2014.

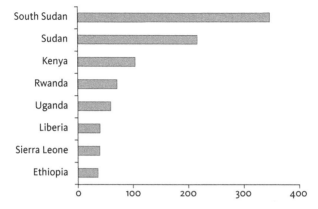

3.1 Government per capita current expenditures (current USD) 2011 or last available year (*source*: World Bank 2013: 1)

and services produced). In nearly every East African economy, GNI and GDP were more or less the same (NBS 2011a). The disparity in South Sudan came about because its oil revenue was shared with Khartoum, and because oil company profits were high. These rates of expatriation of profit are comparable to those in Leopoldean Congo (Rodney 1981: 238). The UN's troop-contributing countries had clearly made a sound investment.

Nonetheless, after 2006 government budgets were huge, outstripping those of more populous and more developed neighbours (Figure 3.1 dramatically illustrates this by comparing per capita government spending). About half the government budget was spent on wages, and about 70 per cent of the military budget went on wages (MOFEP 2011: 8 – an unpublished study found that wages made up an even higher proportion of costs). The first government in Juba to enjoy a surplus distributed a significant proportion of that surplus through a huge payroll. Between 2005 and 2013, the SPLM government in Juba used its payroll to build support in its ten states and to incorporate former adversaries.

Post-2006 national accounts are a remarkable testimony to the short-sightedness of South Sudan's twentieth-century administrators. South Sudan's nineteenth-century history of de-development, constructed around racial oppression, helped to generate an influentially pessimistic twentieth-century literature about South Sudan's development potential. Lazurus Leek Mawut's undeservedly obscure reassessment of the historical constraints on South Sudan's development reviews this literature, enumerating many of the pessimists' claims: South Sudan entered the twentieth century devastated by the slave trade, by inter-ethnic wars and by rinderpest; it was too big, too underpopulated, too hot and wet, too multilingual, too angrily resisting, too diverse to administer; and Britain was in any case a reluctant imperialist, preoccupied by much bigger strategies, and it took on this burdensome territory only to save it for Egypt, or from Belgium, or France, or Ethiopia (Mawut 1995: 2–10).

In contrast, Mawut argues that South Sudan's natural and cultural riches had been extensively mapped in the latter half of the nineteenth century, and offered potential for a more peaceful and fair path to development. But pessimism about development was politically useful, masking the multiple contradictions of economic policies which were developed in imperial capitals or in Khartoum, and which reflected political calculations remote from South Sudanese concerns. Pessimism shaped policy. British administrators began their rule in Sudan with three decades of harsh pacifications. They periodically imposed closed districts, which cut off South Sudan from trade, communications, outside ideas and investment. Post-independence governments maintained and expanded these closed districts. Closed districts were justified in the name of security or 'protection'. They were intensified during crises – the outbreak of Sudanese nationalism and the great depression in the third decade of the twentieth century; the onset of repression that prefigured the first Sudanese civil war in 1961. These deliberate disconnections were evidence that outside forces were indeed reshaping South Sudan in the twentieth century. As in the nineteenth century, outside forces were simultaneously incorporating and marginalizing South Sudan. For most of the nineteenth century, South Sudan was ruled by military expedition and by privateers. In the twentieth century, South Sudan had administrations and budgets. Because avenues to economic development were closed off by closed districts and war, the region's financial resources came from outside. The tiny governing class in South Sudan was directly dependent on Khartoum, and economically autonomous of the productive resources of South Sudanese society. Budgetary information, which dates from the 1860s, is an underused resource for understanding the processes of incorporation, marginalization and dependency. As governments began claiming to represent society, rather than just rule it, their dependency on external resources raised many questions about allocation of state resources which were generated independently of society. Critiques of these historic processes shaped revolutionary theories and also shaped decisions about the allocation of South Sudan's first surpluses, in 2006.

A history of postponed development

Mawut's account of British colonialism carefully lists the reasons which colonialists gave to explain their decision not to invest in development in South Sudan. That is not to say that planning did not happen; on the contrary, development planning in South Sudan began in the nineteenth century. Emin Pasha, the last Turkiya governor of Equatoria, presciently considered bringing Chinese labour to develop its enormous wealth (Emin Pasha 1888: 417). British development planning for South Sudan was among the most advanced in Africa. Mawut's sources, mostly British officials in South Sudan, played no part in that planning, however. It was conducted by imperial strategists in Cairo and London, who viewed South Sudan as a leaky pipeline for Nile waters (about half the White Nile's discharge is lost to evaporation in the Sudd). Planners aimed to reduce evaporation by building a canal across Jonglei, the area to the east of the White Nile. Terje Tvedt argues that the non-implementation of these ambitious plans prevented consideration of more modest alternative developments: ports scheduled for inundation under the canal plans were not improved; roads and railways were not built because the future of waterways was not secure. Even the tribalization schemes of the 1930–46 Southern Policy were implicated in the decision to postpone development: a Jonglei canal would redevelop the entire flood plain unrecognizably, and keeping South Sudanese societies defenceless against such schemes required British planners to oppose the influx of European capital and discourage the formation of cities, or of a class of capitalists with a need for an efficient supra-ethnic state (Tvedt 2004: 157–8, 227).

Changed strategic calculations at the end of empire required the southern provinces to be integrated with northern Sudan, and that integration was hampered by southern underdevelopment. Investigation teams came up with detailed plans for developing communications, cash crops, livestock, mineral resources and of course water resources, with a focus on substituting southern produce for northern exports, thereby promoting the unity of Sudan (SDIT 1955: 176). After Sudan's independence in 1956, Khartoum governments did not implement these plans, but they invested in education projects in South Sudan. On the face of it, this was an appropriate starting point for development: for many years of colonial rule, education policy had aimed at manufacturing ignorance and division in the periphery and manufacturing inequality at the centre. But post-1956, Southern education policy did not address these distortions. Instead, it was preoccupied with a project to coercively incorporate Southern cultures into a unified national identity, based on an idealized version of the Arab and Muslim culture of the economic heartland of the state, which alienated many students (IBRD 1973: 5f.).

Southern politicians who tried and failed to secure federalist arrangements through parliamentary means went into exile after a right-wing military coup in Khartoum; fugitives from the disturbances of the 1950s kept up local acts of resistance; students and junior government personnel joined them as they saw their hopes of getting a post recede; and all these groups coalesced into an armed resistance movement which went through many names and splits but is often called Anya-nya, a name for its armed wing. The movement was not able to negotiate a peace deal with the parliamentary regime that succeeded the dictatorship in 1964/65, and the failure of peace negotiations led to an intensification of war. But when the parliamentary regime, which largely represented the interests of the bureaucratic and commercial elites of the northern Nile valley, fell to a leftist military regime, Khartoum revolutionaries and Southern rebels were both positioned for peace.

The war ended in a 1972 peace deal, organized by a new revolutionary government in Khartoum which sought alliances in Sudan's diverse and impoverished peripheries as a counterweight to the Khartoum elites that it had deposed. It invested in the peripheries too, seeking to reverse the spatial concentration of wealth and development in the northern Nile valley that had been fostered by colonialism. The peace deal established a Southern Regional Government with a parliament and an executive, and with budgets allocated from central revenues, executed by ministers who were themselves Southerners in ministries staffed by Southerners. After the 1972 Addis Ababa peace agreement that ended the civil war in the south, the development plans of the late colonial period were revisited, although development planning was hampered by low resource commitments and even lower execution rates (Yongo-Bure 1989). Development plans were still initiated in Khartoum and Cairo – a significant proportion of development expenditure was allocated to the excavation of the Jonglei canal. After 1974, development planning was further internationalized with the start of oil exploration in Upper Nile: commercial exploitation began four years later, and major decisions about the location of oil infrastructure and with it the spatial distribution of development were announced at the headquarters of the Chevron oil company in California (Alier 2003: 262). These attempts to keep development planning, and development, out of the south accelerated the drift towards a rekindling of civil war. In any case, development planning for the whole of Sudan fell apart as the global financial crisis of the 1970s and 1980s engulfed Khartoum, Sudan and the continent in a long debt crisis. The debt crisis made investment in Sudan's southern and western peripheries unrealizable, and disinvestment from the periphery set it on course for a long war with Sudan's centre, which is still being fought in places like Darfur and South Kordofan.

Underdevelopment and the economic autonomy of the state

A consequence of South Sudan's twentieth-century under-development was the economic dependence of the state on external resources, and economic autonomy vis-à-vis the productive capacities of southern society. Nineteenth-century exploiters of the south yielded a profit, but for the entire twentieth century governments ran the southern provinces of Sudan at a loss. Local revenues often covered no more than 10 or 15 per cent of expenditures, and state accountability was accordingly directed outwards towards the source of its funding. The state's economic autonomy had powerful consequences for the state's ability to wield its violence against society – a Nuer saying describes the government as 'a group of people who have decided to come together to eat people'. But it also affected expectations of state patronage, in a situation where South Sudanese constituencies could exert relatively little economic pressure on the state. A Dinka saying describes government services as the 'things of the Creator' – because the government's blessings are so mysteriously bestowed (Howell et al. 1988: 275). As the century progressed, popular expectations of these blessings hardened into demands from liberation movements for a share of those blessings. Some-times, this was a demand for fair allocations of state patronage;

and sometimes this was a wider demand for a developmental state – a state of hospitals and schools and five-year plans. Autonomy worked both ways – South Sudan is still a country full of remoteness, and people living far away from centres of state power can still live independently of state resources and power, their economic lives unintelligible to statisticians.

The changing basis of the state's economic autonomy from society

The state's economic autonomy has lasted into the twenty-first century, although the scope and basis of that autonomy have changed. During the twentieth century, state activities in South Sudan were mostly financed by parsimonious subventions and grants from central governments in Khartoum. Since 2005, state activities have been financed by revenue from South Sudanese oil, but because South Sudan still shares its oil infrastructure with Sudan, revenue comes through Khartoum ministries to Juba ones. The oil economy lies outside the influence of South Sudanese economic actors, just as the subventions economy once did, and it has therefore maintained the state's economic autonomy vis-à-vis society. From the 2005 establishment of the Government of Southern Sudan until 2012, when the new Republic of South Sudan shut down its oil infrastructure during negotiations on oil transit fees and linked economic and border issues, over 95 per cent of government revenues came from oil. South Sudanese economic actors of today cannot influence the oil economy any more than past economic actors could influence the subventions economy: oil dependence prolonged economic autonomy of the state vis-à-vis society.

Colonial budgets

The economic autonomy of successive governments operating in South Sudan contrasts strikingly with that of its neighbours. Most African colonies were acquired swiftly after the 1885

Berlin conference that began the scramble for Africa, and by the second decade of the twentieth century, Sudan and all but one of the neighbouring French, British and Belgian possessions were paying the costs of their own administration and generating a surplus (Suret-Canale 1971: 342; Gardner 2012: 32; Gardner 2013). Even the tax system of the Ethiopian state had penetrated its agrarian economy as far as its southern and south-western hinterlands, on the borders with South Sudan, which were incorporated only in the late nineteenth century (Pankhurst 1967). Sudan's revenues exceeded expenditure for the first time in 1913 (Daly 1986: 458).

Before 1850, South Sudan was 'administered' by seasonal slave raids and ivory trade missions organized by the Turkiya government, which yielded meagre profits. The private slavery entrepreneurs who ran many areas of Bahr al-Ghazal and Equatoria from the 1850s until the 1870s made rich profits for their Khartoum financiers (Hill 1959: 63; Gray 1961: 50). The first Turkiya *muhafiza* or administrative district was established at Fashoda in 1855, and administration was then extended southwards in the 1860s and 1870s. Its formal objective was to end the slave trade, and in 1874 the newly created southern provinces were made a closed district, and all kinds of trade were discouraged (Hill 1959: 145, 154; Mawut 1995: 21). In spite of active discouragement of trade, individual governors were sometimes able to generate a surplus. Romolo Gessi, the Turkiya governor of Bahr al-Ghazal between 1878 and 1880, covered all his expenses from ivory and rubber sales. He promoted copper and iron working; experimented with rice, sugar, timber, cotton and cloth production; and opened a school for the sons of chiefs from where he expected to draw his clerks (Emin Pasha 1888: 269, 421, 424; Mawut 1995: 25). Gessi and Emin Pasha, the governor of Equatoria, led the only governments in the history of South Sudan that were able to finance administration from local development and even send a minor surplus to Khartoum. But the economic dominance of state's geographical centre was already established: Sudan's finances depended on revenues from the northern Nile valley, Kordofan and the east (Giegler Pasha 1984: Map 2).

The Mahdist state exercised relatively little control over South Sudan and budgetary information on South Sudan in the period awaits research. South Sudan had some kind of surplus, though: farmers in the Shilluk areas of the White Nile sold surplus grain to Khartoum (Ohrwalder 1892: 285). But as the famines worsened in the 1890s, Khartoum replaced this market with armed raids against cultivators in the upper White Nile and Sobat (Johnson 1993: 46). These coercive policies of surplus expropriation continued under early twentieth-century British administrators. But British colonialists could barely meet the costs of subjugation, sometimes postponing their campaigns against local people because of lack of resources: revenue never matched administrative expenditures (Badal 1977: 26). Administration was paid for by development activity in the northern Nile valley, the monetized zone that had become the state's heartland. There, the colonial government used slave labour to revive the grain surplus and then used international finance and wage labour to set up commercial cotton cultivation (Sikainga 1996: 43; Serels 2012: 243ff.).

The debt-financed cotton export economy around Khartoum was a mainstay of government revenue. It paid the costs of pacification and administration in South Sudan and it drew the whole of Sudan deeper into the global financial system. In 1930, when pacification belatedly ended in the south, the possibility for southern development re-emerged, but these plans were shelved after returns from the indebted cotton sector contracted sharply in the global financial crisis of 1929. Austerity measures ensured that Sudan as a whole still produced a surplus, but the administration of the southern provinces still operated at a loss. There was no money to invest in southern development, and in any case the government decided to repress economic development in the non-monetized, peripheral areas of Sudan, fearing that development might lead to uncontainable nationalist sentiment. The Southern Policy was instituted in 1930 and lasted until 1946; it was the culmination of a series of measures aimed at closing off the South and other peripheral areas to trade and influence from the country's economic centre and dividing southern societies, in the words of an influential memorandum, into 'self-contained racial and tribal units'.

The Southern deficit outlived the 1930–46 Southern Policy. For the rest of the twentieth century, available information suggests that the economic autonomy of the state, expressed as the gap between revenue and expenditure, remained constant. In 1951/52, when the colonial government promoted the development of the south for the first time, revenues were estimated to make up about 14 per cent of total expenditures (SDIT 1955: 31). In 1961/62, the south was on the brink of war, and budgets had shrunk: revenues amounted to about 11 per cent of expenditures (IBRD 1973: 5). After the 1972 Addis Ababa peace agreement, development expenditures increased, but overall dependence on external resources was constant (Rondinelli 1981: 620). A 1981 study found that tax revenue as a percentage of total government revenue in South Sudan was about 15 per cent in 1975/76, as compared to 75 per cent in Kenya, 82 per cent in Zaire, 87 per cent in Ethiopia and 89 per cent in Uganda (Tvedt 1994: 79). By this time, Khartoum governments were deliberately maintaining Southern revenues at a low level. Khartoum politicians were reluctant to support oil exploration in South Sudan, fearing that it might encourage separatism there. The Addis Ababa agreement gave the Southern Regional Government control over taxes on Southern production and profits, and according to Abel Alier, Khartoum governments fiddled boundaries, peace agreements and production systems to ensure that those revenues would not come under regional control (Alier 2003: 263–4). These machinations were a factor in the political breakdown that led to civil war in

1983, and shaped negotiations on wealth-sharing in the 2005 Comprehensive Peace Agreement.

Dilemmas of allocation and representation

The state's economic autonomy vis-à-vis society has shaped many of the choices of rulers and ruled. It exacerbated the dilemmas of allocation and distribution faced by governing elites – how should they plan development, when plans meant choosing the social groups or geographic regions that were to benefit from the wealth which they had amassed independently of local productive efforts? It also created dilemmas of representation for everyone else. How could people from one community, or economic sector, or geographical region, persuade the economically autonomous government to direct allocations towards them? How could these constituencies of people, with almost no ability to exert economic pressure on the government, make their case for allocation seem more plausible than those of other constituencies? Analysis of twentieth-century budgets suggests that the most reliable way to attract government resources was to obtain a government post: up to 96 per cent of expenditures went on government salaries and wages.

There was little planned development in South Sudan in the second half of the twentieth century, and South Sudanese with modern educations could not hope to use their capabilities in modern productive sectors. Instead, they looked to employment in state bureaucracies. Sudan's first general elections in 1953 came three years before independence. In 1954, the government established two commissions to 'Sudanize' administration – that is, to allocate government jobs previously held by foreign colonial officers to Sudanese citizens. At the time, Southerners held few government posts. The Southern Corps of the army employed about a thousand men; government offices had a few Southern clerks and messengers. Government posts for Southerners were seen as a precondition for long overdue development. Post allocations to Southerners were central to party electioneering, and to the closely linked Egyptian campaign for the unification of Egypt and Sudan. Southerners were offered only six of the 800 posts to be filled and their disillusionment and anger were palpable in Southern manifestos and position statements for decades to come (Ruay 1994: 70ff.; Wawa 2008).

Post allocation and patronage

Most South Sudanese politicians wanted the administration in South Sudan to be largely in the hands of Southerners. But after independence, the Khartoum government replaced Southern administrators in South Sudan with Northern officials – many Southern administrators went into exile. The policy of 'Northernizing' Southern administration began in 1955, and the insensitivity of its execution led to mutinies, strikes and urban violence which set the stage for Sudan's first civil war, in the early 1960s. The 1972 Addis Ababa peace deal that ended the war set up a Southern Regional Government, led and staffed by Southerners, which expanded government employment. In 1973 the public service establishment of the new Southern Region was 284 administrative and professional personnel, 383 sub-professional and technical personnel and 384 clerical personnel. An estimated twenty thousand additional classified posts were to be filled by former Anya-nya personnel (IBRD 1973: 7). Expenditure on wages and salaries was estimated to absorb about 70 per cent of recurrent expenditures in the 1973 budget (ibid.: 57–8). Wage and salary costs in the national budget were also increasing, as the government began employing the increasing number of graduates that their education system was producing (IBRD 1969: Table 22). But wages made up a much smaller proportion of the national budget: in 1967/68, they amounted to only 38 per cent of recurrent expenditure (ibid.: 26–7). Sudan's route to development was being built around government employment, but this was starker in the south. There, patronage was made explicit in proposed premium pay rates for former Anya-nya personnel (IBRD 1973: 58). Anya-nya personnel benefited little from these plans: over thirty thousand were laid off two years after the signing of the peace agreement (Akuany 1990: 407). Central government failed to finance budgets as its own financial situation deteriorated during the 1970s, and the Southern Regional Government failed to execute them. Nonetheless, the budgets set precedents and expectations for the state's relationship with society.

The emergence of 'minorities'

Sudan achieved political independence in 1956. Post-independence governments were led by the nationalist movement in Khartoum, dominated by the bureaucratic and commercial beneficiaries of the cotton export economy that Britain had established around Sudan's capital. They inherited the state from Sudan's co-domini without a fight: they did not need to build a mass movement that might have worked through some of Sudan's contradictions. Instead, they needed only to play on Anglo-Egyptian rivalries, and the state would fall into their laps. They rejected the possibility of investing in the periphery to correct the regional imbalances that the cotton economy had created, leaving that task to 'market forces' (Khalid 1990: 152). Nonetheless, the notion of popular sovereignty changed expectations of the state across many social groups in the periphery. The state was now supposed to represent people, and when building constituencies to contest the fairness of that representation, or to claim a share in the state's resources, political leaders often fell back on the social differences on which colonialism had built its rule (White 2011). Sudan's twentieth century is so complex because colonial states cut social difference from more than one cloth. The nineteenth-century slave trade had used religiously coloured notions of race to create a Sudan with a monetized, Islamically administered centre dependent for labour on a violent slave-catchment zone in its southern periphery. Twentieth-century colonialists maintained north and south as distinct economic zones. But instead of being governed by slave armies, they were governed indirectly, by the refashioning of ethnic communities into self-contained tribal units, whose collective responsibility for taxation and social services was enforced by government-appointed chiefs with armed police.

These chiefs were not, for the most part, *traditional* authorities: not the persuaders, mediators and nature experts who shared the leadership of South Sudan's many democratic societies. Rather, they were neo-traditional chiefs, given police and guns to implement a coercive economic policy: forced labour, forced villagization and compulsory crops. Colonialists were not in-clined to develop a money economy that would integrate South Sudan into the system of rents, debts and wages of the monetized northern zone. Instead, economic policy was built on the notion of the 'tribe'. Access to land and productive resources was on the basis of notions of kinship. Taxation and labour systems pushed people into identification with tribes, which were built on notions of kinship, and the state made a role for itself in policing intercommunal boundaries, which at the time marked the extent of government-appointed chiefs' powers to compel labour or tribute. Outside a few small urban areas, tax was levied in kind and communally (SDIT 1955: 30). Even taxpayers found this identification of individual and group liability surprising – in 1939 administrators recorded the views of Dinka chiefs as follows:

The suggestion that Government tax should be communal and not individual seemed to them ridiculous. When asked why, if the clan was willing to protect a cattleless member who had killed another by payment of blood cattle [in compensation for crimes or injuries], should not the rich assist the poor in the matter of taxation, the unanimous reply was that such assis-tance was only given for the good of the clan … The payment of Government taxes however benefited nobody but the Government and was therefore a matter between the Government and the individual. They argued that the communal payment of cattle was an indigenous system of insurance evolved by their forefathers. (Lienhardt 1982: 29)

British colonialists sought to provide conditions for capitalist production to develop in the central heartlands of Sudan, but pursued a neo-primordialist economic policy in the south that baffled taxpayers. The method of governance was chosen, in part, because it would repress the development of representative bodies in South Sudan. But in the 1950s, when South Sudan began to be unified with the north, the question of representation became a possibility. Assemblies of chiefs petitioned Khartoum ministries for the appointment of Southern bureaucrats and ministers. In 1954, the decision of the Sudanization committees led politicians and chiefs to write a letter of complaint:

> SUDANIZATION. We were promised that southerners would be promoted in the Police, Administration, S.D.F. [Sudan Defence Force] and any other department where there are qualified southerners, but the result of the Sudanization is MOST DISAPPOINTING. (1954 petition to the Council of Ministers, quoted in Wawa 2008: 111)

Thus wrote the chiefs of Gogrial District (in present-day Warrap state) to the Khartoum Council of Ministers in 1954, copying the British foreign ministry and the president of Egypt. Chiefs who called for these appointments emphasized their role as representatives of wider groups, signing memoranda to the government as follows: 'Ch. GIR THIIK of Apuk [Dinka] section representing 55.000 people'. Although they described themselves as sectional, or 'tribal', representatives, their demands were nationalist, and addressed to international audiences.

The Southern Regional Government, which came into being about two decades after Chief Gir Thiik and his fellow-chiefs wrote their petition, shifted the nature of popular sovereignty in South Sudan and with it notions of representation. Rather than calling for adequate representation of Southerners in a system racially constructed against them, people began to aggregate and articulate local interests. The 'local' in South Sudan had been constructed around ethnicity. People began to call for representation on the basis of sectional groupings or ethno-linguistic communities – the tribes of the colonial era. In 1974, the Southern Regional Government set up a committee to look into the redivision of South Sudan's three enormous provinces (Upper Nile, Bahr al-Ghazal and Equatoria) to allow for the government to bring services closer to people.[2] In many places visited by the committee – particularly in present-day Jonglei, then a part of the vast and largely inaccessible Upper Nile province – the committee's interlocutors mostly focused dispassionately on the economic viability of new administrative units. But the committee was alert to the risks of ethnic fragmentation and the need to protect 'minorities' from larger groups. Some of these minorities sought to align administrative boundaries with ethnic groups:

> There is an influential stream of thinking that we should not encourage ethnic grouping by considering the demands of ethnic groups to have separate provinces ... They think that such an attempt will work against Regional [Southern] unity as well as that of the whole country and that the May Revolution seeks to discourage ethnic and regional fragmentation. (CRSP c. 1975: 46)

Less than a decade later, dozens of people died in the small Jonglei town of Akobo, in disturbances linked to questions of

---

2 The committee established in 1974 created new administrative subdivisions within the three provinces of the newly unified Southern Region. It had no relevance to the debate in the early 1980s that led to the abolition of the Southern Region and the reversion to the three colonial-era provinces of Bahr al-Ghazal, Upper Nile and Equatoria.

boundaries and ethnicity (see Chapter 5). The question of representation was getting enmeshed in questions of ethnicity there and in other areas of greater Upper Nile. Secondary schools were another arena for these questions to emerge – in the days when Chief Gir Thiik was petitioning the cabinet, there were only two secondary schools in the south, but school building and enrolment increased thereafter. Before the Addis Ababa peace agreement, schools never witnessed ethnic conflicts. But in 1978, schools in many parts of Upper Nile were riven by conflicts between Dinka and Shilluk, for example; or Nilotic and Equatorian groups. A committee of investigation attributed the disturbances to the discontent of losing candidates in the elections (Arou 1989).

The Southern Regional Government included a regional assembly and a cabinet which had a fairly good record on ethnic inclusion, and men from each of the three main provinces and from major ethno-linguistic groups successively held the government's top post, the presidency of the Higher Executive Council. But in seeking to create a political system for a unified southern territory, the government opened up the question of representation. Government activity did not go far beyond the payroll and the delineation of administrative boundaries; it was not able to create new economic sectors and interests that might have implied new structures for representation. Administrative boundaries had never before implied access to state resources. One local administrative officer in Jonglei state whose career began in this period pointed out that the alignment of these boundaries with ethnicity harked back to the time when colonial government used chiefly intermediaries to mobilize forced labour for road clearance: 'The borders were those of chiefs when they cleaned the roads ... It wasn't to impress tribalism, it was about roads ... Is it now a problem?' (interview 106/2012).

Post allocation and ethnic boundaries became much more important as the global financial crisis of the 1970s and 1980s ended the Khartoum revolutionary regime's experiment in representative government and socio-economic development in the peripheries. When the crisis broke, Sudan and other African countries sought to shore up their modernization schemes with debt finance, not realizing that modernization itself had changed for good. In their first major post-crisis report on Sudan, World Bank economists set out the new orthodoxy with some asperity:

> Economic mismanagement since the early 1970s has left Sudan with a declining economy and severe structural problems. Unfortunately the root causes of the decline have not been eliminated. These root causes are a pervasive lack of financial discipline in the public sector combined with a deep seated belief by Government and public alike that the Government can and should improve overall welfare by direct interventions in the markets and productive sectors of the economy. (World Bank 1987: 1)

The notion that states should refrain from intervention has only recently been discarded, and in the early 1980s it brought bread riots to the national capital and forced Khartoum governments to divest rapidly from the periphery. Jaafer Nimeiri, the president who had initiated the peace deal in Addis Ababa, partly as a means to use southern support to buttress his position in the north, now needed to reshuffle domestic alliances. He shifted from his southern constituency to a new and well-endowed Islamist one in the north, and managed the resulting southern protests by fostering social divisions there.

'Minority' is a useful word for ordinary people in debates around national identity and representation. It can be even more useful for governments deciding how to allocate the pain of a financial crisis, as they did in the 1980s. In welfare states, governments began constructing 'vulnerable' minorities as a means of rationing formally universal social services. In developmental states, like Sudan, governments fomented antagonisms between different groups, and the notion of 'minority' and 'majority' played an important role. When the Khartoum government decided to end its experiment in Southern autonomy, in order to build new alliances at the centre, it began by turning South Sudan into minorities and a Dinka plurality. The government organized minorities to call for a redivision of the unified Southern Region into three.

Social divisions were played out in a debate about 'Dinka domination' that pitted the region's most prominent Dinka politician, Abel Alier, against its most prominent Equatorian one, Joseph Lagu (Alier 2003; Johnson 2003; Lagu 2006). Dinka people were dominant in the sense that Dinka language-speakers, if aggregated into a single ethnic community, would make up the largest such group in the south. There were no historical grounds to believe that Dinka people could be aggregated into a unified political constituency. But the emergence of a representative Southern political order had opened up the question of the construction of majorities, pluralities, minorities and the fair allocation of government resources. In adversity, the government could use these constructs against people.

The main resource that the government had to offer was the salaried post. This period saw the emergence of a Sudanese pamphleteering genre that presented tables showing the under-representation of particular ethnic communities in cabinets or bureaucracies. The genre was taken up by other peripheral insurgents – one appeared just before several decades of insecurity in Darfur turned to outright rebellion (Seekers of Truth and Justice 2004). In the South, one of these pamphlets was also a portent of war: 'Decentralization: a necessity for the Southern Provinces of the Sudan' was written by Joseph Lagu and included a table entitled 'Number of Dinka and non-Dinka who hold senior posts in the region' (quoted in Ali 1987: 236). In a thoughtful response to Lagu's pamphlet, a group of national parliamentarians calling themselves the Solidarity Committee of the Southern Members of the Fourth People's National Assembly acknowledged that non-Dinka perceptions about Dinka over-representation might have some basis, but stressed that economic, not tribal, differences were at the root of the South's problems.

> Everybody looks upon the government as the sole source of redemption from these evils. Every tribe therefore fights to attain a place in the High Executive Council to earn services should its son become a minister. It is this that caused this row against the Dinka. But under Abel [Alier] and Lagu neither Bor [Alier's home town] nor Nimule [Lagu's home town] has turned into paradise. (Quoted in Wawa 2008: 308)

Southern politicians and, even more importantly, ex-politicians played an important role in fomenting division, in part because it offered new opportunities for posts. Their tribalist demands were a striking counterpoint to the proto-nationalist petitions for southern posts submitted by chiefs in the 1950s. In the view of the Solidarity Committee, the remedy for tribalism lies in 'sitting together and working out acceptable guidelines and laws protecting minority rights' (quoted in ibid.: 302). Redivision went ahead without this dialogue about the meaning of representation and minorities. Redivision required an unconstitutional abrogation of the Addis Ababa agreement, taking the south back to war (Alier 2003: 269).

Government posts and the drift towards war

Once again, a Khartoum government deployed tribalism to address a crisis in the state that was enmeshed in a global financial crisis. As the southern provinces of Sudan drifted back to war in 1983, Kunijwok Gwado Ayoker, a political scientist from Khartoum University, wrote an angry reflection on the way that the creation of a Southern salariat had frustrated the liberation of the south:

> There was no real power (economic, political, cultural or social) delegated to the supposedly autonomous government of

black people. What seems to have happened is that a new way has been opened for any politically conscious Black to enter and to become economically Awalad [boys, or houseboys, an Arabic term that in northern Sudan connotes slavery] of some established military, political, business or any other national interests in the North. Once inside the state's superstructure of power circles, the individual black person is systematically made to lose their basic freedoms ... The salary (which is paid to employees in state business, even if the latter evidently do nothing that may be called economically productive) is therefore an insurance policy against freedom of speech and thought: the good walad [boy/houseboy, singular] is a silent and obedient black man ... Almost all Black elites in the Southern Sudan ... are tied down to the salary system as members of the High Executive Council, Member of Parliament, members of the Sudanese Socialist Union or as regular service officials, clerks. (Ayoker 1983: 26–7)

The 'economic autonomy' of the Southern Regional Government – the fact that its budgets were not financed from revenue generated by the productive capacities of South Sudanese society – meant that underdevelopment continued in South Sudan, as did its economic dependence on Khartoum. Khartoum duly transmitted the pain of its debt crisis southwards.

Although many retrospective judgements of the Southern Regional Government dwell on its failures, it was not without successes. In the aftermath of the peace agreement, a million refugees resettled in South Sudan, and school enrolment increased dramatically. Elections were held, and the standards of political debate in the Juba regional assembly compared favourably with those of the obsequious national assembly in Khartoum. But many negative evaluations of the regional government stress the fact that major schemes were not implemented, or were insensitively transferred to the north for implementation. The development schemes of the period, for sugar, tea, tobacco or

Irish potatoes, had been originally proposed by the Southern Development Investigation Team (SDIT 1955) – at the demise of the Southern Regional Government some thirty years after the report was written, a gloomy political scientist described them as 'the Bible of unrealised Development prophecies for Sudan' (Ayoker 1983: 16). The government had some success with less conspicuous projects such as rural water supply and refugee resettlement, but many South Sudanese retrospective evaluations of the period stress the unbuilt factories that might have demonstrated the transformative power of state-led development a bit more theatrically (Yongo-Bure 1989; Nyaba 1997; Malok 2009). This points to one achievement of the regional government – it succeeded in spreading faith in the potential of the developmental state, and the hope of representation in it. The failure of developmentalism was often attributed to Khartoum governments, even though the developmental state in Africa was being dismantled by the same forces dismantling the welfare state in Europe at the time (Mkandawire 2001). But this hope in the state's capacity to change society nonetheless survived the demise of the regional government.

The Southern Regional Government's experiment in representative government revealed many of the dilemmas of political liberation combined with economic dependency. These dilemmas made the task of liberation movements more complicated. They had to mobilize a rapidly changing society internally structured around ethnicity. They sought political participation in a Sudanese state that was constructed around the racism of the colonial era, but they were not able to address the economic basis of that racism – the concentration of resources at the centre of the Sudanese state. They had almost no economic pressure which they could bring to bear on the central state, other than starting a war that might make the untapped resources of South Sudan unexploitable.

This chapter has looked primarily at the way that twentieth-century budgets set patterns for development and representative government until 1983, which saw the demise of the Southern Regional Government and the SPLA's rebellion against Khartoum. These patterns have persisted. Abraham Matoc Dhal's study of local government financing in Southern Sudan in the 1980s after the demise of the Southern Regional Government shows that dependence on central government transfers was maintained during wartime, as was the overwhelming importance of the payroll (Dhal 2002). A 2003 study, covering only Western Equatoria state, indicated that locally generated revenue was negligible, ranging from 0 to 2 per cent of expenditures in the period from 1996 to 2001 (World Bank 2003: vol. 2, 71).[3] And a recent study from the International Monetary Fund, which reviewed the Sudanese experience of fiscal decentralization in the twenty-first century, found that the peripheral dependency on the centre was increasing and states' ability to generate revenue was decreasing, for reasons that appear to be self-perpetuating: lack of infrastructure and staff; insecurity; depressed economic activity; a weak private sector (IMF 2012: 60).

The next chapter looks at the way that centralization, dependency and patronage politics shaped the SPLA/M's revolutionary thinking in Sudan at the end of the Addis Ababa period. The SPLA/M's manifesto angrily (and sometimes carelessly) denounced the mechanisms of dependency in which Southern elites had got themselves entrammelled. Chapter 5 looks at the SPLM's inability to change these resilient and dysfunctional fiscal and administrative systems when they inherited power.

---

3 Figures in this paragraph are taken from cited reports which listed province- or state-level revenues and expenditures, a practice not observed in every budget or financial report. They are not strictly comparable: some do not include expenditure from central ministry budgets and some probably do.

4 | THEORIES OF REVOLUTION

Understanding South Sudan's path to development

South Sudan's jagged path to development is difficult to summarize. The south was dramatically exposed to global forces much earlier than other parts of the African interior. The deepening penetration of the Egyptian economy by the international trade system set the scope and pace for economic change in South Sudan. Signals from international capital were transmitted rapidly to South Sudan. But they were garbled in the process: agreements to end Egyptian monopolies and liberate international capital led to a debt-financing system for the slave trade that dramatically expanded it. By the end of the nineteenth century, much of the production of northern Sudan was carried out by slaves, and up to a third of its population was enslaved. Before its second, Anglo-Egyptian (or British) colonial era began, it came under the partial control of the proto-national Mahdist state that was supposed to be the midwife for the Day of Judgement, but in fact became the midwife for a gigantic, racially bifurcated twentieth-century state. It provided a prototype for Sudanese revolt that was much emulated but never repeated – the Mahdi rallied a military coalition from a chaotically violent periphery to take control of the centre, which had enriched itself from the divisions it had foisted on the periphery.

For most of the British period, South Sudan was a closed district – not a reservoir of labour, like the districts controlled by pass laws in South Africa or Kenya, but a watery reservoir of imperial pressure on the Egyptian government. Its people were boxed up into tribes in order to retard their political consciousness and make them the poorest, most underdeveloped and diverse periphery of Khartoum. After independence, 'development' worked against people: southern development was concentrated in the education sector. But education became a form of cultural warfare waged against the south, an attempt to impose an idealized version of Arab and Muslim culture on a diverse and culturally confident group of peoples. It was the kind of education that acted as a prelude to a decade of closed districts and civil war. The alternation of war and closure, of crisis and neglect, is a well-established feature of global peripheries and it became South Sudan's experience.

That alternation happened spatially as well as temporally – some areas were permanently in crisis and others were inaccessible and forgotten. Post-independence wars ensured money flowed around garrison towns, which drew in new populations; but towns would empty after massacres or sieges. But outside the garrisons, governments were unable to refashion land and labour systems into an economy of money, wages, rents and debt that would allow a government to finance itself or penetrate society.

The inability to monetize the economy lasted into peacetime. The 1972 peace deal that ended the war began an unprecedented experiment in representative government, but did not change the economic basis of government in South Sudan, which relied for its revenues on externally generated resources that flowed through global systems of credit and debt. When the global system faced crisis in the 1980s, Khartoum governments refinanced themselves through Islamic banks that were able to attract Gulf capital. They emphatically asserted Sudan's religious differences, which had been deeply coloured by the nineteenth-century construction of racism, and retribalized the south.

South Sudan's experience of states and markets is difficult to decode. Samir Amin (1972) proposed an influential typology of colonial economic systems: the colonial trade economy (such as the West African export economies or the big cotton estates of the northern Nile valley); the colonial concessions (areas administered by commercial entities, such as French Equatorial Africa); the labour reserves (such as the closed districts surrounding the settler economies of East and southern Africa). South Sudan's historical experience does not quite fit with any of these types, although it echoes all of them. For theorists of revolution, this concatenation presented diagnostic and prognostic challenges.

Anya-nya's aims

During the first civil war, southern liberation movements emerged in exile after a long period in insecurity and parliamentarianism that failed to address the questions of representation and development. Their spokespersons produced a succession of memorandums that were often prepared for specific audiences, such as the Organization of African Unity. They borrowed from the ideas of other African liberation movements: 'Negritude and Progress' was the slogan of the *Voice of Southern Sudan*, the London newsletter of the Sudan African National Union, a leading South Sudan opposition party. These groups represented the army's presence in South Sudan as an example of Arab settler colonialism (Oduho and Deng 1963). Using what Joseph Ukel Garang (1971) described as a 'racial thesis' of Afro-Arab irreconcilability, they called for Southern separation, rather than a transformation of relationships between different Sudanese people.

Anya-nya and the communist movement

Joseph Ukel Garang was an orthodox Marxist-Leninist and the leading southerner in the Sudanese Communist Party. Like his party, he believed that South Sudan's best chance lay in an alliance with the forces of progress, which lay in the developed centre of Sudan. His most-quoted work, *The Dilemma of the Southern Intellectual*, sets out a periodization of African liberation that reflected the communist mainstream of the time. The slave trade had been smashed by British capitalism. British colonialism had fallen to a national bourgeois liberation movement. The national bourgeoisie sought to exploit the underdeveloped south and the northern worker, just as the British colonialists did, but it was a weak social force, constantly squeezed out of its profits by imperialism. Southern liberation should not aim at getting rid of the national bourgeoisie – the 'Arabs' – but at getting rid of imperialism. And the only way of doing so was by an alliance with the most progressive social force in the country. That was the northern proletariat – the waged railway and factory workers of the towns of the northern Nile valley. The mistake of many Southern intellectuals, he argued, was to think that the south could ally with imperialism to win its own liberation: 'If the South were to separate today, then tomorrow it would be an imperialist colony' (ibid.).

Joseph Ukel Garang followed the party into an alliance with Nimeiri and was executed after an attempted communist coup in 1971. The party had not followed its own advice: rather than building a movement for national liberation it had taken advantage of an army coup and died by the sword. The Anya-nya movement, in contrast to the communists, was able to prevail, forcing the north into an unprecedented set of concessions to Sudan's poorest periphery. Its analysis was not based on Joseph Ukel Garang's programmatic view of history so much as its ability to mobilize from the southern populace 'its hatred and its spirit of sacrifice, for both are nourished by the image of enslaved ancestors rather than that of liberated grandchildren' – to quote a famous aphorism from the German critic Walter Benjamin (1968: 260). But in the Addis Ababa agreement, the Anya-nya chose an alliance with Nimeiri, who saw in the south a counterweight to the traditional forces that his revolution had overthrown. He promised the south the agreement's mix of concessions on development and representation. The success of development thus depended on the alliance with Khartoum: Anya-nya did not build up a social or economic alternative to alliance with Khartoum, only a military and administrative one.

The rapid formulation of the SPLM/A's objectives

In contrast to Anya-nya, the SPLM/A was quick to articulate its political objective. The SPLM/A manifesto appeared in July 1983, within a few months of the mutinies in Jonglei state that began the war – a sharp contrast to the experience of the first civil war, which took almost a decade to switch from localized mutinies and resistance to a war with defined political objectives.

The immediate cause of the 1983 mutinies was the Khartoum government's military preparations for the abrogation of the 1972 Addis Ababa agreement and the abolition of the Southern Regional Government it had established. The wider context for the mutinies was the global economic crisis of the late 1970s, which marked an end to the long boom that followed the Second World War. Khartoum's repudiation of the 1972 peace deal was part of a reshuffling of domestic alliances in response to a global economic crisis for which Sudan was ineptly positioned (Thomas 2010: 109ff.). Before abolishing the Juba government, Khartoum needed to rework its military position in South Sudan. About six thousand former Anya-nya rebels had been absorbed into the Southern Command of the Sudanese Armed Forces, and Khartoum now wanted to move the absorbed forces out of the south (SPLM 1983: 14). The 1983 manifesto was written by members of the Southern Command, and recounted these changes bitterly. But it was much more than a mutineers' list of grievances. And it derided the Southern Regional Government and the Anya-nya movement that had helped establish it and whose elite (said the manifesto) had become the regional government's principal beneficiary.

The manifesto was an ambitious attempt to reframe the problem of South Sudan away from the historical Arab–African cultural divide, which preoccupied much of the written propaganda of the Anya-nya movement, to an analysis that linked South Sudan's underdevelopment to the colonial development of northern Sudan and oriented it towards a future unified socialist Sudan, rather than an independent South. Instead of promoting Southern independence from Khartoum's 'settler colonialism', the SPLM argued for all-Sudan transformation. In part, this was a pragmatic decision. Anya-nya separatism emerged at an untimely moment when the Organization of African Unity had embraced the principles of territorial integrity and state sovereignty and with it the borders which colonialists had drawn across the continent. The SPLM could not promote separatism and maintain alliances with neighbouring states that had their own separatist movements, such as Ethiopia and Kenya. Commitment to state transformation rather than southern separation was an absolute precondition of Ethiopian support.

Ethiopian support meant that the rebels could fight a conventional war, rather than a long guerrilla war. The rebellion started near the Ethiopian border and soon slotted itself into the proxy war between Ethiopia and Sudan. The manifesto certainly shows the influence of the militarist and centralist orientation of Ethiopian socialism – its main strategy is to make the Sudan People's Liberation Army (SPLA) into a 'conventional force that will be able to destroy Sudan's reactionary army' (ibid.: 18). Most of its short chapters are taken up with the histories of military and political organization in South Sudan: one chapter unwisely entitled 'Real and potential enemies of the SPLA/SPLM' takes a paranoid swipe at Sudanese elites, African and Arab reactionary countries and imperialism. The document has more to say about enemies than about South Sudanese people or the possibility of transforming Southern society through armed struggle. Instead, it sees territory as the subject of liberation and people as its instrument: 'Politicization, organization and militarization of the peasantry shall follow as areas become liberated.' The manifesto aimed to create from this militarized 'peasantry' a conventional army that would fight from the country's least-developed periphery to transform its centre (ibid.: 28).

Conventional war

But the SPLM/A operated in a very different social terrain to that of its Ethiopian sponsors, who were able to address the interests of Ethiopian people directly through reform of feudal land tenure (Markakis 1979; Clapham 1989). The manifesto's commitment to territorial control through conventional warfare was made good in the conflict that followed. Liberated territory was not used as a base to set up an alternative version of Sudan. The SPLM/A succeeded in a very rapid conventionalization of the war, mobilizing and deploying huge armies against Khartoum and capturing most South Sudanese territory in a few short years. It succeeded in postponing development of the south's vast natural resources in the absence of a political settlement in the south – its attacks on the giant excavator digging the canal in Jonglei and the Upper Nile oilfields were intended for economic effect. But its conventional war strategy meant that it neglected the social and economic functions of a liberation movement (Nyaba 1997: 54–60). Instead, the SPLA sometimes functioned as a conservative force, maintaining the system of chiefly administration, customary law and communal rights in land that drew heavily on British colonial administrative rules (Kuol 1997). It harnessed local grievances against cultural and economic attack from Khartoum (Johnson 1998: 71). Its transformations of social and economic relations were bound up with its conventional war strategy and its need for provisions. Like Anya-nya, the SPLA often relied for provisioning on local populations. Under Anya-nya, rebels had no alternative to local food, and they developed compulsory food cultivation systems that taxed local labour, and other systems to avoid food confiscations, which had undermined relationships between the rebels and the local population (Ga'le 2002: 47f.; McColl 1969: 10; Wakoson 1984: 164). The SPLA, in contrast, was able to use foreign aid destined for refugees and for the civilian population. In the civil war that followed the 1983 mutiny and manifesto, control over relief supplies was a central aim of the

SPLA and factions which broke off from it. The SPLA's military centralism was supposed to have helped it avoid factionalization: it did not. But the rebels' ability to influence access to foreign food allowed it some autonomy vis-à-vis local populations. This autonomy estranged the movement from many local communities: like the Sudanese army, the SPLA would attack subsistence resources and basic infrastructure of the rural population in order to control territory (Karim et al. 1996; Nyaba 1997).

Dependency theory

Ethiopian notions of military strategy overshadowed the SPLM/A's practice of revolutionary warfare, but the SPLM/A could not readily replicate other elements of its revolutionary strategy, because Ethiopia's economic structure was so different to South Sudan's. Pre-revolutionary Ethiopia had feudal land magnates and commercial landlords that were overturned by the revolutionary land reforms of 1975 (Clapham 1989). Some areas of Sudan had a comparable set of revolutionary possibilities. In the Nuba mountains of South Kordofan national governments had begun alienating land from traditional cultivators in the 1960s. In the 1970s, supported by the World Bank, mechanized cotton farming schemes were set up on alienated, commercially leased lands, pitching the area into the volatile cotton markets of that decade (African Rights 1995: 38; Komey 2007). Displaced cultivators had sought out different forms of resistance, such as peasant unions and political associations (El-Battahani 2009). The Sudanese Communist Party had organized in the area and in the 1960s a dissident communist faction had tried to organize for a Maoist-inspired peasant revolution there. 'Maoism' in this context meant the primacy of armed struggle, and the leading role of the 'peasantry' or rural poor, rather than that of the waged workers or proletarians that Joseph Ukel Garang promoted before his untimely death. According to Magdi El Gizouli, a journalist and academic, the Maoist wing also recognized the importance of ethnicity, of the negritude that Joseph Ukel Garang sometimes appeared to consider misplaced (interview 4/2014). The movement was unsuccessful, but it prefigured the SPLM/A. Although the revolutionary terrain in the Nuba mountains was radically different from that of South Sudan, many Nuba people joined the SPLM/A in 1985 as it brought the war in the South to South Kordofan.

But in South Sudan, the SPLM/A had relatively little to offer people in the subsistence economy, because communities still owned their land and organized their own labour. In South Sudan, as elsewhere in Africa, the liberation movement could not adopt the slogan of 'land to the tiller' that was so important for Latin American revolutions (Mkandawire 2002). The movement looked elsewhere for its economic and social analysis, to a collection of critiques of capitalist development that were partially inspired by twentieth-century Marxism, called dependency theory. Dependency theory helped explain the persistence of underdevelopment in countries that were trying and failing to modernize in the 1960s. Dependency theory argues against the notion that societies progress through uniform stages of development en route to an idealized market or a society free of class division. Instead, it shifts perspective to envisage development in spatial terms – boom towns whose fortunes are tied to ghost towns, or glittering citadels surrounded by storm zones. It argues that colonialism divided the world into a developed core which established a self-perpetuating pattern of peripheral underdevelopment and unequal exchange that was managed by a 'dependent bourgeoisie' – that is, local intermediaries for international capital.

The African academic centre of this theoretical school was at Dar es Salaam University in Tanzania, where John Garang had held a fellowship in 1969, immediately before leaving academia to join Anya-nya. The manifesto he authored in 1983 had 'the fingerprints of the Dar es Salaam school of thought' (Deng 2013: 115). This attachment to the 'Dar es Salaam school' is not evident in all of John Garang's work: his PhD thesis, written in the American Midwest, briefly and diffidently reviewed key texts of dependency theorists. At the time, he was an ambitious officer with privileged opportunities to influence policy development in South Sudan, and his thesis (a study of livelihoods in the flood plains, in the Jonglei canal area) calls for state-led modernization of production systems in the flood plains: replacing subsistence systems with irrigated, mechanized farming; villagization; and reworking of traditional land tenure, which chimed with government policy at the time (Garang de Mabior 1981: 163).

But in 1983, dependency theory's critique of unfair distribution of development between centre and periphery and unfair terms of exchange offered a promising starting point for South Sudanese revolutionaries. They reframed the problem of Sudan away from the problem of racism (John Garang deliberately substituted the term 'minority clique' for 'Arab' throughout the document) to the problem of uneven development. The SPLM/A manifesto argues that South Sudan's problems lie in the way that colonialism aggravated existing differences between societies at different levels of socio-economic development in Sudan and concentrated wealth at the centre. Independence did not correct this skewed development, it just passed responsibility for administering it to African intermediaries, the 'bourgeoisified bureaucratic elite'. But Southern Sudanese were largely excluded from membership of this elite, because they had not been educated, because colonialists educated only a small minority of people in the areas of Sudan that generated quick surplus, leaving other areas of Sudan educationally and otherwise underdeveloped. Rather than addressing the causes of underdevelopment, the Anya-nya sought to promote its leaders into the state elite:

When Sudan became 'independent' in January 1956, colonial jobs were 'unfairly' divided between the North and the South. The Southern elite felt cheated and betrayed by British colonialism. However, the unfair distribution of colonial jobs between North and South, as pointed out earlier, was a historical necessity rooted in the unequal peripheral development of the North and South during the colonial period. As Northernization of the Civil Service became imminent in the South, the Southern Army Garrison at Torit mutinied in August 1955, four months before 'independence'. This mutiny marks the beginning of Anya-nya I and 17 years of war (1955–1972). Anya-nya I was thus precipitated by dissatisfaction with Sudanization, that is, by the unfair distribution between the Southern and Northern bourgeoisified bureaucratic elites. The objective and aims of Anya-nya I therefore centred around jobs and job titles. The jobbist character of Anya-nya I forms an important experience from which the present Movement (SPLM) has a great deal to learn. (SPLM 1983: 7–8)

The manifesto uses the lumberingly alliterative formulation 'bourgeoisified bureaucratic elite' several times. Some Dar es Salaam thinkers of the time had used the term 'bureaucratic bourgeoisie' to describe the workings of the colonial state in places like Tanzania or elsewhere in Africa (Issa Shivji, quoted in Saul 1974; Meillassoux 1970). But this usage may alarm conventional Marxists, who identify the bourgeoisie with groups who own the means of production through the institution of private property – an institution that has not spread widely in South Sudan.

The Dar es Salaam theorists used ideas drawn from Marxism to explain why newly independent African states were dominated by military-bureaucratic elites, prone to coups, and unsuccessful in raising the living standards of their population – questions that are still relevant and, in many respects, unanswered. They argued that the post-colonial state was uniquely unsuccessful because of the role of state elites in managing the private-property system that colonialism had instituted in many parts of Africa. In the Communist Manifesto (1848), Karl Marx and Friedrich Engels described the state as a 'committee for managing the common affairs of the whole bourgeoisie'. It was a pithy way of describing political representation in many European states of the time, which limited voting and membership of parliament to property owners. Those states had all accepted private property, capital accumulation and economic growth as their central political objectives – objectives culminating from over a century of development of new systems of production and trade. The state need only act as a managing committee for these objectives – its job was not politics but 'governance'. In the event, the Communist Manifesto's definition was too much of a simplification to describe the factional flux in the property-owning classes during the European coups and revolutions that followed. Marx subsequently developed a notion of the state as an autonomous alliance of forces that protected the interests of the property-owning classes, rather than just an instrument in their hands (Marx 1963). But in either case, the state protected a system of private property and development which was relatively new, but already beginning to be seen as part of the natural order.

'Marxist analysis should always be slightly stretched every time we have to do with the colonial problem,' said Frantz Fanon (1963: 40), a theorist of revolutions and of violence, whose book *The Wretched of the Earth* was the top of John Garang's list of recommended reading for his commanders (Deng 2013: 116). Much of that analysis-stretching took place in Dar es Salaam. There, left theorists argued that the Marx and Engels description of the state could not apply in Africa. Pre-colonial African states did not aim at entrenching private property, capital accumulation and economic growth. They tolerated communal property systems. The task of the colonial state was to violently transform African communal property systems into private property. And that private property was not intended to lead to capital accumulation in Africa, but to be bought and sold in European stock exchanges. In Europe, property owners used the state to protect their property rights – but in Africa, the state created the possibility of the private ownership of land and other means of production, ownership that in many cases had previously been shared. Colonial militaries and bureaucracies imposed a new productive order, of mines and plantations that did not belong to the people working on them, but instead belonged to distant stockholders. The new military-bureaucratic system that colonialism brought to Africa was able to conjure up private property through violence, and it was entirely autonomous from the productive efforts of people working together to grow and make things. When the colonial state was replaced by the independent African state, the military-bureaucratic system of coercion retained its importance (Alavi 1972; Saul 1974).

The post-colonial states were different from the colonizing state because of the vital role of this military-bureaucratic elite. The military-bureaucratic elite is economically autonomous from the 'indigenous bourgeoisie' – the local factory and plantation owners. These local magnates are not able to accumulate enough financial resources to set prices or make major investments; as Fanon puts it: 'The national bourgeoisie of underdeveloped countries is not engaged in production, nor in invention, nor building, nor labor … Under the colonial system, a middle class which accumulates capital is an impossible phenomenon' (Fanon 1963: 149–50).

Economic power lies with the capital markets in rich countries, and in order for the system to work, the post-colonial military-bureaucratic elite has to represent their interests (Saul 1974). The Anya-nya elites, thought John Garang, started from the awareness that they were excluded from this military-bureaucratic elite because, as South Sudanese, they were from 'Backward Areas' (SPLM 1983: 1). These areas had been violently incorporated into the world system, so that crises in Egypt or Wall Street reverberated violently in the remotest settlements of South Sudan. But they got no investment, no factories, plantations or schools, as a result of this incorporation, and racist ideologies were invented to justify their 'backwardness'. The 'bourgeoisified bureaucratic elites' were there to maintain this system, which kept decision-making in the capital markets of rich countries, and concentrated factories, plantations and schools in areas of Sudan where quick returns were to be had. But the Anya-nya elites only wanted a bigger slice of the bourgeoisified bureaucratic pie. Nothing more.

Orthodox Khartoum communists still flinch at John Garang's 'bourgeoisified bureaucratic' phrase. But although the SPLM/A manifesto makes the case for dependency theory in a way that is sometimes lumbering and tone deaf, the document is often very quotable. The opening paragraph is a fine example:

> The so-called 'Problem of Southern Sudan' is really a general problem in the Sudan. It is generally a 'problem of Backward Areas' in the whole country that is particularized and exacerbated in the South by successive oppressive minority clique regimes in Khartoum. In fact, the problem has its origins in the spread of capitalism and colonialism towards the end of the last century ... (ibid.)

Almost thirty years later, former South African president Thabo Mbeki, himself influenced by the Dar es Salaam school, used the same opener in an influential African Union report:

> During its extensive interactions with its Sudanese interlocutors ... the Panel repeatedly heard that the [Darfur] conflict was in reality a manifestation of a broader crisis affecting the whole of Sudan. This larger problem was described as the consequence of the development of a colonial and post-colonial socio-economic system in which a minority of the population, concentrated in and around Khartoum, maintained a stranglehold over political power and economic resources. (AUPD 2009: vii)

So there is something tenacious about the phrasing of the manifesto, although its content is little studied and often dismissed.

Foreign commentators represent it as a juvenile misreading of Marxist theory, or as an expedient to mobilize support from socialist Ethiopia (Collins 2008; Rolandsen 2005). Peter Adwok Nyaba, a South Sudanese politician with a more supple understanding of Marxist thought, concurs with this analysis: SPLM/A leaders did not believe that they were engaged in a struggle between capitalism and socialism. The Sudanese Communist Party concurred with this analysis too. John Garang shared the text with Su'ad Ibrahim, a brilliant and sympathetic member of the party's politburo, for comment, and she criticized its careless use of Marxist terminology (interview 2/2013, Lam Akol). The party's underground newspaper cautiously welcomed the manifesto almost a year later. It commended the SPLM/A's commitment to a unified socialist Sudan, but criticized its militarism and its invalidation of the role of mass movements in northern Sudan in the transformation of the country (Ahmad 2005: 268–70).

Nonetheless, John Garang came up with an analysis of Sudan's crisis which stretched Marxist orthodoxy and resonated across the country. For the first time, the Sudanese Communist Party lost cadres (educated, cosmopolitan Khartoum cadres!) to a southern armed group (ibid.: 271). But the new analysis had some limitations.

The limitations of dependency theory

Dependency theory offered catchy phrasings that helped to frame Garang's analysis: 'core–periphery', 'incorporation', 'development of underdevelopment'. The theory offered explanations for the spatial distribution of underdevelopment and its persistence during the optimism of 1960s modernization, a movement which sought unsuccessfully to replicate First World models of development in South America, Africa and Asia. But the theory went out of favour for several reasons, some set out by Paul Tiyambe Zeleza: it emphasized external economic linkages and ignored internal processes, having more to say about unequal exchange than about production. It idealizes pre-incorporated development and pushes post-incorporation economic history into an unrelenting saga of deepening underdevelopment (Zeleza 2002: 4).

The possibilities and limitations of dependency theory resonated with Khartoum University radicals in the 1980s, and John Garang's phrasings still resonate today with undergraduates in the new universities in Darfur and South Kordofan. But they were difficult to explain to people in South Sudanese villages: the theory did not prompt reflection on the possibility of local change. Instead of trying to use liberated territory to set up a fairer or richer version of Sudan, the SPLM/A built a reputation for plunder, which set its cadres apart from local people. In a well-known SPLM joke, a villager is startled by being addressed as a member of the movement: 'I'm not a comrade! I didn't steal the goat!'

As rebel movements succeeded in getting control over the distribution of humanitarian supplies and ultimately over oil revenues, the difference between their leadership and the people who refused to steal goats became more pronounced. Like Khartoum governments and the Southern Regional Government established after the 1972 peace agreement, the SPLM/A became economically autonomous from society and dependent on outside patrons. The process by which the SPLM/A achieved this economic autonomy vis-à-vis society during wartime has been much studied (African Rights 1997). Through the 1980s, the United States and Sudan's other creditors pressured the weakened parliamentary regime in Khartoum to allow relief food to rebel-held areas through a distribution system managed by the United Nations, called Operation Lifeline Sudan. For the first time in post-colonial Africa, armed opposition forces were given a role as intermediaries between the populations they controlled and an international humanitarian system. In 1991, things got worse when the SPLM/A split in two. New factions built ethnic constituencies, and used relief food to help them manage those constituencies. Recognition by the international humanitarian system was almost as important as arms supplies. Relief food meant that the subsistence economy did not survive the war intact. Factions targeted the livelihoods of the real or potential or perceived constituencies of the adversaries, and a distribution system structured around factions aggravated the crisis (Scott Villiers and Banggol 1991: 14; Hutchinson 1996: 342; African Rights 1997: 294ff.; Badal 2006: 85).

Dependency theory saw exploitation in terms of unequal exchange, not in terms of the way that societies are organized to produce wealth and accumulate it. The theory did not encourage critical reflection on the transformations that were taking place as a result of the war. The theory's pessimism and its blind spots – its inability to propose a change to the production systems that keep some areas and groups underdeveloped – have shaped the SPLM just as much as its resonant dichotomies, such as the core and the periphery, that remain irresistible for most Sudan/South Sudan analysts.

The manifesto was 'revised in line with changing realities within, and outside, Sudan' during the SPLM's first national convention in 1994 (Kiir Mayardit 2008). The convention switched the centre of the SPLM's discourse towards the idea of the New Sudan, which stood both for the liberated areas and the future of the Old Sudan. Nonetheless, the manifesto's critique of the spatial maldistribution of development reappeared in John Garang's speeches to the convention:

> The very economic system of the 'Jellaba' is responsible for deepening the inherited disparities among the regions of our country in favour of the relatively developed Central Northern Sudan. Because this class has kept the peripheral regions, i.e. Southern, Western and Eastern Sudan as areas of reservoirs of labour and primitive accumulation of capital. (Garang de Mabior 1994: 17)

But by this point, with the Cold War ended, John Garang no longer blamed the colonial regime, or neocolonialism, for Sudan's predicament. Sudan's brutal geography of underdevelopment was the fault of the Khartoum regime alone – the use of the term 'Jellaba', a term for northern merchants in South Sudan with echoes of the slave trade, may have been a belated concession to the 'racial thesis' that Joseph Ukel Garang had rejected. The SPLM/A began openly to consider the possibility of self-determination for South Sudan, as an alternative to the transformation of the whole of Sudan. This reflected the moment: for many groups in Sudan, the 1990s were a period when 'racial' and 'tribal' theses became more compelling, as the Khartoum government divested from the peripheries to help pay its debts, and fostered ethnic conflicts there instead. The 1994 convention came three years after a devastating split in the SPLM/A, and that split took on an ethnic character very quickly.

Perhaps the drift away from the certainties of the 1983 manifesto also reflected the complexity of South Sudan's predicament. The Khartoum government made an unprecedented sacrifice of national sovereignty in allowing the establishment of Operation Lifeline Sudan – no previous African war had seen control over relief supplies shared between adversaries in this way (Karshoum 2004). The sacrifice was to have many implications for the way that the state was constituted in Africa as the Cold War ended. The economic autonomy of South Sudan's elites from society widened, and their dependency on external resources (now denominated as relief food and transport) deepened. A military elite replaced the bureaucratic one, and local food economies that had functioned outside the international system were drawn into it. The developments echoed the chaotic incorporation/marginalization of the nineteenth century, but in some respects the historical processes were even more inscrutable, because incorporation/marginalization was rephrased in the language of humanitarian concern.

But even after distancing himself from some of the insights of dependency theory that were invoked at the start of the armed struggle that he led, John Garang kept firmly to a key principle of

his 1983 manifesto: the primacy of armed struggle. The revolutionary task was to rework the geography of underdevelopment by
seizing control of the state. This primacy was reaffirmed even as
the convention began a yet-unfinished development of a political
wing. John Garang's formulation of the Sudanese crisis in terms
of the unhappy relationship between centre and the periphery
was very clear. But the formulation was inattentive to local possibility, and it was part of the SPLA's decision not to invest
effort in creating an alternative system in South Sudan. Instead,
it made good its manifesto commitment to massive, conventional
warfare that postponed liberation until after state capture. Like
the dependency theorists, John Garang did not bother to offer
tangible social or economic change for the SPLA's recruits or
for its supporters in the here-and-now.

John Garang may have retained a belief in a transformation
of the whole Sudan, but this did not necessarily represent the
views of his movement, and he sometimes implicitly acknowledged
this. Many Southerners were fighting for an independent South,
but they went along with a movement that aimed primarily for
liberation of all Sudan. They may have understood that their
leaders might need to adopt positions that satisfied their foreign
supporters. In a brilliant analysis of the political shyness of South
Sudanese leaders, Nyaba says:

> There is a marked tendency on the part of the South Sudanese
> political elite to shy away from clearly naming what they and
> the people wanted. There is always a tendency to hide behind
> a facade suggestive of some degree of lack [of] self-confidence
> in the cause being undertaken. More attention was paid to
> what others will say about us than what we want ourselves.
> (1997: 32)

When SPLA foot soldiers were asked about the aims of their
struggle, or their commitment to the national unity of twentieth-
century Sudan, they would typically deploy a terse evasion: 'We

know what we are fighting for' – the expulsion of the oppressor (Deng 2005). Or as Walter Benjamin put it: 'Not man or men but the struggling, oppressed class itself is the depository of historical knowledge ... the avenger that completes the revolution in the name of generations of the downtrodden' (1968: 260).

5 | STATE AND SOCIETY IN JONGLEI AFTER THE COMPREHENSIVE PEACE AGREEMENT

An evening with the ambassadors

On 18 March 2012, the keynote speaker at a reception to celebrate the appointment of five ambassadors from Greater Nasir in Upper Nile state was the vice-president, Riek Machar. Speaking in English to the largely Nuer-speaking audience, the vice-president and other speakers stressed that all the ambassadors were from the Gaajak section of the Jikainy Nuer, whose territorial base lies around Nasir, a border town on the Sobat river. Machar presented their appointments as a mark of Gaajak achievement and participation in the state. The audience wore bulky-shouldered business suits and lustrous white shirts; women wore *ketenga*s (African ballgowns or *boubou*s) in glittering Javanese batiks and Nigerian waxies (wax-print fabric), with tresses and weaves in their hair, and lipgloss catching the blazing neon lighting. The audience drifted up to greet the politicians and ambassadors, and over to the buffet of *kisra* and *weika* – sorghum flatbread with a lamb and fermented okra stew – food from the peripheral areas of northern Sudan that was popular in Khartoum settlements to which many of the people in the audience had probably moved during wartime. An elegant bureaucrat, from a nearby Nuer section, bemoaned the precedent: 'People are going to complain, we don't have ambassadors, we don't have generals' (interview 19/2012).

The stews, the English-language speeches and the suits all suggested to the bystander that the SPLM's intention of ridding the country of a bureaucratic elite had not survived the war. The whole evening suggested that ethnicity was being put to new uses in the system that, after a long war, the SPLM had inherited. This chapter looks at the ways in which the new government in Juba has structured its relationship to South Sudanese society, and the importance of ethnicity to that structuring. The chapter starts by looking at the advantages that the SPLM-led government enjoyed when it took power. It then looks at the way that the government has dealt with the dilemmas of representation and allocation that were identified in Chapter 3. That chapter argued that, once the idea of representative government emerged in South Sudan in the 1970s, powerful structures impelled people to use ethnicity as the basis for representation. This chapter examines how these structures have endured in rural politics through the civil war and into the independence era, looking at several local conflicts over administrative and ethnic borders, and at local budgets in Jonglei and greater Upper Nile. A local approach is needed to appreciate the way that the spatial distribution of ethnicity interacts with the spatial distribution of economic development. The chapter goes on to look at the way that diaspora and urban politics have also been caught up in the politics of ethnic allocation and representation. Finally, it looks at some of the implications of this social structure to the workings of the SPLM and the SPLA.

The SPLM's inheritance

The SPLM became the overwhelmingly dominant party in what is nominally a ruling coalition that led the Government of Southern Sudan in 2005, and led the country to independence in 2011. Since 2005, the SPLM sought to consolidate a South Sudanese state from unpromising legacies that were set out in some detail in previous chapters. It enjoyed considerable advantages over previous regimes – a long liberation struggle which mobilized near-universal support for its objectives (if not for its methods); a widely recognized (Christian) religious identity; and in the unloved Arabic language, a lingua franca that draws many

South Sudanese into a single linguistic community. Most of all, it had a huge budget. The last government in South Sudan that could pay its own costs came at the end of the Turkiya.

After the 2005 peace deal, South Sudan's government had budgets running to billions of dollars, all from the country's oil resources. Although it has financial resources that are the envy of its neighbours, the resources come from an oil infrastructure that is shared with Khartoum. The huge budgets of today exhibit some continuities with those of the twentieth century, in that they are still based on external rents, rather than a strong domestic product. These rents are generated by a very small proportion of the population and the government is the principal recipient. This has created the same imbalances between the centre and an underdeveloped periphery that characterized the relationship of Khartoum with its vast and diverse hinterland. It has also given the government the same dilemmas of allocation and representation that caused problems in the Southern Regional Government of 1972–83, and like the Southern Regional Government, the new Juba system has often used ethnicity as a basis for addressing these dilemmas and for organizing its relationships with rural Sudan. The SPLM used much of its wealth to set up a huge payroll, and ethnicity was one of the key means to claim a place on the payroll.

This use of ethnicity was another bequest to the SPLM. During the 1983–2005 civil war, the Khartoum government followed a strategy of intensifying ethnic differences in the peripheries of Darfur, Kordofan and Southern Sudan (Takana 2008). This system of an ethnically structured periphery managed by a relatively powerful centre is being partially replicated in South Sudan. The parallels were frequently mentioned in the interviews on which this book is based, but they are not precise. South Sudan, unlike Sudan, had no experience of colonial development, and has no obvious state centre or state culture to impose on other cultures – no inherited system of dominance to be implicated in future wars. The SPLM's use of ethnicity to organize rural Sudan is not entirely driven by parsimony or by the malicious intention to profit from turning South Sudan's diversity into a source for division between people – the motivations of most previous regimes. Its liberation struggle was partially justified as a form of cultural self-defence. This conservativism was to a certain extent unavoidable – the SPLM's conventional war aimed to instrumentalize local social systems and subsistence economies in order to defeat the Khartoum army, not to transform society. But in government, the SPLM has kept the political order in the countryside to a model developed in the colonial period. At the same time, it has rapidly built up urban centres that monopolize financial resources. In many respects, the national capital relates to rural South Sudan in a manner that many ordinary people compare to Khartoum. The distances from the South Sudanese periphery to the new centre at Juba have not got much shorter since South Sudan's independence.

Ethnic competition for state posts

South Sudan's ethnic diversity gives it many advantages, and in everyday experience, people's ethnic affiliations generally provide them with language, cultural resources and social networks and the means to produce and share wealth. There's nothing wrong with ethnicity. South Sudan's ethnic problem lies in the fact that inequality is often experienced in ethnic terms, and the government's principal means of redistribution of wealth and mitigating these inequalities has been the state payroll. The review of South Sudan's fiscal and financial history in Chapter 3 showed how governments in South Sudan disbursed most of their financial resources to the state payroll, and that access to and exclusion from the payroll often set the stage for ethnic antagonisms. 'Arab' or 'Dinka' domination was set out in tables that purported to show government posts assigned to people embodying and representing apparently bounded ethnic communities.

Administrative boundaries and ethnic boundaries

Chapter 3 argued that ethnicity acquired new ideological functions in the 1970s, and that this may have been linked to the
emergence of the notions of popular sovereignty, representative
government and a developmental state in a country where the
colonial state's relationship with rural communities had been
structured around ethnicity. People advanced their claims on the
state by invoking ethnicity; and because so much of the state
budget went on salaries, they often sought government posts. In
urban areas, people could make a claim that their community
was under-represented at a particular level – one of the reasons
for the appointment of Gaajak ambassadors.

But in rural areas, the possibility of non-military appointment
scarcely existed. Most rural government jobs were in county
headquarters. This fact led rural people seeking a place in the
new order to agitate for the creation of new counties or *payam*s
(sub-counties), often using urban ethnic networks to press their
case at the centre. This agitation led sometimes to serious disputes
around administrative boundaries. These disputes appear to be
linked to the emergence of representative government in South
Sudan in the 1970s, when rural people began to consider their
participation in the state.

In 1974, the Juba government adopted a policy of decentralization and established a Committee for the Redivision of the [three
vast] Southern Provinces, which toured South Sudan to conduct
hearings with local people to decide on the establishment of
smaller administrative units which might bring development closer
to people. Discussions in Upper Nile province, briefly related in
Chapter 3, were mostly concerned with the economic viability of
new administrative units, and the location of new administrative
capitals, which had many implications for the economic life of
its immediate environs: 'Redivision would mean more salaries
for the provinces' (CRSP c. 1975: 42). Outside Upper Nile, the
question of creating ethnically homogeneous administrative units

was discussed and gently resisted by the committee: 'We do not call for ethnic provinces or for encouraging ethnic movements but we think that consideration should be given to the ethnic element when calculations for the setting up of the new provinces are made' (ibid.: 46).

By the beginning of the 1980s, however, Upper Nile was the scene of political contests over the ethnic homogeneity of administrative units. Before the nineteenth-century Nuer migrations, the Sobat river and its tributary the Akobo had been areas of settlement for Anuak people, a Luo-speaking group. Anuak and Nuer tradition both agree that the ancient founder of the Jikainy Nuer as a people was an Anuak prince whose mother floated him west on a gourd (Jal 1987: 15). Nineteenth-century Nuer migrations pushed Anuak people eastwards into retreat. In the early 1930s, there were only four Nuer villages in Akobo district, an area historically associated with Anuak people. But after Sudan's independence, the Nuer population of the area increased, as war displacement and cattle diseases reworked the ethnic demography of the area (Evans-Pritchard 1940b: 10–11; Willis 1995: 199; Johnson 1988).

By the 1980s, Akobo town was predominantly populated by people from the Lou Nuer section. It became part of a competition over administrative borders and ethnicity. A local government official from the time explained:

This decentralization brought about ambition for people to have a separate administrative centre. This prompted memories from Anuak that this place was theirs originally and they should get it back ... [previously] people were not educated and not serious about jobs. But as things grew up, they found that to be an official in government is a big privilege. So everyone wanted a position. Every ethnic group wanted a share of their own. (Interview 61/2012)

By 1983, dozens of Anuak and Nuer people had been killed

in lynchings and massacres and the Anuak population of Akobo were moved to Pochalla and Malakal (interview 61/2012).

Boundary changes in the 1990s intensified ethnic and sectional differences. Soon after taking power, the current government in Khartoum began a new process of administrative redivision that led in 1994 to the division of pre-secession Sudan into twenty-six states – a figure later reduced to twenty-five (Takana 2008: 7). Around the same time, the government began a fiscal stabilization programme, which aimed at addressing Sudan's debts arising from 1970s public investment programmes and re-establishing its relationship with international financial institutions. The stabilization programme halved public expenditure as a proportion of GDP: reduced transfers to states accounted for about half of these reductions (World Bank 2003: 46). The states had responsibility for basic services, which faced heavy cuts. The policy of fostering ethnic divisions within these newly impoverished states was necessary to manage these economic changes, as one Khartoum-appointed governor from the period explained:

> The creation of counties around ethnic boundaries started
> with National Salvation [the regime established after the 1989
> coup in Khartoum]. In order to have power in the centre, they
> must engage the peripheries in power struggles. The federal
> structure was really to protect the grip on central power ...
> Then it came down to county levels, that the county was
> based on sections. Then the localities ... I tendered another
> proposal, when Riek Machar was president of the coordinating
> council, to rearrange the counties [in order to combine Nuer
> and Dinka people in administrative units] ... This was in
> 1998. The motivation was that you cannot solve these tribal
> sentiments – you have to arrest them earlier by establishing
> geographical administration, not ethnicity ... I was trying to
> mix people because I knew the undeclared policy of ethniciza-
> tion of peripheries was against the interests of the South. I've
> never shared this with anyone, but when I came to the south

I told people not to share this path, of ethnic identities. What happened in University of Juba yesterday [the closure of the university in March 2012 after inter-ethnic clashes between students] is a clear manifestation of this policy. (Interview 19/2012)

Administrative boundaries and land disputes after 2005

Since colonial times, Khartoum regimes had fostered power struggles in the peripheries in order to maintain their grip. Instability was often fostered in times of austerity: the government transmitted the costs of economic crises at the centre to the periphery by cutting the local development budgets. Local antagonisms diverted attention from disinvestment (World Bank 2003: 46). The 2005–11 Government of Southern Sudan and the Republic of South Sudan that succeeded it did not need to ingratiate themselves with international financial institutions by the savagery of their austerity measures – with their oil revenues, they did not need international finance at all. But they maintained and in some respects deepened the linkage between ethnicity and administration. In Jonglei, aligning administration with ethnicity meant the creation of new counties and new paramount chiefs. Paramount chiefs sit at the apex of a chiefly hierarchy imposed by colonialism on more complex and diffuse pre-existing systems of authority. For example, after Lou Nuer people were bombed into submission to colonial authority in 1930, they were concentrated and classified by *cieng* or section. At independence, there was one Lou Nuer paramount chief, but during the rearrangements of the 1990s, they were given another county, which meant that the two main Lou subsections, Gun and Mor, were each given a paramount chief, in Nyirol and Akobo respectively. After the signing of the Comprehensive Peace Agreement (CPA), the westernmost Gun section was given an additional county, based on the two major Gun subsections, Baal in Nyirol and Dak in Wuror (senior local government official, interview 32/2012).

The leaders of South Sudan's liberation struggle formally rejected tribalism, but South Sudan's 2005 and 2011 constitutions put the customs of ethnic communities and what they describe as their traditional authorities at the centre of rural governance. There were several reasons why the SPLM/A decided to perpetuate the model of peripheral governance that had been developed as a colonial expedient. One was the absence of an alternative: like many African liberation movements, the SPLM/A was operating in a social terrain that did not lend itself to revolutionary change. Access to natural resources like land and water was locally managed by customary laws: there were no landlords to depose. Another was the legitimacy of Africanism: the liberation movement aimed for a transformation of the whole Sudan from Khartoum regimes that had long promoted the Arab and Muslim culture of the heartland of the state as the basis for a unified national identity. The SPLM/A invoked African custom in opposition to Arab and Muslim culture. A third reason for maintaining an ethnic model for rural governance was hope: South Sudan's ethnic communities have long traditions of vernacular democracy, which some in the movement hoped might counterbalance the militarism and authoritarianism of the liberation movement. Perhaps more important than hope was suspicion: Khartoum's use of civil administration to proliferate social divisions and structure them around ethnicity was accompanied by a militia policy, described in Chapter 7, which proliferated militias, also structured around ethnicity. That pushed the SPLM/A towards reliance on the military, rather than the civil administration proposed by the movement's conferences in the 1990s. Local authorities whose legitimacy lay in ethnic or kinship structures were an appropriately weak partner for a military administration.

But maintaining a model of governance that organized state–society relationships around ethnicity raised unexpected political dilemmas for governments that claimed to represent that society. The number of Gaajak people in the diplomatic corps is one such dilemma. Another set of dilemmas were bound up in administrative boundaries, which increasingly became seen as ethnic boundaries too.

In 2012, when many of the interviews on which this chapter is based were conducted, Jonglei state was caught up in a war of massive raids and counter-raids that mobilized and killed thousands of people. This war led people to retreat from county boundaries, to towns and hinterland pastures, and this reduced tensions at the borders between the predominantly Murle area of Pibor, predominantly Dinka Bor, and predominantly Nuer Akobo and Wuror. 'They don't have dispute now, because insecurity has pushed people away from contact areas. Between Pibor and other places, nobody is talking about the land now. This is what will happen later,' said one senior local government official (interview 32/2012). In the states of Warrap and Lakes, similar processes entangling administration and ethnicity in the aftermath of a long war have led to conflicts along county and *payam* borders (Zoe Cormack, researcher, interview 3/2014).

Similar processes happened in the fertile and populous areas of Upper Nile state. There, state ceremonial became an arena for contest over ethnic boundaries. State ceremonies often begin with dancing, and groups dance in styles associated with particular ethnic groups. In the state capital Malakal, the order in which different ethnic dance troupes performed on state occasions had a political meaning. Many Shilluk people believe that a tradition emerged that would have Shilluk dancers leading the ceremonial, in acknowledgement of the importance of Shilluk people and culture in the town. During a 1981 presidential visit to Malakal, the Southern Regional Government, led by Abel Alier, brought Dinka women to dance at the president's reception. Thirty years later, at the independence celebrations for South Sudan, Dinka dancers led the celebrations and Shilluk dancers came later (anonymous, interview 156/2012). This relegation had political resonance, because Shilluk people in the 1980s and today believed that boundary changes marked Dinka encroachment on traditionally Shilluk lands on the east bank of the White Nile.

Shilluk people inhabit a mostly contiguous territory along the banks of the White Nile and Sobat rivers that begins near their junction south of Malakal. Tonga is a Shilluk town on the west bank of the White Nile, and in the 1970s the administration of Shilluk villages on the east bank of the White Nile came under the new Jonglei province, which had been set up by the work of the 1974 Redivision Committee.[1] In 1981, as the Southern Region drifted back towards war, administrative boundaries became sources of insecurity. This happened at a regional level: Jaafer Nimeiri's government changed the boundaries of the Southern region in order to ensure that the regional government did not control the new oil industry (SPLM 1983; Badal 1986). Khartoum fostered local antagonisms in the run-up to the abolition of the Southern Regional Government, and tensions between Shilluk villagers in Jonglei and their Dinka neighbours increased. Police intervention led to the burning of Shilluk villages and fears that Shilluk people were to be pushed off the east bank spread. According to Nyaba, 'The politics of borders created such bitterness that it led to arms trafficking in Upper Nile and Jonglei provinces. Ethnic groups started arming themselves ... to resolve the question of these boundaries by physical means' (Nyaba 1997: 25). Nyaba argues that contests over ethnic boundaries that emerged at this time were postponed because of the civil war: 'The people had been completely disoriented and pitted against each other over issues that did not matter much in their lives ... many of the youths, who left their homes to join the SPLA/M, did so initially in the hope [of] acquiring arms and [coming] back to resolve the local conflict' (ibid.: 26).

However irrelevant, these boundary questions have survived

---

1 The White Nile flows northwards, but in the Tonga area it flows almost due east at a bend in the river. Tonga is conventionally described as west bank, although it would be as accurate to describe it as north bank.

a devastating war and still complicate daily life in Shilluk lands. Dinka encroachment on Shilluk lands is imaginatively linked to the ethnicity of leaders like Alier and Kiir. In the allegedly encroaching Padang Dinka areas of Fangak and Khor Fulluth/Pigi that lie just south of the Shilluk lands in Jonglei state, boundary issues were even more complicated. But before addressing these complexities, here is a brief summary of human development in the area, taken from the 2010 statistical yearbook, which helpfully aggregates a huge amount of statistical information from surveys conducted between 2006 and 2009. The population of the two counties was just over 200,000. Although the area is associated with cattle keeping, 90 per cent of households were engaged in farming, and yields in the two counties were under 0.4 tons per hectare, one of the lowest yields in the whole of South Sudan. For every 100,000 completed pregnancies, 1,861 mothers died. This dreadful figure was not the worst in the country, but figures for contraceptive use – 0.1 per cent – certainly were. About a third of children were malnourished and primary net enrolment was 52 per cent. Only five of forty-seven schools in Fangak had toilets, a sure way of depressing female enrolment (SSCCSE 2010).

Why Khor Fulluth/Pigi? The statistical yearbook uses both names for the same place. The county, which lies just south of the Bahr al-Ghazal before it reaches the Sobat, was also called Canal because it was the route for the Jonglei canal. The county is home to four Dinka sections: Ruweng, Rut, Thoi and Luaic. Two of the leading sons of the area were George Athor (Luaic) and Gier Chuang (Ruweng). George Athor led the SPLA response to the Khartoum-aligned militias in his home area during the 1990s. But he started a rebellion in 2010 after failing to win the governorship of Jonglei, and he died mysteriously the following year (see Chapter 8). Gier Chuang, another general, was at the time the minister of interior in Juba. Both were high-ranking SPLA insiders, but they apparently had a personal rivalry, which may have played out in the appointment of rival commissioners,

rival names for the county and arguments about subdividing it.
One observer explained:

> How can you have two commissioners? One is Khor Fulluth
> and one is Pigi. It was partly about the relationship between
> Gier and George ... I have no idea. It was just a leadership
> kind of thing. Does the problem reflect a real division in the
> society or was it about ambitious politicians? I wouldn't be
> surprised if they were working against each other. (Interview
> 181/2012)

The politics of boundaries could thus incomprehensibly shift
from a question of Dinka encroachment on Shilluk lands to an
argument between two Dinka generals over the leadership of one
of those ethnic communities. The argument and the rebellion did
nothing for the everyday concerns of people in the area. They
did not even make sense to the Pigi commissioner, who told a
press conference marking his resignation that he was leaving his
post to spend time with his beautiful children. 'Subdivision of the
counties is not the solution at all. I believe politicians need to
sit down and try to make a new formula on how to govern this
country' (James Aleu Majak, quoted in Sudan Tribune 2012b).

Counties as a means to manage state patronage

In some cases, boundary politics have an economic rationale:
this is the case on the populous, fertile and well-connected Nile
banks. But in many cases, county boundaries do not demarcate
territory with any realizable value: changes to county boundaries
are economically useful only if they attract state jobs and state
investment in infrastructure, such as the building or repair of a
school or office. This is the way that local people can make claims
on the oil rents concentrated in the capital Juba.

In 2005, South Sudan's enormous budgetary expansion took
place as the new government adopted a constitution with a chapter devoted to 'decentralized democracy' – meaning that some

of the new resources would be assigned to the ten states and seventy-nine counties (that at least was the number of counties in 2010). States and counties generate little revenue, and are heavily dependent on transfers from central government. Local budgets are spent on wages. When oil revenues brought an end to austerity budgets in the peripheries, from 2005, the new financial resources went on payroll, which suggests a policy of developing clientelist networks. Clientelism is a relatively low-budget means of managing stark inequalities of power and wealth. It is one possible model of development for South Sudan and Sudan: it distributes scarce resources over a vast territory while building loyalty to the government through the installation of a cadre of government employees across the states. When he was vice-president, Riek Machar promoted this model – he argued that multiplying counties and county towns is a way of distributing state resources more widely across the country, fostering urban-ization, and moving people away from traditional economic life. In a speech in March 2012, he said: 'Having more counties is development. We are trying to urbanize our people. In fifty years most people will be in towns. Agriculture will be much, it will be the end of pastoralist migration.' However, in the lineage societies of Upper Nile, these counties are configured around smaller and smaller subsections, and they are means for people of a subsection to get posts and basic services, and be able to keep up with the people of the next county town, who would be of another subsection.

Some politicians have taken this argument a step farther, calling for the division of Jonglei into two states. This seems an obvious solution to the violence in Jonglei, which has pitted large populations against each other. According to current policy, it would double central transfers to the same population: all states currently get exactly the same share of national revenue regardless of area or population. Two possible divisions of Jonglei are north–south, or east–west. These proposed divisions, according to one parliamentarian and historian from Greater Bor, sometimes reflect past ethnic alliances and antagonisms reflecting intercommunity tensions or confected by political leaderships. An east–west division would unite Lou Nuer, Murle and Anuak people, but separate them from Dinka people and the Nuer groups of Zeraf island, the tract of land lying between the Bahr al-Jebel and the Bahr al-Zeraf. A north–south division would unite Dinka people with Murle and Anuak people and unite Nuer people who live mostly in the north of the state (interview 100/2012). The leaderships of smaller ethnic groups want smaller divisions. In 2005, some Murle people called for a state uniting Nuer and Murle people, before the current violence in Jonglei began. Throughout the Jonglei crises that followed South Sudan's independence, the leading Murle politician Ismail Kony called for Pibor and Pochalla counties – Murle and Anuak areas respectively – to be made a state. Their population was less than 215,000, according to the 2008 census, and such a state would have no all-season river. Some Anuak politicians reject all of these formulas, believing they would divide the Anuak population, and call for a state to be made up of Pibor, Pochalla and Akobo, with another two states in the rest of Jonglei (see page 291).

These discussions about division are really a discussion within leaderships – state posts go to only a handful of people. There is no discussion about administrative division among ordinary people, according to the same local government worker: 'No discussion. Discussion is with leaderships' (interview 93/2012). Politicians are motivated by the hope that they may establish deeper and more reliable constituencies from the powers of patronage than a state budget would confer; and their anxieties are fed, in part, by the unexplored but presumably considerable subterranean resources in the state, the largest oil concession still under exploration in the new republic. 'Everyone wants land because they don't know what's under it,' said one Akobo politician (interview 139/2012).

The policy of proliferating counties and aligning them around ethnicity had a powerful supporter in the former vice-president. Local politicians found the policy attractive because it provided a framework for negotiation with central government with relatively modest financial implications. A new county costs less than an all-weather road (over $1 million a kilometre) or a power station. But the returns on such a policy diminish over time. Calling for a moratorium on the creation of new counties, former cabinet minister Peter Adwok Nyaba points out that 'the proliferation of counties drawn along ethnic, clan and political lines encourages centrifugal forces and has a destabilising impact on national integration' (Nyaba 2011: 30). Fragmenting the periphery along ethnic lines keeps financial resources in Juba.

Concentrating wealth in Juba

Chapter 3 addressed in some detail the composition of state budgets to argue that governments in southern Sudan were historically dependent on external resources; they spent little of these resources on development, and most of them on payroll, and Chapter 4 argued that the resultant impotent bureaucracy was for the SPLM an argument for revolutionary change. Making the government in South Sudan smaller and more impotent was an aim of Khartoum governments in the 1990s: they divested from the peripheries in order to strengthen the economic position of the centre. But the oil boom that began in 1999 allowed for a reconsideration of this policy: transfers from Khartoum to the peripheries increased dramatically from 2000 (DJAM 2012). The 2005 Comprehensive Peace Agreement enshrined South Sudan's share of the federal budget in constitutional law, requiring Khartoum to transfer half of the revenue from South Sudan's oil to the Juba government (Interim National Constitution [2005], Article 192).

'The budget is the skeleton of the state, stripped of all misleading ideologies,' runs the famous dictum of Austrian sociologist Rudolf Goldscheid. What does the enormous budgetary expansion arising from the oil boom and peace agreement tell us about the

TABLE 5.1 South Sudan budgets in Sudanese pounds, 2005–11

	2005 outturn	2006 outturn	2007 outturn	2008 outturn	2009 outturn	2010 outturn provisional	2011 approved
Revenue	1,869,722,079	2,736,099,414	2,977,805,178	6,789,576,441	4,239,803,630	5,756,840,579	5,767,110,495
Expenditure	452,286,139	3,581,548,512	2,936,495,552	5,712,662,066	4,234,653,769	5,576,100,547	5,767,110,495
Salaries	35,456,486	1,185,733,716	1,479,751,066	1,873,440,153	1,977,349,566	2,205,676,172	2,433,391,475
Operating	402,176,606	1,438,197,773	1,058,416,888	2,227,295,738	1,255,266,702	2,279,567,567	2,075,522,856
Capital	14,653,047	957,617,023	398,327,598	1,611,926,175	1,002,037,501	1,090,856,808	1,258,196,164
Salaries as percentage of total expenditures	8	33	50	33	47	40	42
Transfers to states	231,121,152	525,546,238	631,610,393	637,602,757	1,089,895,729	1,219,072,203	1,526,950,618
Transfers to states as a percentage of total expenditures	51	15	22	11	26	22	26

Source: MOFEP (2011)

meaning of the state in South Sudan? South Sudan's record in distributing resources outside the capital is poor – worse than that of the Khartoum government. According to the Ministry of Finance and Economic Planning figures, transfers to states made up between 11 and 26 per cent of all expenditure in the period from 2006 to 2011 (see Table 5.1) – the average (mean) for those years was just over 20 per cent.

These official figures were challenged by an unpublished 2012 study commissioned by the government and conducted by the Sudd Institute, a Juba think tank, which found that just 17 per cent of the national budget is transferred from Juba to the states (report contributor, interview 191/2012). These figures suggest that South Sudan compares unfavourably with Sudan when it comes to the centralization of national wealth. In Sudan as a whole, 36 per cent of the national budget was transferred to northern and southern states in 2006, the last year for which an aggregate figure was made available (World Bank 2007). Subsequent official figures on federal–state transfers indicate that the proportion of Sudan's budget transferred away from the centre to the periphery grew over the period from 2005 to 2010 (DJAM 2012). In South Sudan the aggregate transfer between 2006 and 2011 was significantly lower and more volatile – fluctuating between 11 and 26 per cent. At state level, the pattern of concentration at the centre is repeated: most state revenue stays in state capitals. Jonglei state revenue was 194,040,587 Sudanese pounds in 2011 (senior state finance ministry official, interview 36/2012). About 90 per cent of this stays in the state capital. A county receives about one million pounds a year, with no allowance for operational costs, only payroll (senior county official, interview 79/2012). In 2012, South Sudan decided to shut down oil production, from which about 88 per cent of its revenues are drawn. The first cuts to be announced were in transfers to states (senior state finance ministry official, interview 36/2012).

The spatial distribution of resources in South Sudan's budgets suggests that the state is a highly centralizing one. Expenditure breakdowns suggest that the state is a clientelist one. According to official figures, about 40 per cent of the total budget was spent on wages in the period from 2006 to 2010. At a state level, the proportion is much higher. In Jonglei, the state government spent 78 per cent of total expenditures on the payroll in 2012. Operating and capital expenditures made up the rest of the budget, and there were almost no resources for development (ibid.). In Upper Nile state, official figures for 2008 and 2009 put spending on salaries lower, at around half of budget (World Bank 2009: 126).

The system of allocating a small amount of money to rural areas and spending it mostly on salaries is a venerable one in South Sudan. The evidence presented in Chapter 3 indicates considerable continuity in the structure of rural public finances – dependence on external transfers for revenue, and significant expenditures on wages. The fact that ambitious political operators in Juba want a proliferation of ethnically based counties that will expand this clientelist system is evidence of its workability. But this ethnic clientelism has risks, as Nyaba points out above. In a study of clientelism in Ethiopia's post-1991 system of ethnic decentralization, Paulos Chanie (2007) suggests that excessively lopsided distributions of resources can lead to mutinies; and that the overlap between clientelism and ethnicity can go awry. This may be happening in Jonglei, where most people live in a subsistence economy where raiding has become part of production systems. Government clients in the salary system are not able to dissuade young people from their own kinship groups that this raiding is counterproductive. The clientelist system is unlikely to offer development opportunities that might absorb the productive energies of these young people: the logic of the system is to manage rural affairs by judicious selection of weak allies in exchange for relatively small sums. The mass violence of armed young men in Jonglei may be an angry articulation of excluded rural interests, which exposes the limitations of the ethnic community as a structure for organizing relations between the state and the rural population.

The importance of towns in the creation of new ideas about ethnicity

One of the problems of ruling South Sudan is the government's autonomy from the productive efforts of its people. From 2005 to 2012, the government lived off oil rents, and its main means of wealth distribution is the government payroll. The government's autonomous economic power is scattered in uneven concentrations across South Sudan's territory in the towns and barracks where the government payroll is the basis of economic activity. Before the establishment of an oil-financed government in 2005, these towns had been centres for South Sudan's tiny monetized sector, which slowly and often violently extended its power over the subsistence sector of the countryside. At first, slave raiders would use local intermediaries to secure provisions and porterage from local communities, or raid or levy slaves from them. Throughout the twentieth century, rural South Sudan had low-budget governance systems that drew rural people into the money economy of the towns by creating tax and judicial authorities there from existing structures that were based on kinship, ethnicity or shared histories of migration. The taxes and fines of these local authorities drew people into the money systems of the towns. People also moved to the towns because they were displaced by war, or because warring parties deliberately destroyed systems of subsistence; or because they were seeking participation in urban social services or markets (Leonardi 2013).

South Sudan probably has the fastest urbanization rate of all its neighbours. Under 2 per cent of the population of the southern provinces lived in urban areas in the 1955/56 census: the 2009 census found 18 per cent of the population in towns. Juba's population in 1956 was 10,660. A municipal survey in 1973 enumerated 56,737 people; at the start of the 1983 civil war, another survey enumerated 83,787. The 2009 census enumerated 372,000 people in Juba. The only time that Juba's population dropped in all those years was 1965, when it fell to 7,000 in the wake of government massacres in the town (PCO 1957; Henin 1958: 56; Wakoson 1984; McMichael 2010).

Urbanization helps to stratify South Sudan in two ways. First, towns organize their populations into social hierarchies. Nineteenth-century towns were forts which divided people into slave raiders, farmers and slaves. Twentieth-century towns were constructed to emphasize social differences too, with first-class housing for white colonialists, second-class housing for northern Sudanese and Egyptians, third-class housing for South Sudanese in government service, and fourth-class housing for temporary workers (Ga'le 2002: 140). Today, instead of fourth-class housing managed by pass laws, towns like Juba have informal settlements managed by evictions: informal settlers are bulldozed out of their mud and grass *tukul*s or huts and pushed into the rent system at the edge of the town (McMichael 2010). An equally important means of stratification is spatial. Spatial stratification operates as follows: the central government dominates the economy through its control of oil rents. It allocates most resources to Juba and to the army: only about 10 per cent goes to state capitals (this does not include the financial resources which go to provincial army barracks in wages). The government's financial transfers mostly remain in state capitals. A very small proportion of allocations to states, perhaps 10 per cent, goes to rural areas. Sometimes, these spatial and social hierarchies have an ethnic colouring. Rural ethnic groups that are nearer towns or road infrastructure are more likely to participate in the money economy than those remote from them. The spatial hierarchies caused by South Sudan's model of development are sometimes experienced as ethnic hierarchies because of the spatial distribution of ethnic difference. These imbalances can sometimes be the cause of tension, and in Jonglei state that tension has led to war.

Ethnicity in diasporas and towns

Ethnicity is often presented as a framework for organizing relationships between the state and rural society. Rural South Sudan is where one can find chiefs and customary courts and other institutions that are based in ethnic communities. But the functions of ethnicity are expanding. Ambassadors sometimes organize around ethnicity, as the opening paragraph of this chapter suggests. Diasporas may organize around ethnicity too, as the blood-curdling press releases quoted in the Introduction suggest. And many townspeople participate in urban ethnic associations – groups of people from one linguistic and cultural community that help members of kinship societies negotiate the tough process of migration to the towns. The government may even encourage this kind of urban association: in a political order overwhelmingly dominated by a single party, particularist groups can play a useful role in articulating local interests – and in fragmenting opposition too. These groups provide social networks and welfare but they also link the politics of the periphery to that of the centre. The following section looks at the role of diasporas and urban associations in making ethnicity a more tangible part of the state's relationship with society, influencing the state's behaviour when faced with dilemmas of allocation and representation.

Diasporas: prestige schools and prestige brides

Bor College High is one of three private schools in Jonglei's capital: it opened in 2012 with twenty-one students in three breeze-block classrooms that were still waiting to be plastered a few months later. Its director is from Jalle *payam* in Bor county. In 1991, Riek Machar's faction of the SPLA attacked his area and he fled to a Kenyan refugee camp. From there, he was resettled as a Lost Boy (see below) in the United States, where he got an MBA from a Jesuit university. He set up his school when he came back to Bor in 2010, in the belief that education quality in state schools was 'not that good: teachers are not there and salaries are low'. Although not all the school's teachers agree that its commercial approach is improving standards, the director hopes that South Sudanese private education will discourage the widespread expatriation of South Sudanese capital to private schools in Nairobi:

> All three partners in school are [from the] diaspora. Their shared interest is community benefit, social responsibility, to give back to community. Politically, they want more private sector ... In discussions with government, we ask for the government to subsidize the private sector, ultimately the kids are the government's responsibility. Because people are sending kids to neighbouring counties because education is better. From a financial or economic standpoint, the money is going overseas. (Interview 90/2012)

A young woman student at John Garang Memorial University in Bor stresses diaspora social networks: 'All my family are here and I'm glad that I'm back home again. People who have lived overseas like to socialize together ... They have a lot in common.' She is happy to be back, she is young and looking for love, but return has brought its share of problems. People like her, people from the diaspora, are driving up bridewealth for young women. This is a development with many social implications.

Although some people monetized bridewealth during the war, returnees now denominate the bridewealth in cattle, said one economist and politician (interview 177/2012). Educated returnees have no taste for cattle-keeping and buy up cattle from the market, sometimes over a hundred head, for the most desirable young women. Bridewealth inflation shifts power to cash-rich males, and it also shifts power from younger to older generations. Cattle ownership is complicated and patriarchs have a great deal of influence over bridewealth or other decisions to dispose of family herds.

The bridewealth system was supposed to symbolize an exchange of wealth and obligations to create a fair alliance between two families, not a commercial transaction, but the dollar-fuelled inflation in bridewealth is changing things. Young people do not like it: 'Young women we have no say. It's a buy-off. We don't get what we expect, like love. If we love someone and he doesn't have enough dowry we don't get him' (interview 90/2012). Other interviewees saw bridewealth inflation as an attempt by people to recoup cattle lost in wartime by trading off daughters (former Red Army soldier, interview 92/2012).

Like many other returnees investing in Jonglei, Bor College High's director describes himself as a Lost Boy. 'Lost Boys' was a name given to the young cadets of the Red Army, an SPLA initiative from the 1980s aimed at creating a disciplined and in-doctrinated army and to prevent desertion (Red Army logistician, interview 165/2012). The Red Army brought boys from across South Sudan to training camps in Ethiopia. Some girls were also recruited and organized in what was known as *katiba banat* or Girls Unit (Berger 2010). Many were coerced, but many sought active participation in the SPLA's liberation struggle. After the 1991 split in the SPLA, many moved to refugee camps in Kenya; and from there many were resettled in the United States, in one of the country's most successful resettlement programmes (HRW 1994; Office of Refugee Resettlement 2003). In the process, the Red Army cadets were renamed Lost Boys – a name stressing their vulnerability rather than their agency: 'Red Army was a name given by Garang. Lost Boys was a name given by the international community' (former Red Army member, interview 92/2012). Their reinvention as Lost Boys was a way of translating South Sudan's trauma into something comprehensible to the international officials making decisions about South Sudanese people's lives – much as the language of Muslim persecution of Christians has helped to link South Sudanese traumas to the War Against Terror. Lost Boys may have been successful because they were fluent interpreters of their country's trauma to foreign audiences (Bok 2003; Nhial and Mills 2004; Deng et al. 2005; McKinnon 2008). Some of them are now trying to transform their societies of origin through remittances or return. One Bor academic described their objectives as follows:

> *What are the objectives of diaspora remittances?* The Lost Boys built a hospital in Duk ... There are others who remit money to improve the business of their relatives ... Also building – the houses built here. It's the money coming from abroad. It's a positive impact of the diaspora.
>
> *Is there a political objective for diaspora investment?* I would not call it political in the sense of someone trying to get elected. It's more the need to change society. I know a business person who has built a church. He's a good business man and he has a supermarket. There are people who have built schools ... They are bringing money in and doing developmental things ... But they go in for support to their own, not [the] South. (Interview 87/2012)

'Going in for support to their own [society]' means that many in the diaspora invest in the kinship systems that are the basis of most agro-pastoralist societies in Upper Nile. The Lost Boys phenomenon grew out of a 1991 split in the SPLA, a split which soon acquired an ethnic colouring, and for that reason, many Lost Boys are Dinka. Some interviewees from the diaspora argued that diaspora commitment to the promotion of an entire ethnic group was an attempt to go beyond family support to something bigger – that is, the beginnings of a contribution to a national identity. One Akobo politician believed that diaspora identification with a major sectional grouping was evidence that people were imagining themselves as part of larger-order communities.

> [Among the] diaspora – the big social change is education. Some of them, from nothing, have bachelors' [degrees].

They are becoming an inspiration to others … They had that tendency of rewarding the community. Only a few may think of their immediate families. They think of wider basis. That's why they form Lou Nuer society. Not a Gun or Mor society – we've been resisting this thing. Because people feel insecure. Wherever you go you get Lou, Lou, Lou. Lou are unique in regards to other Nuer. The only society that have identified themselves as Lou – ethnically, not geographically. (Interview 19/2012)

This particularism means that different diasporas play different roles in different contexts: bridewealth is increasing in Murle society, but Murle diasporas play no role in bidding it up, according to one Murle leader (interview 105/2012). In contrast, diasporas can play an important role in debates over state and county borders. One Jonglei politician explained that there was a delegation of Murle and Anuak people from the diaspora coming to discuss state division:

These people influence the politicians, 'We can contribute from the US to you'. They want politicians to take [more] land, otherwise the Nuer in diaspora will not stand with them, they will stand with someone who is serious about taking land. Diaspora people communicate with people on the ground and you become a bad man.

Is this going to lead to conflict? Absolutely.

Why are the diaspora powerful? As a member of the ruling party, there are some areas I won't touch. But diaspora can say anything. (Interview 139/2012)

The diaspora played a role in the recent violence between Murle and Lou Nuer communities. Lou Nuer websites based in the United States incited violence against Murle people, and inhibited peaceful resolution. One local government official, with US connections, said: 'Nuer in the US want to buy ammunition, not to make peace' (interview 79/2012). Not all Lou Nuer people in the diaspora supported this aggressive stance; and those that did probably had relatively little influence. They added fuel to an existing sense of injustice rather than influencing tactics or strategy: in December 2011, their genocidal rhetoric was reproduced in graffiti on the walls of Likongwele hospital, but was readily disavowed in the peace conferences that followed the attack on Pibor county (anonymous, interview 123/2012).

Diasporas from (northern) Sudan and East Africa

Returning Lost Boys in Greater Bor and Nuer bloggers in Nebraska are the most visible members of the diaspora. But the biggest diasporas were in (northern) Sudan and East African countries. Up to four and a half million Southerners were displaced by the war, according to some estimates, and at the end of the war, the southern population of northern Sudan was estimated at around one or two million and mostly occupying the lower ranks of the labour market there (IDMC 2010). Nearly all Southerners left Sudan after the referendum that led to the establishment of an independent South Sudan, under pressure from the Khartoum government, which saw them as a potential opposition constituency. After the first civil war, South Sudanese societies with limited assistance from government commissions and international funds welcomed the return of a million refugees (Alier 2003; Malok 2009). A similar reintegration process got under way after the 2005 Comprehensive Peace Agreement.

Up to half of Jonglei state's population left during the war years. Their place of displacement was often determined by available escape routes. Many people from the north-west corner of Jonglei state – Lak, Thiang and Gaawar Nuer; and Rut, Thoi, Ruweng and Luaic Dinka – moved to Malakal and the north. Many people from the south-west – Bor, Twic and Nyaraweng/Ghol (also called Duk) Dinka – moved to Equatoria and Kenya, although some moved to northern Sudan. Many from the eastern half of the state – Lou Nuer, Murle, Jieh and Kachippo people – moved to Ethiopia, although substantial numbers also moved north. A 2008 report estimated that about 200,000 returned to the state in the aftermath of the CPA: the report estimated that Bor town had a population of 50,000–70,000 people, approximately 75 per cent of whom were returnees – in 2012, Bor's population was nearer 300,000 people (Pantuliano et al. 2008).

The scale of the displacement and return is so wide ranging that it is difficult to summarize. In Pibor market, ladies make sugary spiced tea in the Khartoum way. In Bor, groups of women manage restaurants selling northern stews and flatbreads (*mulah* and *kisra*) and the Nilotic classic *wal wal*, a sorghum couscous served with a thin yoghurt and flavoured with *lalob*, a bitter and nutritious kernel. They sell this recently commodified rural cuisine to soldiers, office workers and students in neat shacks of corrugated iron in the market, transforming the informal economy and local gender orders in the process. Many of these returnees did not understand the violence:

> It was the people returning from the north who were killed [in the December 2011 attack on Pibor; unlike local people] they didn't know how to run … There were many women because women returnees from northern Sudan were separated from their husbands, who were mostly [former Sudanese army] soldiers in Juba looking for work or papers. (Pibor politician, interview 89/2012)

But the experience of moving to northern Sudan does not necessarily lead to a facility for market exchange or a lack of familiarity with violence – the paths to modernity in South Sudan are jagged, after all. Two Nuer men in their late twenties or early thirties described their time in northern Sudan: studying and working in construction and agriculture. They said that they did not learn much Arabic and were not able to feed their children every day, and had gone back to 'running after cows' and being 'white soldiers' (part of a group of armed rural youth) (young Nuer men reportedly in the White Army, interviews 47/2012 and 77/2012). In spite of explicit denials, they probably participated in or led the 2011 attack on Pibor.

Sara Pantuliano and her colleagues (2008) found that only 10 per cent of the returnees in the period from 2005 to 2008 received any form of government or international assistance. This probably indicates the resilience of kinship systems, which took the strain of much of these returns. Sometimes, people reconnect with these kinship systems by returning to rural settlements and villages that have not changed much physically since the start of the war (social relations have been violently modernized by phenomena like the White Army – see Chapter 7). But probably more often, returnees are connecting with kinship systems in urban areas, where associations play a role in bringing people from the same areas or ethnic communities together.

Urban ethnic associations

Much of South Sudan's urbanization was a traumatic response to rural conflict. But as people became accustomed to the services and opportunities available in towns, many chose to stay. People moving from the diaspora after the peace agreement or the referendum had also become open to urban life. However, the move to towns is costly: most water supply is privatized, and government services like education and health are not free at the point of delivery. People arriving from villages or returning from the diaspora have few safety nets unless they are eligible for a few weeks of the World Food Programme's half-kilo daily grain rations. So they need to use their existing social networks to survive the transition, and these are largely configured around kinship. As well as providing a welfare system for people, kinship forms the basis of many urban communities. Family status laws – governing divorce and adoption – are mostly customary, and this gives a role to the traditional authorities of ethnic communities in the towns.

In South Sudan and across Africa, townspeople began to form ethnic community associations shortly after the development of towns. 'They are not a survival from pre-European society,' wrote Thomas Hodgkin towards the end of the colonial era (Hodgkin 1956: 86). Although based on traditional social structures, African urban ethnic associations were mostly led by educated young men who used the associations to maintain influence at home. Severino Fuli Boke Tombe Ga'le reports the existence of a Madi community association in Juba in 1938, which linked Madi intellectuals in the capital with Madi people in the centre of Madi culture in South Sudan around Nimule, on the Ugandan border (Ga'le 2002: 96). Ga'le describes their roles in the early 1950s as follows: 'The Madi civil servants in Juba formed an association called the Madi Community Council (which still exists). Its Central Executive Committee was subject to the approval of all the Madi working-class throughout the southern districts, and was recognised by the bulk of the Madi in the country' (ibid.: 46).

The chiefs of one Madi group, Madi-Lukayi, are drawn from a leading or royal clan, and Ga'le describes how during a succession crisis in 1950, the Madi Community Council secretly nominated a civil servant from that clan to become chief: 'If Mr. Okumu [the Council's nominee] won the confidence of the majority at home, then he would become the head-chief … and allow swift channeling of development projects for the whole of Madi.' The leading clan accepted the nomination and submitted it to the district commissioner and governor for approval '(with secret copy to Madi Community Council-Central Executive Committee)'. Okumu was chief for over two decades, making an alliance with the Khartoum government against Anya-nya during the first civil war, and surviving as chief thanks to the amnesty contained in the 1972 Addis Ababa agreement. The Anya-nya movement appointed alternative chiefs to manage the displacement of the

Madi population during the war, and Ga'le, by then an exiled politician, re-established the Council: 'When in 1965 the Madi moved out of their homes and settled either in liberated areas or in exile along the borders in response to an ANYA-NYA call, I rejuvenated the Madi community council amongst them, which turned the Madi into horses willing to shoulder any national revolutionary functions' (ibid.: 50).

Ga'le's account is given at some length because his is a unique documentary record of vernacular connections between town and rural structures of authority and the role of ethnicity in those connections. His account of secret letters under the nose of the [British] district commissioner; 'modern' structures such as a central executive committee; chiefly openness to the interventions of educated intellectuals promising development; and the way that intellectuals could end up on different sides of the revolutionary struggle but nonetheless maintain their leading roles in wartime and peace – all would be recognizable today. His description of his compatriots as 'horses' suggests respectful consideration of people who are seen as slightly less than comrades. One Jonglei politician, discussing these groups today, described the distinction between a political figure and his ethnic community in paternalist terms: 'You are not acting in the same wavelength. It is very difficult for you to update them for your level, or to sacrifice/forsake them' (interview 19/2012).

Urban ethnic associations are diverse, ranging from small groups of minor officials raising funds to repair hospitals and schools, to the glittering supporters of the Gaajak ambassadors mentioned earlier. They are often democratically organized – the presence of executive committees usually denotes an electing membership. They have different meanings in the capital and in the periphery. A young state parliamentarian from Nasir, the major Gaajak capital near the Ethiopian border, earnestly defended the appointments:

During all those wars, most of the rebel groups were in the

Jikainy Nuer area [Gaajak are part of the Jikainy Nuer]. When John Garang went to the Jikainy area, he established his movement there. He mobilized the youth to be trained in camps … we thought we have helped a lot. The food which is eaten by the forces, they get it from us. The labour – they even forced the young boys to carry the bullets. Then you will say, let me be a military rather than a labourer without pay. [Recruits] from Bahr al-Ghazal did not bring enough ladies and they married from [Jikainy areas] … During war, Arabs cannot come. So that was a liberated area, no development at all. In the representation we are not represented. Upper Nile has four ministers from Shilluk, one from Dinka and one from Nuer in Juba. When they went to Salva Kiir, he said I have noticed you are not represented, that's why five ambassadors came, it was even through struggle. (Interview 157/2012)

Politicians can use these groups as a means of communicating with their rural constituencies. Most politicians spend relatively little time in their home areas, but these extended networks allow for wide communication and the formulation of interests (senior state parliament office-holder, interview 38/2012). These urban ethnic communities are even influencing urban development patterns, as one politician from Greater Bahr al-Ghazal commented:

There is a lot of villagization of the towns. You can see some of our homes. I'm comparing with Khartoum, I was brought up in a multicultural space. Everybody here [Juba] is around their section, Agars have their own, the Gaajak [a Lakes state Dinka section and an Upper Nile state Nuer section]. The politicians are the ones running those things, the division of electoral constituencies and *payam*s, so the government has legalized this type of thing, it's becoming entrenched … The people in towns are very much linked to the villages, those people in the suits will go to the *tukul* and talk about petty petty things. (Interview 12/2012)

The interests of the urban salariat and rural pastoralists and cultivators are not synonymous, but the emerging political order in South Sudan links them, and this linkage helps shapes some of South Sudan's political contests, such as the arguments over administrative boundaries. Urban groups participate in these arguments over distant borders in underpopulated peripheries – because of awareness of subterranean resources there, and because new counties mean new posts for which they or their families might compete.

So these networks are not just a welfare system: educated people seeking appointments or access to capital need to negotiate them effectively in order to attain their goals. They are also a means of miscommunication:

> Intellectuals and elite in urban centres are living a decent life. Sometimes they may not be well versed in the actual situation on the ground … any decision they make is not really [informed] because they are just getting info as a second- or third-hand information … they make abrupt decisions which in some cases they can fall into trouble without analysis. (Bor politician, interview 142/2012)

Ethnic associations can potentially play a powerful role in state politics. The Lou Community Association in Juba is led by cabinet ministers and, according to one interviewee, it intervenes simultaneously in the politics of Jonglei and the politics of Nuer representation at the centre of the state (SPLA reserve officer, interview 63/2012). But Murle people do not seem to have the same kind of ethnic associations, according to one Murle researcher and activist (interview 124/2012). In part, this is because urban Murle people are routinely associated with rural Murle raiding groups, as members or instigators (one of the problems of ethnic associations that are channels of urban–rural political communication is that they are readily suspected of instigation and collusion when conflicts erupt in polarized areas). In places like Bor, most Murle people have left, and those who remain live in government rest-houses or hotels near state offices.

Another reason for the apparent inability of Murle people to form urban ethnic associations is the age-set system, which organizes male pastoral tasks around age. In times of violence, age sets can form the basis for mobilization for war (Andretta 1985: 124ff.). In other Jonglei societies with age sets, this system was deliberately weakened by the SPLA during wartime. But in the relatively introverted and embattled Murle society it appears to have been strengthened and militarized. According to the researcher and activist interviewed, the Murle age-set system has paradoxically undermined the development of an urban association for all Murle people. After the December 2011 attack on Pibor, the Murle community in Juba contributed food and blankets for children affected by the attack. One thousand children came to the commissioner's compound in Pibor to collect biscuits, and about thirty-six children who had lost contact with their parents stayed in the compound. But the Murle community in Juba seems not to have established an ethnic community association like those of their neighbours: people prefer to organize around age sets rather than in the surprisingly widespread modern idiom of the Community Association with its Central Executive Committee (Murle researcher, interview 124/2012). According to Diana Felix da Costa, a researcher working in Pibor county and among Murle diaspora, those sections of the community using social media are beginning to make new connections (interview 2/2014).

For the SPLM, particularist organizations such as urban ethnic associations are politically useful. In twentieth-century Sudan, they tended to increase in importance during periods of single-party dominance (Thomas 2010: 140). Then, they allowed for the articulation of local interests in a way that could not threaten the dominance of the ruling party. They also made concerted action by ethnically diverse marginalized groups difficult. Today, South

Sudan has no political movement of hunger or resistance – instead, the hungry and the resisting communicate with political leaderships through urban–rural networks based on kinship or ethnicity.

Ethnicity and the state

Ethnicity appears to have acquired an ever-denser tangibility in South Sudanese politics, for a number of reasons. First, economic development has taken place in territories historically divided among different ethnic groups, and partially administered by traditional authorities drawn from those groups – and that economic development happened unevenly. It created spatial as well as social hierarchies, and in South Sudan spatial hierarchies often promote or demote people according to ethnicity. Secondly, rural government systems emphasized ethnicity, drawing administrative borders around sectional and subsectional territories. Thirdly, these territories and the sections that inhabit them are the constituencies for South Sudan's politicians, who were often unable to manage political bases through resource allocation, and have been tempted into mobilizing them by invoking fears of 'ethnic demotion' instead. Fourthly, communities are urbanizing rapidly, and ethnic affiliations have helped many people negotiate tough transitions into towns without welfare systems. Fifthly, the state's financial resources have largely been used for state consolidation rather than redistribution – paying salaries for security forces and a civil service. The main means of ensuring fairness in distribution is the ethnic quota system, whereby different groups are guaranteed government posts, or are given additional posts in response to complaints of under-representation. This forces ambitious people to develop ethnic backing. Finally, many of the military and economic systems during South Sudan's long civil wars manipulated traditional structures and ethnic differences in order to achieve political goals. Ex-adversaries, generally from militias mobilized around ethnicity, went on the state payroll and into ethnically mixed military units, where they and their commanders tried to negotiate their incorporation into South Sudan's new political order.

The SPLM system and ethnicity

South Sudan's political order is overwhelmingly dominated by a single party, the SPLM. It has not achieved this overwhelming dominance through the military defeat of its enemies, but through a mixture of military steadfastness, diplomacy and national consensus-building backed by oil revenues. In the decade after 1991, the movement split into factions. The dissidents publicly called for internal democracy and an independent South Sudan, in opposition to John Garang's authoritarianism and his commitment to a transformed, unified Sudan. But such ideological differences were overshadowed by a 1991 massacre, committed by a largely Nuer army against a largely Dinka populace in Bor town, which deeply implicated the dissidents in the worst kind of ethnic politics. The dissidents, many of them from Nuer groups, allied with Khartoum. Khartoum encouraged these ethnic militias in the belief that they would lead to a quicker or cheaper victory for the Khartoum government. They came to believe that a determined scorched-earth strategy in the oil-rich border areas, mostly home to Nuer people, would transform their economic position, and that fostering intra-Nuer divisions could help them achieve that. The 1997 Khartoum Peace Agreement brought many of these leaders into the Khartoum government. One politician of Nuer origin who was a close ally of Khartoum retrospectively argued in support of this policy: 'We pledged our full support to defend the oil exploration ... It was possible but not an easy task. The SPLA and the West did not like it. But we took a political decision: we cannot have peace without financial resources' (interview 19/2012).

But the devastating oil wars in Nuer areas helped push some SPLM/A dissidents back to John Garang's mainstream faction. Riek Machar, who had reached the office of Sudanese vice-president as a result of his agreement with Khartoum, defected from Khartoum in 1999 and rejoined John Garang's movement in 2002. With US prompting, the SPLA/M and the Khartoum government began peace talks, signing a cessation-of-hostilities agreement.

The reconciliation between Riek Machar and John Garang was driven by military and diplomatic realities, and it proved to be a model for the incorporation of other South Sudanese political and military forces which had dallied with Khartoum after the 2005 Comprehensive Peace Agreement was signed. By then, there was plenty of oil money to lubricate the new spendthrift consensus, which ensured the SPLM's dominance of the political scene. But it was not enough to manage the wider contradictions of South Sudanese society.

The 2010 elections showed the limitations of the SPLM's system of consensus. The SPLM candidate, Salva Kiir, got 97 per cent of presidential votes, and his party took 94 per cent of seats in the Southern parliament (the composition of the legislature was modified after independence). South Sudan's formally pluralist political order is effectively a single-party system. Such systems may work if the party is agile enough to negotiate or resolve social and economic contradictions within its own structures. In some periods of African history, single-party systems were seen as preferable to multiparty systems, which it was feared would aggravate those contradictions. But in 2010, the SPLM was not yet a locus for negotiating and resolving the country's contradictions.

Instead of addressing South Sudanese contradictions, the SPLM moved them into the arguments about administrative boundaries and government post allocations, which are at the centre of real politics in South Sudan. The 2010 elections were a moment when the SPLM could have used its potential as a mass movement to start to address the dilemmas of representation and allocation of resources in a society increasingly structured around ethnicity. The SPLM entered those elections as the dominant political movement with overwhelming powers of resource allocation. It was bound to win the elections: what mattered more than the vote was the nomination process. A nominations process based on local consultations and attentive readings of local personalities and priorities might have allowed the party to address some of the contradictions arising from South Sudan's diversity. The elections in northern Sudan (Sudan was one country in 2010) took place in a comparable situation, with the dominant National Congress Party holding all the cards and taking all the votes. The National Congress Party's internal consultation mechanisms were a central part of the nominations process, and were an occasion for real politics, at least within the party. But in what was then Southern Sudan, the nominations process lacked transparency.

The 2010 elections also saw the emergence of another kind of 'real politics' in South Sudan: the mutiny. After the elections, some failed candidates in Jonglei and Upper Nile turned to insurrection. Unsuccessful candidates were able to mobilize support for insurrection in the remote and peripheral areas of Jonglei, in particular. Generally, they used ethnicity as a basis for mobilization. People turn to violence in these places because peripheries are politically incoherent, economically marginalized, and their militarized populations are desperate enough to risk a costly challenge to the 'single-party system'. These mutinies, as will be seen in Chapters 7 and 8, played lethally into tensions between different ethnic communities, such as those between Nuer and Murle people.

The SPLA system and ethnicity

The government had a limited capacity to defeat insurgents, and relied instead on co-opting former adversaries by putting them on the payroll of the security forces (rather than the county payroll). This system began with the 2006 Juba Declaration, which incorporated most of South Sudan's Khartoum-aligned militias (known as Other Armed Groups) into the SPLA. The deal ate up most of the country's budget, but until the crisis of December 2013, it was the basis for the country's most durable ceasefire.

In 1955, there were 1,770 soldiers in the Southern Corps of the Sudanese army (COI: 1956). Five decades later, when the SPLA's first payroll audit was completed, 177,000 soldiers were enumerated (military official, interview 6/2013). This figure may not even have included the tens of thousands of militia members who were being incorporated into the system at the time, nor the large numbers absorbed into paramilitary forces like the police and the wildlife service. The SPLA served as an expensive mechanism for resolving the contradictions of the long civil war. It united John Garang's guerrilla army and the Khartoum-aligned militias that had fought against them in a single vast structure that in 2013 was the third-largest army in Africa – only Sudan's and Egypt's were bigger (IISS 2014).

The post-2006 SPLA was based on the formation of ethnically mixed units made up of former adversaries. The SPLA was given the unmilitary task of providing a framework for national identity and national reconciliation. The SPLM's route to nation-building was a small county headquarters in a county whose borders were configured around ethnicity: the SPLA's was the creation of a multi-ethnic unit, generally working in Arabic: the nation's unacknowledged lingua franca is often the language of command. The SPLA's powers of patronage are also significant: part of the SPLA's role in greater Upper Nile is to provide an alternative means of inclusion on the state payroll for youth leaders involved in local violence. Another important means by which the SPLA distributes the country's wealth is the location of barracks. Senior commanders set up barracks in their home areas, and payday at the barracks is a significant event for a small town. Traders moved from as far as Darfur to barracks towns in the mud of Khor Fulluth or Owach, homes to two senior generals (anonymous, interview 172/2012).

In the SPLA, the quota system, as well as acting as a means of redistribution, was supposed to act as a means of reconciliation. In interviews in 2010, during the tense run-up to South Sudan's independence, SPLA senior officers acknowledged that national reconciliation was for them an unconventional military task:

> *You see the SPLA as a place for reconciliation?* The SPLA will remain as an example towards the unification of the whole south ... Despite the fact that the army is for an entity called South Sudan not an army of one political party, we believe that the support given to the SPLM is because of the SPLA ... It's an example that can bring the people of South Sudan together – we have all representation within SPLA together. And we've opened up. Whatever damage you have done to SPLA you are forgivable. When you come you are transformed. But that is not the case within SPLM – it's a combination of people with different opinions in one basket and they are fighting in the basket.
>
> *If reconciliation is led by the military, it has a lot of implications for society?* We're aware of that. We are forced by the North [the Khartoum government] to do that. The North has decided to form militias. They are depleting our resources through those militias, whether fighting them or integrating them. (Interview 191/2010)

An enormous map of Jonglei hung on the wall. George Athor had just begun his post-election rebellion there, which was soon networked with another rebellion in Murle-land, and everyone in the SPLA was saying that Khartoum was providing the weapons. Athor was killed a year later, but the rebellions in Murle-land were resolved by incorporating rebel leaders into the SPLA. The strategy deeply distorted the national budget. But it was an almost unavoidable temporary solution to the presence of huge numbers of Khartoum-backed militias in South Sudan, many of which were drawn from Nuer ethnic constituencies.

Incorporating these militias in the military was a costly political achievement for South Sudan. In Jonglei and in other pastoralist areas, the achievement was greatly complicated by the way that guns had infiltrated production systems – most cattle keepers had them, and many used looting as a restocking mechanism. These young men were armed civilians, not soldiers, and they could not readily be integrated into the new system. The next few chapters explain why.

PART TWO
JONGLEI'S MUTINIES

The next three chapters discuss South Sudan's second civil war, and the post-war violence it has shaped. They are not comprehensive accounts of Sudan's civil wars, which have received much attention from historians (Wakoson 1984; Nyaba 1997; Jok 2001; Ga'le 2002; Alier 2003; HRW 2003; Johnson 2003; Poggo 2009; Malok 2009). The wars lasted such a long time, were so entangled in regional and world politics, and moved through such complicated phases, that even the best accounts run the risk of descending into patternless detail, or of shifting dizzily between too many vantage points.

This book tries to avoid the problem of patternlessness by presenting South Sudan's military history in a political context. Part Two begins with a short memorable life story, which illustrates the political history of a fierce and dependent colonial and post-colonial state, which organized its relationship with rural society around ethnicity, and which used posts as a principal means of distributing power and wealth. Chapter 6 tells the story of the tragic miscalculations of a gifted intermediate school graduate from Pibor who made his way through the Sudanization commissions' version of meritocracy to a short government career. Hassan Ngachingol, the protagonist of the story, is part of South Sudan's military history because he helped to reinvent the state-dependent ethnic militia, which had disappeared from South Sudan at the end of colonial pacification campaigns. Their re-emergence dates from the 1960s, and their subsequent growth was temporarily arrested by the post-2006 SPLA, which incorporated all of the most organized ethnic militias into government payroll and created a vast general staff. A crisis in Juba in December 2013 appears to have put an end to that process of unification and apparently has seen a reconfiguration of military power around the political structures of the countryside. Since the emergence of the colonial and post-colonial states, those political structures have been bounded by ethnicity.

Another problem in telling war histories is the vantage point. South Sudanese rebels sought to establish control over 'the bush' – the periphery – and move from there to control provincial towns, state infrastructure and resource-rich areas. Violence was patterned around 'strategic resources' – resources or populations needed for South Sudan to participate in the wider world economy. But it is too simple to say that the long cruel conflict was just about these resources – the violence was also patterned around the (ethnic) political structures of rural South Sudan. Wars in South Sudan are complicated because they fit into different regional and global conflicts too – the Cold War and its aftermath in the Horn of Africa and the Great Lakes, the Arab–Israeli conflict, the War Against Terror and wars in the Sahara. At different points in South Sudan's long wars, people have died as a direct result of these outside conflicts.

A comprehensive narrative needs too many perspectives. As an experimental alternative to a comprehensive approach, Chapters 7 and 8 present the civil war and its aftermath mainly from three hinterland vantage points – starting with Pibor county and moving to Nuerland and Greater Bor. They focus mostly on youth armies, because these were such an important legacy of the wars. The youth structures improvised during these wars were local attempts to deal with the problems of marginalized peripheries. They outlasted the war because marginalization did – they continued as a marker of the violent contradictions and diminished possibility in South Sudan's hinterlands.

6 | THE LIFE AND DEATH OF HASSAN NGACHINGOL

In 1954, committees were formed to replace the eight hundred British personnel in the Sudan government with Sudanese civil servants. The committees made decisions on merit – that is, the facility to pass civil service examinations. They paid no attention to the question of regional representation, appointing only six people from Sudan's southern provinces and two from Darfur (Ruay 1994: 70ff.). Many people interviewed for this study said that Hassan Ngachingol was one of the six appointed from the south, although the Sudan Government List of 1959 says that he was first appointed in April 1956, as the *mamur* of Pibor district (*mamur* was a senior administrative post which in the late colonial period was usually held by locally appointed, rather than British, personnel).

Ngachingol was one of five boys from his age group who were sent to the American mission school in Nasir, on the River Sobat near the Ethiopian border. Steven Babanen Tonga, the first Pibor MP, was in his class too (government official, interview 91/2012). Ngachingol was from the Murle community and when he went to mission school, he was called David. He took the name Hassan when he became a Muslim. A handful of educated Murle people converted to Islam, perhaps seeing it as a means to improve communications with the new independent government in Khartoum (pastor, interview 105/2012).

The government was led by the nationalist movement in Khartoum, dominated by the bureaucratic and commercial beneficiaries of the cotton export economy that Britain had established around Sudan's capital. They inherited the state from Sudan's co-domini without a fight: they did not need to build a mass movement that might have worked through some of Sudan's contradictions, when they could play on Anglo-Egyptian rivalries instead. They rejected the possibility of investing in the periphery to correct the regional imbalances that the cotton economy had created. Instead, they selected idealized versions of Arab culture and Islamic religion as the basis for a unified national identity, and they began to impose that culture and religion on southern provinces (Khalid 1990: 152).

South Sudan's modernized sectors were tiny – the army, the graduates of a few English-medium schools, a cotton plant in Western Equatoria. In the *dirigiste* colonial economy, cotton workers had often been paid lower wages for the same work as cotton workers in the north, and in the run-up to independence, hundreds were sacked and replaced by northerners. Southern soldiers in the Southern Corps mutinied when they were ordered to Khartoum. These protests were ferociously repressed. Southern parliamentarians organized against the dominance of the centre over the periphery, often in concert with groups from the closed districts in northern provinces, such as Darfur, Kordofan and Blue Nile. The parliament's inability to deal with this challenge to the structure of the new state was one of the factors behind a military takeover in 1958. The new regime countered federalist demands by intensifying the Arabization and Islamization of the southern provinces. In response, civil servants and politicians established an opposition in exile with an armed wing, Anya-nya, in the early 1960s. From 1963, isolated skirmishes turned into a rebellion with a name. School students and remnants of the 1955 mutinies began armed opposition within the south.

One of Anya-nya's first attacks was on 9 September 1963, against the police post in Pochalla, a village in what was then Pibor district on the Ethiopian border that was home to the Anuak king (Ruay 1994: 106). The Khartoum army's violence eventually pushed most of the south into support for the rebels, but at the outset the rebels were concentrated in the schools and military structures of the south's small modern sector. Chiefs had sat on the judges' benches when mutineers were hanged, and uneducated people working in the subsistence economy were not likely to have an understanding of the aims of the rebellion: Sister Ermello Cariolato, a nurse at Malakal hospital, treated seven young men dying of their tortures after being arrested by the army, and she doubted that they were 'freedom fighters': 'They seemed to be simple villagers to me as they spoke neither Arabic or English. Only one of the seven could say "moya", the Arabic word for water' (Sudan Informazioni News Agency n.d.: 51).

Students, in contrast, played a leading role, and were encouraged to do so by older politicians and intellectuals who had gone into exile. Education – in an Arabic-language, nationalist curriculum and often in Islamic schools – was the mainstay of the government's development policy for the south, and the schools in Upper Nile were Islamized most quickly (Sanderson and Sanderson 1981: 366; IBRD 1973: 5–7). But school graduates feared that they would not get government jobs, which were dominated by northern officials: 'there was ... the realisation that racism would limit their prospects', said one student of the time (interview 61/2012; Oduho and Deng 1963: 18). The Pochalla attack on Pibor was led by Paul Nyingore, an Anuak school student, who may have persuaded a young educated member of the Anuak royal family to provide the rebels with a small stash of firearms, which were an inheritance from the early twentieth-century trade in arms, grain and ivory organized around the Ethiopian border. Within a year of Nyingore's attack, boys began to desert schools and drift into armed opposition in the bush: boy student enrolment went down from 12.6 per cent in 1964 to 2.0 per cent in 1965 (IBRD 1973: Table C-3).

Some educated Murle men joined the rebels, including the MP Steven Babanen Tonga, John Tholomuthe and John Kireru.

Several ordinary Murle people joined too. But Ngachingol tried to prevent Murle people from joining the rebellion. One Murle civil servant said: 'Hassan Ngachingol prevented Murle from joining Anya-nya I. He said, you are not educated. If there is a liberation, and you're not educated, what will you be? He was encouraging education. After you are educated join the movement' (government official, interview 91/2012). Instead, Ngachingol invested his community in the government's survival. The government set up local militias called *al-haras al-watani*, the National Guard, in 1963 or 1965. The militias distributed small arms to villagers.

Local National Guard militias were under the command of the local district commissioner, according to one interviewee, a senior army officer. Ngachingol's force used superior government guns against Anuak areas, even killing the Anuak king, he said (Jonglei politician, interview 137/2012). The importance of a local militia in Pibor for managing a troublesome border was stressed by a politician from Akobo:

> Hassan Ngachingol influenced the relationship between Murle and the government. He was trusted by the government. When the rebellion took place, Hassan adhered to the government, including arming the tribes. So he armed his own people under the pretext of local protection, from Dinka, Nuer, Anuak and Jieh people. But the government interest was to fight to rebellion, because Pochalla was very near. (Jonglei politician, interview 19/2012)

The National Guard was not everywhere based on the creation of ethnic antagonism, or the identification of Islamized allies in the south. In Shilluk areas, a paramount chief named Edward Amum Okiech established a National Guard after the local Anya-nya commander killed three of his brothers in a dispute related to the chief's participation in a national conference. On the east bank of the Bahr al-Zeraf a Gaawar Nuer prophet named Gony Yut got government arms too. Another prophet on Zeraf Island called Ruei Kuic, in contrast, sided with Anya-nya and began killing tribal chiefs on the island, calling them government people (Upper Nile academic, interview 149/2012; Jonglei politician, interview 165/2012; Johnson 1994: 300). Maker Thijok, a Lou Nuer man from near Waat in central Jonglei, joined the National Guard after his cattle were stolen by Samuel Gai Tut, one of the first leaders of Anya-nya and himself a Lou Nuer.

> Maker Thijok – the first Lou to become *haras al-watani* – his cattle camp was attacked by Samuel Gai Tut [an Anya-nya commander] and his cattle were taken. They were being driven to Bor [now capital of Jonglei state]. When he got the news that his cattle have been taken, he asked his children, how many of you have been killed. They said, none. He said, these are girls, these are not my boys. He called them and said, it is better for you to lose your sons than to lose your cattle. Because having cattle the family will grow and the dead will have a wife [a reference to the system of ghost marriage, whereby a deceased man is legally married to a living woman, and her children by another man are legally his]. So he said, please go back. They went and followed the Anya-nya force and clashed between Duk and Yuai [north of Bor]. Most of his sons, about nine, got killed, but the cows were retrieved. So when the cows reached his home area between Pieri and Waat, he moved to Waat, made his agreement with the army, and became *haras al-watani*. He was armed, and his cattle used to graze between Walgak and Waat in an open area under army surveillance. They married for those who got killed, now Maker is a large family, the area is now called after him instead of his father. (Jonglei politician, interview 19/2012)

The National Guard, in some accounts, were small fry, men recruited by chiefs and district commissioners at the behest of the army. There was an army and a police post in Pibor at the time. One Pibor man, who was reportedly a member of Ngachingol's force, said: 'They were not many – fifty or so. They had *abu khamsa* [outdated rifles]. They didn't go on operations. They were community police. They had no military barracks, they stayed at home only. They didn't have khaki either. They were in the city. They didn't go out' (interview 187/2012). In Nuer-land, some people called them *kiyadit* – snitches – a Nuerized word for the CID or Criminal Investigation Department (Upper Nile politician, interview 97/2012).

Ngachingol was one of the highest-ranking Southerners in the civil service. He took his alliance with Khartoum much more personally than other people in the National Guard system – apparently, his disappointment with the alliance led to his suicide, which seems to have been tied up with his support for army and police recruitment. As the war progressed, Ngachingol became a district commissioner, and his district was enlarged to cover both Akobo and Pibor, a vast stretch along the Ethiopian border. He encouraged young Murle men to join regular forces:

> He became DC of Akobo and Pibor. They invited him to
> army barracks there and *jallaba* [Northern Sudanese] soldiers
> said they had taken the Murle boys and killed them. Hassan
> Ngachingol heard this, he was a Muslim and he tended
> towards Arab. Murle themselves didn't want Muslims. When
> Hassan Ngachingol heard this he got angry that he had helped
> the *jallaba* government and he went out and took his pistol
> and killed himself. In 1965, June or May. He demanded
> pistol from his driver, he was a rough man [that you had to
> obey] ... The *jallaba* soldiers were right, more than twenty
> [Murle] police in Yambio had been killed, in 1964. But they
> kept recruiting. That was the first recruitment. It's kept up.
> (Government official, interview 91/2012)

Suicide is a very unusual ending for a South Sudanese, or for an ambitious politician anywhere. The details of Ngachingol's life are difficult to piece together at this distance, but his story is an important one for Murle history. 'Hassan Ngachingol had a big effect on the politics of Murle. He killed himself for that reason,' said the Murle intellectual quoted above (interview 91/2012). One contemporary recalls that his suicide might have been linked to an affair between his wife and an army officer from the north. But now, his alliance with Khartoum is remembered as the start of a history of Murle collaboration (even though non-Murle groups also joined the National Guard, and even though many Murle joined Anya-nya). The belief in Murle complicity and the belief that a small local force in Pibor could help Khartoum's army secure the Ethiopian border or disrupt Jonglei state is still alive today.

His story is also important for understanding the way that hopes for development and participation in the state began to be transmitted to rural South Sudan. Ngachingol was seeking education and participation in the government for Murle people. He appears to have seen the army as the best hope for his people, and the recruitment which he helped promote became an important route for Murle participation in the salaried and superannuated military economy. Anya-nya's schoolboy rebels were also bringing rural people face to face with their aspirations for education and participation in the government. They retreated to their villages and the forests around them because political changes in towns and schools were undermining their futures. Going to the village, they needed to explain the relevance of town politics and government posts to local community interests. Chiefs had mediated between town and rural politics for many years previously (Leonardi 2013). But things were changing: a Khartoum minister visiting the southern provinces shortly before the outset of the conflict noted a shift from the authority of chiefs to the authority of intellectuals (Sanderson and Sanderson 1981: 379). The civil war that moved to villages from urban state institutions such as barracks and schools meant that the question of modern education and participation in government was being posed by younger voices with different hopes. Even though students and government personnel were still part of the kinship system and may even have come from chiefly families – like the Anauk prince at Pochalla – they were emerging as a social group.

The rebellion required this emerging social group to engage with rural South Sudan. As the rebellion grew, the problem of supplying forces with food led to crises such as the one that led Maker Thijok into the National Guard. Civil administration was established in 1966, and based on colonial precedent (Ga'le 2002: 47f., 282). Many areas had a system of taxation based on compulsory food cultivation, and the end of military food confiscations reportedly improved relationships between the rebel army and local populations (ibid.: 47f.; McColl 1969: 10). Sometimes, the aims of taxation went beyond army provisioning into development: Anya-nya set up 200 schools in the areas it controlled (IBRD 1973: 45).

Ngachingol's story also marks the beginning of independent Sudan's long history of using local communities as the basis of militia recruitment – itself a continuation of colonial practice. Hassan Ngachingol worked through the Murle paramount chief Jakor to recruit people (anonymous, interview 15/2012). The civil administration set up by Anya-nya would also recruit locally: one Anya-nya administrator from present-day Warrap state, Abel Choul, described how he would hold meetings with young people and with the heads of Dinka sectional groups and Dinka religious leaders, to explain the reasons for the struggle and send them to a military headquarters at Teetadol on the route to Congo for training (interview 3/2013).

The National Guard system for organizing local communities for military purposes may have been a way for local communities to protect their social, cultural and production systems from much larger forces sweeping the country. 'The [first] civil war did not deeply fragment the community, the kinship system,' said one politician whose career began in the Anya-nya era (interview

165/2012). But in allowing for temporary conservations of local systems, the National Guard emphasized local differences too. This is clear from its afterlife in the disarmament programme after the Addis Ababa agreement, which was implemented by Anya-nya officers who had been integrated into Khartoum's national army. Some interviewees implicated the National Guard in the breakdown of order in the mid-1970s in places like Akobo, and in a series of clashes between Nuer and Anuak people in the early 1980s that led to most Anuak people leaving Akobo (former local government official, interview 61/2012; Anuak leader, interview 65/2012). In Jonglei's current climate of violence and intercommunal tensions, interviewees often relate the stories of Anya-nya, its adversaries and heirs, in starkly ethnic terms – for Anuak leaders today, the National Guard was a way for Nuer people to use state structures to advance ethnic objectives. This development was not new – ethnicized militias were part of the slave trade that transformed Sudan in the nineteenth century, and part of violent British 'pacification' campaigns in the twentieth, and they exacerbated social divisions. Ngachingol's tiny National Guard helped give the entire Murle people an unwarranted reputation as ethnic collaborators with a hostile Khartoum regime, and was an important milestone in the adoption of these ethnicized, militarized colonial systems of governance for local ends. It is to this story that this book now turns.

7 | THE CIVIL WARS IN JONGLEI

Overview of the 1983–2005 civil war

The remoteness of Jonglei's hinterland from unlistening centres of power gave many of its communities a different experience of wars, states and markets to that of the rest of the flood plains and the remainder of South Sudan. Its remoteness made it a place of mutiny and insurgency, and its proximity to the unsettled and little-known Ethiopian border meant that mutinies and insurgencies often turned into wars. In 1963, an attack on the police station in Pochalla, on the border with Ethiopia, came at the start of the war between Anya-nya and the Khartoum government that lasted until the Addis Ababa peace agreement in 1972. Some Anya-nya forces were incorporated into the Sudanese Armed Forces, and their discontents played out in a series of 'Anya-nya 2' mutinies in the 1970s, many in the garrisons of the eastern flood plains. These mutinies, and the guns and repressions that they spread across the state, were entangled in ethnic tensions, such as that between Anuak and Nuer people in Akobo in the early 1980s; and in the 1983 mutinies in Jonglei barracks such as Bor, which began the SPLA's twenty-two years of war with the Khartoum government.

The SPLA's strategy of defeating its enemy through conventional warfare was described in Chapter 4. The strategy paid off in Jonglei: the SPLA soon controlled most of the eastern flood plains. It also controlled access to the government's two big projects in the region: the Jonglei canal and the oilfields of Upper Nile. The SPLA's war helped to bring down Jaafer Nimeiri's regime, which collapsed in 1985. Nimeiri was replaced by a parliamentary regime that was unable to meet the military challenge from the south. The parliamentary regime began arming irregulars drawn from the marginalized ethnic communities that Nimeiri's debt-financed modernization schemes had tried and failed to include in a new Sudanese political order. In 1989, the parliamentary regime fell to an astute alliance of Islamists, security men and financiers who intensified the war in the south. In 1991, with the end of the Cold War and the fall of the socialist-military regime in Ethiopia, the SPLA faced crisis. It split and its armed struggle was transformed into a war of factions, militias and raiders that began in Jonglei and spread across greater Upper Nile. The split created the conditions for the government army to mount dry-season campaigns deep into Jonglei's hinterland, and to emerge as the main supplier of money and guns to militias, which proliferated in greater Upper Nile.

Militia proliferation fragmented military efforts and pushed the violence along diverging trajectories. In the north–south borderlands a 1980s war of cattle theft, abduction and plunder turned into a 1990s war for control of oilfields (HRW 2003). In the eastern hinterlands of Jonglei and Upper Nile states, fighting between and within ethnic communities turned into multiple and interlinked wars over ethnic boundaries, water and pastures. These military stalemates lengthened the war, and diplomacy and politics began to overshadow strategy. The divided southern leaderships exploited post-Cold War opportunities and the Horn of Africa's rough-and-tumble interstate system. They set up civil adminis-trations, or militia coalitions; they made peace agreements with Khartoum and temporary reconciliations with each other. Many ordinary people participated generously in these frail precedents for a wider peace. But in the end, the tempo for peace was unexpectedly set by the War Against Terror and the related oil boom that began in 2001. That global war terrified Khartoum's ruling coalition of Islamists, security men and financiers, who had welcomed al-Qaeda's Osama bin Laden to Sudan in the 1990s. In the first five years of the twenty-first century, Khartoum signed security agreements with the United States and repackaged itself as a bulwark against Islamic extremism in north-east Africa. Khartoum's rulers transformed their financial situation through oil exports to East Asian markets. Under international pressure, they concluded a pragmatic and astonishing alliance with their bitterest adversaries, the SPLA.

The 2005 peace agreement was an ambitious attempt to come to terms with Sudan's many contradictions and to redress the imbalances of wealth and power that Sudan's unipolar development model had wrought. But it was also an exclusive deal, between two security elites. It envisaged the incorporation of all other armed groups into the SPLA or the Sudanese Armed Forces, the two armies it recognized. South Sudan had dozens of armed groups, some of which had recognizable structures of command that would allow for incorporation. Many Jonglei groups were different: locally organized and decentralized groups of armed young men who did not fit into the political order set up by the 2005 agreement. They were often drawn from kinship structures or age sets of a group defined by ethnicity or language. But like the urban ethnic associations encountered in Chapter 4, they were not 'traditional' structures. They were mostly young, and mostly lived in remote peripheries whose liberation is proving to be so slow. And many, perhaps most, lived in the eastern hinterlands of Jonglei.

Pibor as vantage point

The version of the civil war presented here takes Pibor county in Jonglei as its first vantage point. It is a spot isolated by its ecological conditions, predominantly inhabited by Murle people. People living in the counties to the north are predominantly Lou Nuer, and those to the west are mostly Bor Dinka. Smaller and much less well-known groups lie to the east and south. The Anuak centre of Pochalla is on the border with Ethiopia. To the

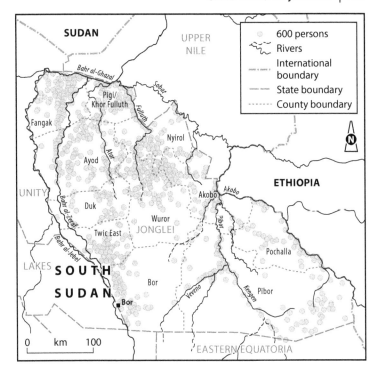

7.1 Counties and population density in Jonglei, 2008 (*source*: SSCCSE 2010: 14)

south-west lies the Kidepo valley of Eastern Equatoria, home to a complex of agro-pastoral communities including groups speaking languages linked to Murle (Didinga, Tenet, Longarim/Boya) as well as Toposa and other Equatorian languages. The Boma plateau, to the south-east of Pibor, is home to Kachippo people: farmers and hunters who speak a Surmic language related to Murle. South of the Boma plateau live Jieh (Jié or Jiye) people, a small group linked to Equatoria and the Toposa language and culture. They keep cattle, and probably began moving to the area in the twentieth century (Kafi 1988; Bader 2000; Harrigan and Arou Man 2005; Walraet 2008). The civil war began with a mutiny in Pibor, Bor and Pochalla in 1983; the first liberated territory was in Pibor county; and in late 2006 the last Khartoum-aligned militia to join the SPLA was the Brigade, also known as the Pibor Defence Force. Even after the Brigade's incorporation, conflict continued in Pibor county. That is why the civil war story is mostly related from Pibor and its surrounding counties.

Setting people against each other

Hassan Ngachingol's life and death introduced a section of the book that deals with military history because of his strangely prototypical life. A bright youngster from a remote and little-known ethnic community, he overcame the enormous obstacles preventing South Sudanese from preferment in the civil service. He became a Muslim to demonstrate, perhaps, his cultural affinity with the post-colonial state in Khartoum. He worked up his ethnic community into a political constituency, and turned some of them into a military force which he put at the service of the state. In doing so, he sometimes brought his people into conflict with their neighbours.

Hassan Ngachingol's National Guard was one of the first militias in post-independence South Sudan. The British had also used ethnicity as a basis for military recruitment in Jonglei. They first occupied Murle-land in 1912, and their troops brought at least 1,600 porters with them. All the porters were from the Dinka population along the river, who paid taxes to British administrators and who demanded protection in return, from the Murle raiders who had been carrying out annual dry-season attacks on people and cattle (Collins 1960: 37). Using ethnic communities to discipline and occupy their neighbours was a policy followed during the harsh pacifications that marked the first decades of British rule. Colonialists subsequently tried to repress interactions between different ethnic communities. They were not able to penetrate South Sudanese society deeply: Murle people had shown little interest in allying with state power before Sudan's independence.

In 1930, British officials had found it difficult to raise a force of twenty-six chiefs' police in Pibor (Willis 1995: 202).

So Hassan Ngachingol's doomed alliance with Khartoum represented something of a new departure. The Home Guard was a military structure established by central government, drawn from his ethnic community to manage local insecurity and repress dissent, and it widened access to firearms in a place that would help trigger off South Sudan's next few wars. According to one historian from Anyidi in Bor county, Murle raids on his area began almost immediately:

> The peace between Murle and Bor [Dinka] held [from 1912] till 1962 when they were armed by the Arabs to fight Anya-nya 1. So the first attack, I was in school, was on the seventeenth of March 1962, Bec Dyang cattle camp was attacked. People got surprised. The hostilities came up and Murle withdrew to Pibor and raiding was happening, until 1972 ... After 1972, Murle attacks on Bor subsided. There was a government in Juba, the Jallaba [northern Sudanese] were far, there was disarmament ... After the 1983 rebellion, Murle attacked cattle camps in Bor in June. It was the first attack since 1972: hostilities always intensify when a North–South war is on. In Nayaj they killed at least thirty-five fighting youth. In Anyidi on the fifteenth of June they killed ninety-six. This was their own decision, but may have been supported by government – but targets were cattle camps. (Interview 43/2012)

This historian's argument, that national politics began to set the pace and scope of violence in Jonglei, is borne out elsewhere. The relative quiet in south-eastern Jonglei following the 1972 Addis Ababa peace agreement may have been the result of government intervention. After the killing of several police and army personnel in Murle-land in 1973, William Nyoun Bany, an Anya-nya officer incorporated into the Sudanese army, led a disarmament campaign there (Jonglei politician, interview 187/2012). William

Nyoun was one of a number of army officers managing the security of Jonglei province and who went on to be leading figures in the SPLA and its later factions. As the peace agreement began to break down, the violence started again. A 1984 study found that there had been fourteen raids in the period from 1969 to 1983, resulting in 112 deaths and the theft of about 14,000 cattle. Eight out of the fourteen raids took place in 1983, the year of the mutinies in Bor and Pibor that started the 1983–2005 civil war (Howell et al. 1988: 266). Records of the violence in the 1970s and 1980s suggest that casualty rates were lower than those of the first decade of the twentieth century (Collins 1960).

National politics may not have been the only factor. In the 1900s and 1960s, ecological conditions or cattle diseases may have been an aggravating factor. Drought brought Murle refugees to Bor areas at the beginning of the twentieth century – just after the continent's devastating encounter with rinderpest. And the period from 1961 to 1964, when the Bec Dyang cattle camp attack occurred, saw very high floods along the length of the Bahr al-Jebel, leading to a tense reorganization of grazing systems among formerly cooperative groups (Howell et al. 1988: 300–1). Local tensions may also have played a role: a Murle interviewee who served in the SPLA believed that the 1983 attacks on Anyidi were linked to the killing of a Murle man named Gayein (interview 104/2012). But it is hard to dismiss the claims of the Anyidi historian quoted above, that Jonglei disturbances were part of a national drift towards war.

The 1980s: Jonglei's militias and the national drift towards war

The 1970s were a period of relative calm in South Sudan. Most of the incidents of insecurity were linked to disagreements about the terms of integration of former Anya-nya forces into the Southern Command of the Sudanese Armed Forces. One of the most serious was the mutiny of the Akobo garrison in 1975. The government formed National Guard units in Akobo to counter the threat from mutineers (former senior local government official, interview 61/2012). These groups, in turn, were drawn into the politics of ethnic boundaries that emerged in Akobo during the Addis Ababa period (see Chapter 5). Local communities were beginning to seek arms to defend territory that they scarcely used (Nyaba 1997: 23–6).

These local disturbances were pulled into a national story. The Khartoum government decided to abrogate the 1972 peace deal that had established the Southern Regional Government. It began by ordering forces absorbed from Anya-nya into the Southern Command of the armed forces to move to the north of the country. When the Jonglei battalions refused to move, the army apparently prepared to disarm them in their barracks. In May 1983, a battalion deployed to Bor, Pibor and Pochalla mutinied and moved to Ethiopia, where they established an alliance with Ethiopia, wrote the manifesto and formed the SPLM/A in July (Alier 2003: 283).

The Murle attacks on Greater Bor in June 1983 may have been incited by Khartoum, but the attackers were not acting as representatives of a unified, corporate Murle system. On the contrary: Murle intellectuals and their local recruits began taking Sudanese territory before the SPLM/A had begun fighting. Lokurnyang Lado was the son of Lado Lokurungole, a Bible translator for the missionaries, an Anuak abductee who had become Murle by forced adoption. His son Lokurnyang led a small leftist faction based around the Khartoum branch of Cairo university, called the South Sudan Liberation Movement or Front (Akol 2009: 4; Nyaba 1997: 27). Ngachigak Ngachaluk was another Murle and a fellow student. A Shilluk student named Pagan Amum was also part of their group, and Pagan's sister later married Ngachigak (Arensen 1992: 20; Swart 1998: 73; Pibor intellectual, interview 91/2012; Upper Nile politician, interview 167/2012).

Lokurnyang Lado's student faction set up a base in Ethiopia, just across the border from Boma. They recruited Murle fighters and in July 1983 they took Boma, making it the first 'liberated territory' of the war (the smallest administrative unit in South Sudan is still called a boma council, in honour of the liberation). They kidnapped some missionaries and ecologists but retreated to Ethiopia after an aerial counter-attack by the Sudanese Armed Forces. After the Boma student revolutionaries retreated to Ethiopia, John Garang and his SPLA/M commanders flew to their base across the Ethiopian border from Boma to negotiate with them. Pagan and Ngachigak both joined the SPLM/A. Ngachigak became a senior commander and died in 1986, commanding an attack on Kapoeta. He was recognized by President Salva Kiir Mayardit as a founder of the SPLM (Kiir Mayardit 2008). Pagan Amum went on to be the secretary-general of the SPLM, a post he held until 2013. But Lado refused to join, and was arrested. At the end of 1984, he was executed by firing squad during a passing-out parade for new recruits at Bonga, an SPLA camp in Ethiopia. The SPLA sometimes scheduled executions around parades, in a theatrical demonstration of its gun culture. Lam Akol, later a political adversary of Pagan's, says that Pagan was a member of Lado's firing squad (senior SPLA commanders, interviews 137/2012, 178/2012; Akol 2009: 4).

In Khartoum, Murle students and soldiers were joining the SPLM/A (SPLA soldier, interview 104/2012). But at the same time, Murle raiders were attacking Bor. According to Nyaba, the SPLM/A sought to contain these conflicts by encouraging young people from areas affected by Murle raiders, to get guns to defend themselves from local insecurity (1997: 26). A senior commander from Bor explained the process:

> Some SPLA teams were sent here from Jamous battalion and mobilized [Greater Bor youth] to form Battalion 105. The best way to get people – you would say the arms are over there [in Ethiopia], you go and get them to protect yourselves against Murle ... when they got [to Ethiopia], they were told they would get arms only after training. Then they were politicized.

John Garang said, your enemy is not Murle, your enemy is Khartoum, who is supplying arms and ammunition to Murle ... This was the political work that was being done, we succeeded. (Interview 137/2012)

The strategy did not diminish intercommunal tensions. In 1985, within two years of the capture of Boma, Ismail Kony, a Murle policeman from a lineage of spiritual leaders, set up a Khartoum-aligned force in Pibor, reportedly to defend the area from the SPLA. The Pibor Defence Force, often called the Brigade, was defeated by an SPLA force in 1987, led by Kennedy Gayein, himself a Murle. The Brigade continued fighting from the bush around Pibor: Johnson argues that they targeted Nuer and Dinka civilians (2003: 68). In response SPLA forces, some reportedly led by Salva Kiir, attacked villages in western and eastern Murle-land in 1988 and again in 1989 (McCallum 2013: 41–2).

Why did a liberation movement turn so quickly against a civilian population, and why did it appear to target Murle people on the basis of ethnicity? The SPLA's strategy was to liberate territory by setting up and unleashing a massive territorial army backed by Ethiopian state power. Its first battles were fought against potential rivals within South Sudan, the most prominent of which was Anya-nya 2. Anya-nya 2 was led by officers who had defected from the Sudanese army long before 1983, many of whom operated in the strategic Ethiopian borderlands. The rebels spent five years fighting before unifying their ranks: the fighting drew local (Nuer) communities into a brutal war of provocation and revenge that exacerbated tensions between Nuer people and an ethnically plural SPLA that nonetheless began to be perceived as Dinka (Nyaba 1997: 50).

Khartoum played up ethnic tensions where it found them. Local tensions were played out in cattle raids, and local communities sought out weapons from the Sudanese Armed Forces or the SPLA to defend their livelihoods. Young men and boys, many with responsibilities in the cattle economy, were drawn into the violence. Khartoum's counter-insurgency campaigns, like almost all counter-insurgency campaigns, fostered insecurity among these young men and boys by targeting them routinely as potential rebels. One interviewee from Duk (a largely Dinka area north of Bor) fled his home in 1987 to join the SPLA. He was eleven at the time, and he described the terrors of his youth:

> *Why did you separate from your family?* Most of the older people were not so scared like us. They could hide near the village, then after they would creep back home. So most of them were less afraid, and most of them perished from hunger. It seemed to us that this was not going to be easy, with your *tukul* [hut] being set on fire, and your animals being eaten. If he's burning the *tukul*, and if you see dead bodies of your colleagues, that makes you to flee. There was no time to discuss. I left my dad in 1987 and we next met in 2003 in Nairobi. My younger brother, the two of them followed me, I never saw them again. My mum died when I left.
>
> *Was your decision a political one?* Originally it was out of fear, it was out of attack. When John Garang saw that these young people have come together, they are vulnerable, he has to introduce the philosophy, because young people could think that he as leader is the source of the problem. So he had to explain why he's fighting ... That exposed us to current politics. We had to take sides, composing songs about the struggle, full of history and creating awareness among the young generation that we are backbone of this country and fight for rights, and depend on education not on military alone. (Interview 92/2012)

Together, the counter-insurgency forces and the SPLA militarized boys and young men. Early SPLA training stressed the importance of brutality in achieving the goal of territorial liberation. One slogan said: 'You must live through the barrels of your guns. Food, wife and property wherever you find them are to be acquired through your might' (African Rights 1997: 84). Another notorious slogan was aimed at shifting youth allegiance away from absent parents to the military hierarchy: 'Even my father I will give him a bullet'. These youngsters brought their half-educated fears, their mixed loyalties and harsh training with them to Jonglei and Upper Nile, the gateway to South Sudan (Leonardi 2007). Commanders treated local populations harshly. The SPLA's young soldiers looted cattle from young cattle keepers, and pushed them towards armed resistance. There were massacres on all sides.

1991: the split in the SPLA

By 1989, the SPLA had liberated most of South Sudan. It had penetrated (north) Sudan and was on the offensive in South Kordofan and Blue Nile. The National Salvation Revolution, led by Omer al-Bashir, ousted a defunct parliamentary regime, just as the Cold War drew to a close. In the Horn of Africa, Cold War alignments fostered proxy wars between neighbours, which grew more conspiratorial and vengeful as the old system gave way (De Waal 2004). In May 1991, the socialist government in Ethiopia fell as the Soviet Union neared formal dissolution. The SPLA had based its strategy up to this point on conventional warfare – the construction of a powerful military machine that could transform the political situation through state capture. It had no strategy for social or economic transformation for ordinary people other than conscription (Nyaba 1997: 56). The fall of the Ethiopian regime fatally undermined this strategy. The SPLA was forced to leave its Ethiopian bases, and quickly split into two factions.

The split – some three months after the fall of the Ethiopian regime – reflected differences at the top of the movement over internal democracy; the question of Southern self-determination; and the desire to realign the movement in an emerging post-Cold War order. The dissidents failed to rally the SPLM to their cause. Unable to gain enough momentum to unseat Garang,

Riek Machar, the dissidents' leader, adopted a strategy of militarily defeating Garang's faction, starting with an attack on his largely undefended home area. The dissident faction did not have enough trained soldiers to do so, and Machar sought to recruit untrained personnel for the operation. Unable to build a political constituency for internal democracy or Southern independence, the dissidents created an ethnic constituency from young Nuer men from the eastern flood plains – Riek Machar's origins lie in the Dok Nuer section of the western plains. With the 1991 attack on Bor, Jonglei lurched into a new kind of conflict that was configured around ethnicity, young people's networks and kinship structures – which could astonishingly mobilize up to 10,000 armed youngsters for an attack on a provincial town. They were called the White Army.

The White Army

The term 'White Army' was first used in the 1991 attack on Bor, a military operation that gave an ethnic character to the factional politics at the top of the SPLM. The attack also changed the way that young people organized in South Sudan's remote peripheries. The attack recalled the Dinka–Nuer tensions of the 1983–88 conflict between Anya-nya 2 and the SPLM/A, and bequeathed Jonglei a legacy of youth violence and ethnic violence that was still working mysteriously over two decades later.

The term came to be applied to bands of armed Nuer youth who engaged in feuding, cattle raiding, criminality and community defence. They were not part of the SPLA or the militia system organized by the Sudanese army, but would sometimes fight on behalf of organized forces in return for supplies or booty. Relationships between different generations of males were traditionally organized by the age-set system – new, more autonomous, more militarized styles of organizing youth emerged during the civil war. Armed youth in other South Sudanese communities organized in similar ways, but in Nuer society this style or system of youth organization appeared more tangible and unified to outsiders, in part because of the catchiness of the term 'White Army'.

1991: the attack on Bor

Around 1989, after half a decade of more haphazard recruitment, John Garang established the Red Army, a cadet training system aimed at providing a continuous supply of recruits for a disciplined, indoctrinated army (Jonglei politician, interview 165/2012). In 1991, Riek Machar's new recruits were mobilized much more quickly, without political or military training.

The first major operations began within a month or two of the split. Most participants were from three of the eleven named large territorial/kinship Nuer sections: Lou, Gaawar and Eastern Jikainy sections. Lou are mostly in present-day Nyirol, Wuror and Akobo; Gaawar are based around Ayod; and Jikainy people live along the Sobat river and the Ethiopian border in present-day Upper Nile state. They were mobilized in part by a prophet, Wutnyang Gaarkek (also Gatkek, Gatakek) from the Lak Nuer section of Zeraf island (Nyaba 1997: 97).

At a time when the cattle population in the Jonglei hinterland was under pressure from disease and flooding, recruits were promised that they could keep cattle stolen during raids (Scott Villiers and Banggol 1991: 22–30; Jonglei politician, interview 137/2012). These untrained recruits were called *jaysh mabior* (the Arabic and Nuer words for 'army' and 'white'), a reference to the white ash which cattle keepers spread on themselves to ward off insects in cattle camps (Jonglei politicians, interviews 137/2012, 184/2012). The 'White Army' name may have been chosen to emphasize the cattle-camp culture of its members – and the fact that their political objectives were not articulated, or instinctually oriented towards looting. A readily translatable phrase, the 'White Army' entered the discourse of foreign observers, like that of the Red Army or the Lost Boys.

The new young army, led by SPLA and Anya-nya veterans, began its attack on the Bor area in October 1991. Greater Bor is the home of Nyaraweng, Ghol, Twic and Bor Dinka sections who live along the Bahr al-Jebel river in the present-day counties of Duk, Twic East and Bor. Most of the people from these sections lived on a ridge of high ground that runs roughly parallel to the river. John Garang's home area is near Kongor, in Twic, and this may have influenced motivations. The attackers began in Duk Padiet, in present-day Duk county, and fought and raided their way south through Twic to Bor, killing thousands of people and displacing nearly all of the inhabitants of the area (Guarak 2011: 213). The attack depopulated the area and nearly all its herds were plundered.

The attack also created the illusion of unified Nuer power, which has proved to be one of South Sudan's most tenacious. Neither Nuer nor Dinka people have a political headquarters, nor any history of concerted action for corporate political or military objectives, and members of each group have fought on every side in the wars and political contests of the past two centuries. Nuer and Dinka people have many interconnections too. The Nyareweng and Ghol Dinka groups in Duk county have many marriage and other ties to their Lou and Gaawar neighbours, even adopting the Nuer straight-line forehead scarification in preference to the more conventional Dinka parallel Vs. In the three years previous to the attack, Duk people had supported Lou people with food during a food crisis, and in the years after it Nuer society fell apart in a civil war (Johnson 2003: 117).

1992: the Nuer civil war

The Bor attack emptied the Nuer–Dinka borderlands of civilian population, and cattle in these areas were expropriated to feed militias. This exposed the isolation of Lou people of the Jonglei hinterland, who bordered Dinka areas which had become the front line in the battle between SPLA factions. Lou people have no direct access to the all-season Sobat and Zeraf rivers, which means that much of the economic life of their areas depends on negotiations with neighbours. Relationships with Dinka people who partially controlled access to the Zeraf river were already in crisis. Relationships with Jikainy people, who controlled access to the Sobat river, worsened after the new Ethiopian regime restricted Sudanese access to Ethiopian pastures, which pushed Jikainy herders towards Sobat pastures. In a hungry period, these pressures soon led to a Lou–Jikainy civil war that was fuelled by Khartoum arms. Riek Machar's 1991 attack on Bor militarized and impoverished Jonglei's Dinka–Nuer borderlands and the 1992–94 Lou–Jikainy war exposed the inability of his faction to manage the ethnic constituency they had deployed, and the temporary nature of White Army command structures (Johnson 2003: 116ff.). A 1994 peace conference brought partial resolution and enumerated losses:

TABLE 7.1 Losses in the 1992–94 Lou–Jikainy war

	Jikainy	Lou
Killed	857	482
Cattle raided	26,428	50,817
Homes burned	3,000	

Source: 1994 Akobo peace conference archives, quoted in Lowrey (1996: 160)

These figures suggest a dramatic increase in the lethality of conflicts. In the first two decades of the twentieth century, a large raid might result in thirty or forty fatalities, according to British intelligence reports (Kelly 1985: 44). A 1937 Lou raid on a Murle settlement killed seventeen people and was considered a crisis (Lewis 1972: 10, 12). But without seeking to diminish the tragedy of the deaths in this war between allies and kinfolk, the cattle losses recorded above may have been more historically significant. They indicate a dramatic and not-yet-reversed shift in the cattle economy that saw raiding become part of stock management and production systems in Jonglei. Looted cows were used to acquire weapons, in a development with wide and largely unstudied social implications. Young males diverted their energies into this violent mode of production with its confusing mix of criminality and community defence (Skedsmo et al. 2003; Young 2007). The costs of this shift are dealt with in more detail in Chapter 9.

New youth army

The White Army's composition sometimes bewilders outsiders because it is relatively young and is built on traditional social structures for organizing youth that have been undergoing violent change for over a century. The 1991 Bor attack was memorably brutal and 'tribal' and it has contributed in its way to the vast corpus of ethnicity-first writing about South Sudan. But the emergence of the White Army in Nuer areas, and less catchily named militias elsewhere, was a marker of the many shifts in the relationship between generations that had their roots in the targeting of youth, simultaneously by counter-insurgency operations and by recruiting sergeants from the rebel side.

Traditionally, Nuer society organized generational relationships through the age set (*rić* in Nuer). The six horizontal scars (*gaar* in Nuer) across the forehead are a visible initiation ritual of Nuer males that is historically linked to the age set. A boy would be initiated along with some friends, and after initiation he could participate in adult discussions and he was no longer allowed to milk cows. Every four to ten years, the participants in these local ceremonies would then be aggregated into age sets. A traditional spiritual leader known as the cattle expert (*kuar ghok* in Nuer) was responsible for creating distinct age sets every few years, by declaring a new age set open and closed, and giving it a name. Age sets were organized locally, but the process of opening, closing and naming was coordinated across Nuer-land, so that a member of an age set in one locale could place himself in the generational order in another locale. Age-set relationships cut across lineage and territory, giving individual Nuer men a set of rights and obligations in a wider Nuer community and facilitating migration. Age sets thus helped create a wider Lou or Nuer identity, counteracting the fragmenting character of kinship, which continually creates new 'segments' or family groups (Duany 1992: 62, 113).

Over the last thirty years age-set institutions in Dinka and Nuer society have been changing in response to a number of factors: schools and insecurity kept young men away from cattle camps; initiates were supposed to be fattened on milk in cattle camps, and this practice was hampered by several years of poor yields in the 1980s; churches discouraged age-set institutions; and the SPLA repressed initiation rituals (Hutchinson 1996: 296ff.). 'Riek Machar was a zonal commander in Bentiu. He was ordering people about things, he prohibited marking as a primitive thing, fining fathers with a heifer or two [for scarifying their boys]. Some people would come with a marked boy, saying here, I've done it, here is the cow' (Jonglei academic, interview 22/2012).

Some interviewees categorically stated that the age-set system was alive in Lou and Jikainy communities (Upper Nile politician, interview 182/2012). But many others said that it was disappearing – some even dated the last age set to the 1980s, and said it was called Militia or Koryom – the latter is the name of an SPLA battalion (Jonglei humanitarian worker, interview 56/2012; church pastors, interview 62/2012; politician, interview 135/2012). These are not necessarily inconsistent statements: the initiation ritual of scarification still continues at local levels, and these local groups of initiates may have a name. But the process whereby a recognized spiritual leader aggregates local groups of young initiates into a named structure that is recognized across Nuer-land, or across the Lou territorial grouping, seems to be fading out, and names recognized by some as an age set are recognized by others as a gang of troublemakers.

Although not every Nuer interviewee was aware of the current age set (*ric̆*), everyone talked confidently of a youth category which they called *bunam*. According to Gabrial Gai Riam Weitour, *bunam* 'is a newly established institution in the Nuer governing system, mainly in the eastern Nuer, but [it] plays a very important role in conflict resolution' (Weitour 2008: 183). Interviews with people in Akobo in 2012 suggested that the word had a range of meanings. Some people used *bunam* to denote fighting-age young males, or males as fighters. A young person with a disability can join an age set but he cannot become a *bunam* (Jonglei education officials, interview 76/2012; Jonglei politician, interview 165/2012). *Bunam* is an Anuak loan word which is now part of eastern dialects of the Nuer language. It reportedly entered the language in the 1970s, when tensions between Anuak people in Akobo and Nuer incomers were on the increase. In 1982, after the killing of a Nuer youth leader, Nuer young men from a cattle camp organized a massacre of Anuak people in Akobo town, after which nearly all the historic Anuak population of Akobo was displaced. 'It was a youth initiative, a surprise attack. We didn't know,' said an official working in Akobo at the time (interview 61/2012).

In Anuak, *bunam* or *butnam* denotes a fishing camp. It can be a place where young people go to prepare for a confrontation (bilingual Nuer–Anuak speakers, interview 173/2012). In Nuer youth groups, *bunam* select their own leaders, called *kuar bunam*, in a procedure that mirrors the selection of traditional leaders and chiefs. The *kuar bunam* has to be brave and persuasive, and he is also chosen from families or small sections under-represented in the current traditional leadership systems – Nuer democratic culture requires that everyone has a turn.

> If your community has had the chance to govern, they give the chance [to be *kuar bunam*] to the *cieng* [section or subsection] that has not ruled. They will give the chance even to a specific family. If the family brings the wrong person, they will ask for another person. You start with a chance for Yoal or Nyaak, then

they will go for a third – say a chance for Biliu [the names of smaller Nuer sections or *cieng*s around Akobo town] ... Then it goes to a family [within the smaller section] who did not get a chance. It's the same with traditional leadership. But not with the political leadership. That was the same system in the days of Riek Machar. They can use the leaders selected in this way and incorporate them into military. (Jonglei humanitarian worker, interview 63/2012)

Bunam are not entirely independent of elders: 'They defend the area, property, and all this. But still they listen to people. A Nuer elder can rebuke them, but tomorrow they have their own way,' explained one senior official (interview 135/2012). But whereas age sets are elder-led systems for organizing relationships between different generations – they are opened, closed and led by a traditional leader – the *bunam* system seems to be youth-organized and youth-led. The word *bunam* is used only in the eastern Nuer dialects exposed to Anuak linguistic influence – western Nuer dialects do not have the word, said two pastors, one from eastern and the other from western Nuer (interview 168/2012). It may be significant that this word should have emerged in areas where youth-led armed groups like the so-called White Army were most deeply established.

What is the political/military significance of these linguistic shifts? Nuer society is often represented in a highly militarized way: colonial observers defined 'tribes' as raiding units (groups regularly uniting in warfare) and age sets were organized at the level of the tribe, leading many to present age sets in military terms, even though the age-set system has many non-military aims, and even though Nuer raiding, during the long period of Nuer expansion, was not organized around age sets (Spencer 1998: 168; Evans-Pritchard 1940a: 253ff.). And although one should be cautious about militarized representations of Nuer society, the system established by *bunam* seems to be more militarized and more detached from the influence of traditional leaders than the age set. An interviewee formerly involved in training the Red Army explained:

> So there was the end of *ric* [age set]. *Bunam* was youth-led and Anya-nya 2 co-opted it. Now there isn't a youth movement, only tribal and ethnic youth. Which are very dangerous. The age set instilled children in their social roles and their tribal belonging. The *bunam* word then came in. It united the youth of the tribe. [When in 1983] the SPLA divided itself into two, most of the [Nuer] people thought that the SPLA was a Dinka-dominated movement. [Anya-nya 2 leader] Abdalla Choul took over and used [Nuer] tribal sentiments to discredit the SPLA. So the issue of *bunam* became a very important factor in the fight against the SPLA. The Murle were with the north in terms of militia and they encroached into Lou terri-tory. *Bunam* became effective in defending the Lou. Gaawar became threatened and they adopted the *bunam* system ... where I come from was overrun several times by Lou. The word arrived in Nuer-land in the 1980s. But it existed with Anuak and Murle. Before it came to Lou, it went to the Ethiopian Nuers who were the first to acquire arms. (Jonglei politician, interview 165/2012)

Youth armies in Pibor

The year 1991 witnessed transformations in Pibor that attracted much less attention. Along the borders between Ethiopia and Sudan, the Horn of Africa's dissidents were drawn into small deadly cross-border wars. Across the borders from Jonglei, the SPLA fought in support of Ethiopia's socialist regime until it crumbled. The following year, Ethiopia helped the Khartoum gov-ernment take the Anuak border town of Pochalla. The Sudanese army and Ismail Kony's Brigade attacked Pibor from government bases in Pochalla in the east and Bor in the west, in a major campaign that saw the government recapture many of the towns

Murle age sets (plural forms)

Longoroket, born 1900s–1910s, only two left

Nyakademo, born 1910s–1920s

Nyerza, born 1920s–1930s

Maara, born 1930s–1940s

Dorongwa, born 1940s–1950s. The age set of Ismail Kony

Muden, born 1950s–1960s. An age set that joined Ismail Kony's Brigade. Some took part in post-2010 mutinies

Titi, born 1960s–1970s. An age set that joined Ismail Kony's Brigade. Some took part in post-2010 mutinies

Butotnya, born 1970s–1980s. The first age set to fight younger age sets with guns rather than sticks. Some took part in post-2010 mutinies

Lango, born 1980s–1990s. Now competing with Butotnya over military roles. Some took part in post-2010 mutinies

Nyakorumong, Tagot. Possible names of emerging age sets

it had lost to the SPLA (humanitarian worker, interview 120/2012; senior SPLA commander, interview 178/2012).

For the next fifteen years, Ismail Kony's Brigade had the run of Pibor town and the settlements around it – Boma remained under SPLA control. The social changes that ensued there were different from those that took place in Nuer-land.

The Nuer age-set system apparently decayed during the civil war of 1983–2005, perhaps because of military pressures or because of changes to the organization of restocking and raiding which partially detached some young men from traditional social structures, which may have turned the *rić* age set into the *bunam* fighting group. But under a similar set of pressures, the Murle age set appears to have been entrenched.

In Pibor county, the age set is a named grouping of Murle men whose age range is not more than ten years apart. The youngest age set can come into being only when the members of the oldest age set die – the next age set will open only when the last surviving members of the oldest age set, called Longoroket, all die (local government official, interview 91/2012). Age sets tend to be named in western Murle-land, among the most cattle-dependent groups, and it may take many years for the age set to travel east as far as Boma. In 2013, no Boma natives were Lango, according to Diana Felix da Costa, a researcher working in Pibor county. She also argues that requirements for age-set spacing may be a relatively recent innovation.

> The time range between age sets is shrinking, I have heard many Murle arguing that the reason the Bototnya have become such 'troublemakers' is because they were 'squeezed' between Titi and Lango, and never got the time to become the dominant ones, since now generations are emerging too fast. (Interview 2/2014)

The age-set system has many social functions. It is used to divide labour in the dry season, when younger people are required to start the annual migrations (Andretta 1985, 1989). It has helped to maintain Murle cohesiveness during long displacements. In part, this is because it acts to delay young men's marriage. The second-youngest age set prevents the youngest age set from attending courtship dances by stick fighting and other forms of intimidation. After the 1983–2005 war began, that fighting became more violent. Delaying the marriage of young men is linked to the Murle system of polygyny. Many polygynous marriages are contracted by older men. Delayed marriage helps maintain a pool of workers with no dependants, and it also generates many young widows, some of whom occupy socially precarious niches in Murle society.

The bridewealth system also delays young men's marriage. The minimum bridewealth is (a relatively high) forty-two cows. Bridewealth may be higher in special cases such as elopement (Pibor humanitarian worker, interview 119/2012). Young men may get some cattle from the dowries of their sisters, but responsibility for amassing those cows lies primarily with the young suitor – whereas in Dinka and Nuer society family members all contribute (Andretta 1989).

Raiding allows young men to circumvent marriage delays, and the age-set system is an important factor underlying the cattle raid. And the age set is very resilient in Murle-land. Most Murle interviewees said that they had never heard of a Murle man who did not belong to an age set (one male Murle interviewee said he had not joined). Nonetheless, the church in Pibor opposes the system, and during the SPLM's occupation of Pibor between 1987 and 1992, some commanders tried to repress the system because of the increasing violence associated with it. One commander from that time explained:

> The age-set system, its background is respect for your elders.
> Until 1985, the age set was fine. People didn't fight. But when
> the SPLA/M came in, we did not encourage it. Because it
> brought problems. We banned the age set. I said we would
> not accept it. Our soldiers, we banned them from going to
> age-set events. Sixty lashes for taking part in [an age-set event]
> ... The age-set system is not good, it's reached to the point
> of firearms. We used to hit each other with sticks. (Interview
> 178/2012)

Ismail Kony, the brigadier-general in charge of the Brigade, was also a traditional spiritual leader and government-appointed paramount chief. He became district commissioner and later governor of Jonglei, and appears to have exercised his multiple forms of authority to orient Murle age sets and kinship systems towards societal resistance to outside encroachment. This resistance may have overlapped with a kind of shrewd neo-traditionalism, allowing men of his generation to accumulate cattle and marry frequently, which may have aggravated tensions among younger groups. Ismail Kony married many times, astutely choosing brides from different Murle sections. He also used the age set as the basis of military recruitment, while militia leaders elsewhere tried to smash the age set. The SPLA commander quoted above said that the age-set system was reinstated by Ismail Kony in 1992. One researcher from Jonglei explained:

> Ismail Kony tried to use age-set system … They were his army, his soldiers. They worked according to age-set group. They act as the soldier age group … Ismail Kony is Dorongwa. He collects people by age set. He has Moden and Titi. It was according to age set that he encouraged them. He talked to people according to age set … No way for a leader to say – abandon age set. Many tried to do that. Kennedy Gayein [an SPLA commander between 1987 and 1992] tried to beat people when he was officer commanding Pibor. (Interview 124/2012)

Ismail Kony may have maintained his long incumbencies as a spiritual, military and political leader through a policy of social conservatism. One of his associates argued that Murle politicians from the SPLM/A opposed the age-set system as a means of undermining chiefs and concentrating power in their own hands. Ismail Kony was protecting Murle values that were being shaken by the war (interview 166/2012). But his militia was also a modern phenomenon – it was called 'the Brigade' (sometimes the 'Pibor Defence Forces'), not the *buul*, the Murle word for age set.

The mid-1990s – war reconfigured around militias

Pibor's Brigade and the new White Army military structures were not the same, but they both used traditional age or kinship structures to build their forces. They operated in a military environment and lived off a cattle economy that had been transformed by the 1991 attack on Bor. Initially, Murle isolation kept them out of Jonglei's conflicts – Pibor town was a destination for refugees from the violence between Nuer and Dinka people, and then for refugees from the internecine Lou–Jikainy war of 1992. But by the mid-1990s that had changed. One former SPLA officer in Akobo gave the following account of the relationship between Jonglei's different conflicts.

> The war started between Nuer and Dinka. The layer of
> Lou–Murle started in 1996, after the split of the SPLA in
> 1991. The real historical conflict is Dinka–Nuer, which started
> in 1983, and the SPLA being seen after 1992 as a Dinka affair.
> That caused the split of 1991, the breakdown of traditional
> norms. The militias came after that, and the enemy began to
> infiltrate. The year 1991 brought the movement to its knees
> almost; the SPLA struggling to regain control through youth
> community defence and [Riek Machar's] Nasir faction doing
> the same. The two factions used their communities to fight
> each other ... then the enemy tried to ensure the divide-and-
> rule system ... When [Murle leader] Ismail Kony sees that
> 1991 is like a fight between Nuer and Dinka, he forms his
> militia and ensures that he arms his own community. Before
> 1996, this cattle raiding had been there, it was a normal thing.
> Murle were looking just for the cow, not killing women or
> child abduction. The same with Nuer. And not at a mass
> level. But after 1991, Murle began to have two groups which
> still exist even now. One group led by the militias, very much
> under Ismail Kony, and another group that are ordinary
> people. They raid differently. Ordinary raiders just look for
> cattle. But by December 1996, a major attack was launched by
> Murle on Akobo community, that was suspected militia. It was
> not the ordinary raiding ... Murle community killed over three
> hundred women and children. (Interview 63/2012)

After the 1991 events in Bor, insecurity in Jonglei's hinterland was managed by garrisons of the regular army in towns, supported by militias based on kinship or age groupings with recognizable command structures, carrying out military tasks in the hinterland; which in turn were linked to less formal groups such as the White Army. Militias and less formal groups were shaped by local conditions, not replicas of each other. Although the militias and informal armed groups were dependent on Khartoum, they sometimes fought each other. The war between Murle and Nuer groups was an example of wars between two proxies of the same regime, and it soon overshadowed the smaller opportunistic raids that preceded it.

Why did raids against Nuer people begin in the mid-1990s? It may have been that raids against Dinka herds were no longer possible, as most Bor Dinka people had been displaced, and their herds had been looted or moved to Equatoria or Bahr al-Ghazal. Or it may have been related to political developments at the time – in 1996, Riek Machar signed a political charter with Khartoum beginning a process of constitutional change that eventually made him assistant president of Sudan. Never having been a rebel, Ismail Kony was not a signatory to these peace agreements, which reshaped powers of political patronage in Khartoum, Juba, Malakal, Bor and the areas under the control of the Sudanese army. Perhaps his exclusion affected the situation. One interviewee from near Pibor argued that levels of armament increased at the time: 'Lou got many arms during those years. That's why the number of the raids increased. It was not like before, three guns, non-automatic. It was risky to go for raid in those days' (interview 192/2012).

The political charter and the 1997 Khartoum Peace Agreement that resulted from it were part of a Sudanese tradition of peace agreements between rebel armies and central government at which the National Congress Party regime in Khartoum proved to be particularly adept. Peace was a more urgent aim for local people, and at this time many peace conferences began to be documented across South Sudan (Bradbury et al. 2006). In 1999, a peace conference at Wunlit, on the borders of Western Upper Nile and Bahr al-Ghazal, made concrete steps towards addressing the crisis in Nuer–Dinka relations that had spilled over there from Jonglei. Hutchinson (2000: 12) argues that Lou and Murle women played a role in limiting violence between their two communities, at a time when 'people-to-people' peace conferences were gaining ground.

Youth and militarization in Bor and Bahr al-Ghazal

The youth army that attacked Bor in 1991 was a grouping that was reinventing generational order among Nuer people. Ismail Kony's Brigade exploited traditional age systems. But not every ethnic community in Jonglei started a militia. The 1991 attack on Bor did not lead to young men there reworking their own decaying age-set systems or setting up their own army. Unlike most other areas, Greater Bor had very few militias – John Garang's SPLA set up a militia in Duk called Dukey in 1993, when Duk became a front line between two factions of the SPLA. But the Dukey militia ceased to exist in 1994 after an agreement between Duk and Lou people (Jonglei politician, interview 137/2012). Depopulation meant that there were few pro-government militias – Bor town's population in 2005 was very low, and the local Khartoum-aligned militia (led by an SPLA defector called Deng Kelai) had 400 personnel. Bor and Twic county had no militia at all (Jonglei politician, interview 184/2012).

This absence of militias in Greater Bor is sometimes presented as an example of Dinka passivity, which some colonial anthropologists made much of (Evans-Pritchard 1940a: 125). But Dinka sections elsewhere, such as in Bahr al-Ghazal, were soon drawn into the war of youth militias. Around the time of Riek Machar's 1991 attack on Bor, John Garang dispatched his chief of staff to attack Leer and Adok in present-day Unity state, the home territory of the Riek Machar Dok section of the Nuer people. Nyaba describes what happened:

Cdr. William Nyoun Bany, the SPLA Chief of Staff, himself a Nuer, commanded this attack. This attack was defeated and repulsed. Cdr. William Nyoun was ordered by the SPLA H/Qs to withdraw with his forces through Yirol. The Nasir forces pursued Cdr. William in the Dinka land. This marked the beginning of the armed incursion into Bahr al-Ghazal and the transformation of the inter-SPLA fighting into a Nuer–Dinka conflict.

In the space of five years (1992–1996) there were regular cross-borders raids and cattle rustling between the Nuer and the Dinka (Chiech, Agar and Luaic sections) … In these civilian conflicts, thousands of lives were lost, thousands of heads of cattle looted, women and children abducted and tens of thousands of people … were displaced.

The need to defend themselves and their property pushed many people to acquire firearms. This is how the gun replaced traditional weapons of spears, sticks, bows and arrows. The SPLA occasionally provided weapons either as gifts to the chiefs or in exchange for their food ration. Nevertheless many people purchased their own rifles using their own cattle, while others got their firearms in the battlefield. The armed youths were loosely organised into *vigilante* groups that became known as *'Gel-weng'* [cattle protectors]. (Nyaba 2001: 8)

Over two decades later, armed youth are still part of the pastoralist systems in Dinka areas of Bahr al-Ghazal. But something different happened in Bor. One young Dinka man said: 'they say Dinka are coward because at that time people were engaged in a different war' (interview 136/2012). Nearly all the population were displaced, and over time this displacement forced many Bor Dinka people into greater reliance on SPLA protection and access to markets and services in other areas of South Sudan.

Comprehensive peace and disarmament

The 2005 Comprehensive Peace Agreement set up a new political order that recognized two armies – the Sudanese Armed Forces and the SPLA. It was an attempt to address the contradictions that Sudan had inherited from the colonial era in a decisive and resolute way. But it was an exclusive agreement, between the two most powerful security elites in the country. It was reached in Nairobi, far from the local militias and local attempts at peace. All other armed groups were required to incorporate themselves into one of those two armies.

How were those other armed groups organized? The 1997 Khartoum Peace Agreement envisaged a unified South Sudanese army called the South Sudan Defence Forces (one of many precedents set by the 1997 agreement that appeared in the 2005 peace deal). The SSDF ended up as a weak coordination mechanism for decentralized militias. Gaaluak Deng Garang was a Khartoum politician and soldier from Upper Nile who in the run-up to the 2005 agreement organized meetings between militia leaders that were aimed at unifying them. Deng Garang states that the SSDF did not initially include what he calls 'tribal armed groups [*al-majmūʿāt al-qabiliya al-musallaḥa*]'. These groups – such as the White Army and the Brigade, or Pibor Defence Forces in Murle-land – were mainly involved in defending their crops and livestock (Deng Garang 2006: 158). They were also different from other militias because they had never rebelled against Khartoum, unlike many of the SSDF militias, whose history began in the anti-Khartoum mutinies of the late 1970s and 1980s. The creation of the SSDF eventually allowed for the incorporation of most of South Sudan's militias into the SPLA, when in 2006 the SSDF leader signed the Juba Declaration and was appointed deputy commander-in-chief of the SPLA (Young 2006).

Not all 'tribal armed groups' resisted the peace. The Gaajak section from the Greater Nasir area, near the Ethiopian border, was one of the Eastern Jikainy groups who had participated in the White Army wars of the early 1990s. In 2006, they gave up some of their weapons. In spite of continued tensions with Lou Nuer herders over grazing rights, and in spite of the fact that South Sudan's most venerable and persistent rebel militia leader,

Gordon Koang Choul, is a son of the area, the people of Greater Nasir did not endure a militia war or a war of armed civilians like their Lou neighbours. Riek Machar, then vice-president of South Sudan, sought to explain Gaajak peacefulness, while warming up a predominantly Gaajak audience in Juba:

> The Gaajak area was disarmed in 2006 very peacefully [applause]. They are peaceful with Dinka Padang, Anuak, and other Nuer. They're waiting for development and basic services. The closure of the [oil] pipeline [to Port Sudan] is a blessing to Gaajak [applause] ... Trucks are now coming from Ethiopia to Malakal [through Gaajak areas]. Don't sleep – get into business. Business is the most important thing, nations are not developed by government alone, but by private sector [applause]. Gaajak river bank has a crop [in the dry-season months of] January to March ... so much potential in agriculture. (Near-verbatim transcript of speech on 18 March 2012)

The Ethiopian border was a resource for Gaajak people: their section has lands in Gambella on the Ethiopian side, whereas Lou people live only in Sudan. In wartime, they could live with Ethiopian relatives and reinvent themselves as Ethiopians, and benefit from the educational rights of an Ethiopian citizen, which in Dergue-era Ethiopia were not trivial (Gaajak politician, interview 189/2012; Feyissa 2009). Fifteen of them had PhDs, the vice-president told his audience.

Riek Machar's argument that the possibilities of private sector development may reduce violence and promote disarmament sounds unduly optimistic. Nonetheless, the post-CPA concentration of violence in areas most dependent on the cattle economy, where economic life had been reconfigured around cattle raiding, invites question. Perhaps the need to maintain raiding systems, or to protect from raiding neighbours, was less urgent in areas where infrastructure and alternatives to the cattle economy were becoming available.

The spatial distribution of resistance to disarmament may shed light on local economic imperatives. The first campaign in Jonglei took place in four northern counties whose inhabitants are mostly Nuer. Ayod lies on the Bahr al-Zeraf and is the centre of the Gaawar section. Wuror, Nyirol and Akobo lie to the east of Ayod, and they are the centre of the Lou section. During the 2005/06 dry season, cattle keepers from the Lou and Gaawar Nuer sections made a routine request for access to pasture in Duk county. The traditional authorities of the Dinka Ghol and Dinka Nyaraweng of Duk county asked them to surrender their weapons before grazing; the Nuer cattle keepers refused this unprecedented request. Attempts by the new SPLM governor of Jonglei state to negotiate disarmament broke down in January 2006, just as most Khartoum-backed militias declared their intention to join the SPLA. In the SPLA's view, Nuer armed civilians near Duk attacked an SPLA patrol newly deployed to Jonglei and then pursued them across inhospitable terrain: several hundred died. At the same time, some elements from the Khartoum-backed militias who resisted integration into the SPLA moved into these societies bristling with arms, some of them hoping to negotiate the terms of their integration from there. 'The White Army and the militias were one and the same thing at the time,' said an SPLM official closely involved in the process (interview 184/2012). The SPLA may have decided to target the White Army because loosely organized civilian groups presented fewer political challenges than did organized militias in terms of disarming. The name 'White Army' may even have offered propaganda advantages for the would-be disarmers, by making their target more tangible or digestible for journalists and NGOs.

Many in the SPLA wanted a harsh response to the January 2006 attack by Lou elements in the Duk area. The SPLA had agreed to the Juba Declaration that month, a peace deal which generously incorporated Khartoum-aligned militias into the SPLA. Some militia commanders (such as Simon Gatwich, who had been involved in the 1991 raid on Greater Bor) were forming tactical alliances with armed youth, perhaps to improve the terms of their integration into the SPLA (SPLM official, interview 184/2012). Peter Bol Kon, the Lou Nuer officer from Nyirol who was coordinating the disarmament, was one of those wanting to teach the cattle camp soldiers a lesson for the losses suffered by the SPLA in the January attack (humanitarian worker, interview 73/2012). Peter Bol Kon's forces routed the 'White Army' in the Yuai area, Wuror county, in May 2006, and then looted their area, reportedly taking only one casualty – in the six months to May, an estimated 1,600 people had been killed as a result of the disarmament campaign (Garfield 2007: 17). Armed youth in the neighbouring counties of Nyirol and Akobo moved to conciliate the SPLA and make at least a show of disarmament (Jonglei humanitarian worker, interview 73/2012). Many people believed that the White Army had been destroyed (Young 2007: 17). But Jonglei was on the cusp of a new war.

8 | THE GEOGRAPHY OF CONFLICT IN JONGLEI AFTER THE COMPREHENSIVE PEACE AGREEMENT

In 2005, the signing of the Comprehensive Peace Agreement presented Ismail Kony and the Murle leadership with political dilemmas. His system had used links with the Khartoum government to make the most of Murle isolation, and now Murle political leaders had to negotiate their way into a new order centred at Juba. The January 2006 Juba Declaration brought most of the militias of the greater Upper Nile into the SPLA, but Ismail Kony did not sign a deal with the new government in Juba until December 2006. The terms of that deal required the incorporation of his Brigade into the SPLA, and his incorporated soldiers and officers were subsequently deployed across South Sudan, breaking the link between local militias and local political leaders. In that year, Lou Nuer areas had been badly affected by the violence of disarmament, and Bor's population was increasing dramatically. Some Dinka Bor people were bringing their cattle home, and others were restocking through cattle markets.

The government's first priority was to disarm 'armed civilians' – informal armed youth groupings like the White Army, which had transformed the military and economic order of Jonglei but had no place in the peace agreement. They sequenced this around political realities. Ismail Kony was pressured towards an agreement – pressure may have gone as far as abductions of Murle cattle drovers. But there was no direct confrontation with Ismail Kony's Brigade or with the armed civilians of Pibor county, which were the Brigade's social constituency. In Nuer-land, all the militias were incorporated into the SPLA and the government began a violent and forcible disarmament of what was called the White Army in Wuror. Disarmament was organized ethnically, and that set the stage for further conflict.

Initially, disarmament in Murle-land was relatively non-coercive. In 2007, Ismail Kony led a reasonably modest disarmament campaign, with the urging of Murle neighbours in Jonglei. The next year, a coercive disarmament campaign collected more than eleven thousand weapons, almost three times as many as the previous year. There were many allegations of torture and mistreatment of Murle civilians during the campaign (McCallum 2013: 49ff.). Disarmament of mobile youth is a difficult military task, and often soldiers target instead more sedentary elements in society – families with small assets to protect, which are unprotected by the state. 'Lumping together these different interests as a tribe isn't helping,' commented one disarmament official (interview 183/2012). Ethnically targeted state disarmament campaigns assume that ethnic communities have shared military objectives and may vicariously victimize the least violent members of the community, in a process likely to deepen antagonisms.

In 2007 and 2008, ill-sequenced and ethnically targeted disarmament campaigns stoked violence. The trouble between Murle people and their neighbours played out in two different ways. One was the opportunistic raid, repeated localized attacks that took children and cattle and displaced a large population of Greater Bor westwards, emptying its easternmost settlements (Harrigan 2011: 35ff.). Another was a war pitting two Khartoum-aligned groups against each other. This chapter tries to focus on these two 'modes' of attack and argues that each was deployed on one of two major fronts. Murle raiders stole cattle or children from Greater Bor. Murle and Nuer raiders engaged each other in massive attacks on the hinterland counties of Pibor, Akobo and Wuror.

Some interviewees explained the two modes of attack by reference to difference in military organization between Dinka and Nuer groups, with Dinka people presented as less assiduous pastoralists and less predisposed to fight than Nuer groups. With little inclination for retaliation, runs this argument, Dinka groups exposed themselves to small, opportunistic attacks – the costs of such attacks in Nuer areas would be much higher. Local views sometimes recalled the hierarchies of ethnic ferocity that were a preoccupation of colonial anthropology. But Greater Bor had little in the way of militias or informal armed groups. Bor town's population in 2005 was very low, and the local Khartoum-aligned militia (led by an SPLA defector called Deng Kelai) had 400 personnel. Bor and Twic county had no militia at all (Jonglei politician, interview 184/2012). The low levels of militia formation are linked, like so much in Bor's recent history, to the 1991 attack by Riek Machar's faction of the SPLA. The 1991 attack depopulated the area, forcing displaced local people into greater reliance on the SPLA for protection and access to markets and services in other areas of South Sudan. This reliance may be the origin of the contemporary stereotype of the well-connected Bor security man (Walraet 2008). Lack of militias may have less to do with alleged Dinka passivity and more to do with the radically changed political culture in Greater Bor. Displacement meant that many Bor people were more closely aligned to the national struggle, better educated and (as refugees) more aware of the African and international environment. After the 2005 Comprehensive Peace Agreement, the provincial capital was gradually enriched by the emergence of a huge salariat which dominated the cash economy of the whole state (see Chapter 5). But Dinka groups organized in response to the raiding economy too. In 2007, after Lou people were disarmed, Dinka raiders from Duk Padiet took 20,000 cattle from Lou areas in a single raid (ICG 2009: 3). And in response to the outside raiders, some youth in Twic have mounted defensive formations around cattle camps or mobilized pursuit parties (Harrigan 2011: 50).

Other modes of insecurity – the intra-sectional feud

The main focus of this chapter is on these two modes of conflict and their two fronts, in part because they are central to the depiction of Jonglei today. But Jonglei's insecurity involves more than these two fronts, and cannot readily be reduced to ethnic antagonisms. Before turning to an analysis of the unhappy relationship between Murle people and their neighbours after the 2005 peace deal, the chapter briefly reviews the context of insecurity: feuds, conflicts over cattle, boundaries and elections.

Many people in Jonglei died in local feuds that had no political resonance beyond the villages where they occurred. One state parliamentarian described one such feud in his home area, south of the Sobat river:

> They were fighting about a dance party at night, so one drunk man fired a gun and killed three people including an eleven-year-old boy. It is not intended. The revenge came in the morning, they killed four or five people. This was October 2011. It was not even announced by the commissioner because he doesn't go there. You could not even hear it from Miraya [the radio station with the biggest network of correspondents in South Sudan]. (Interview 157/2012)

This feud took eight lives before it came to the attention of the parliamentarian. In April 2012, a senior local government official in the neighbouring county of Akobo said that he was aware of eighty-nine unresolved feuds in his county, each involving up to five deaths. 'Feuds are the biggest killer,' he said, before correcting himself – over two hundred people had reportedly been killed in cattle raids in his county in the past four months (interview 75/2012). Cattle shortages arising from cattle raiding perpetuate feuding, because customary-law resolutions of cases of homicide and bodily injury are based on an exchange of cattle – the places where Radio Miraya does not reach are the kind of places where the penal code and the statutory courts cannot operate either.

Most such feuds probably did not appear in the Jonglei state ministry of interior's records of conflicts in eight of the state's eleven counties in the dry seasons between 2009 and 2011. Many of the conflicts were between sections of the same ethnic community, and others were between neighbouring ethnic communities, such as a joint Ghol Dinka and Lou Nuer raid on (predominantly Gaawar Nuer) Ayod in June 2010, which took over three thousand cattle. Conflicts were not only about cattle: a major conflict between Twic sections occurred in 2010 and 2011 about county and *payam* boundaries, which in Jonglei are being increasingly configured around sectional differences (see Chapter 5). In Twic, the largest of four major Twic subsections has two *payam*s and the other three sections have one each. The first deaths of local people in the conflict over the delimitation of a new *payam* for the county were in February 2010 (Harrigan 2011: 32).

Jonglei's persistent mutinies

The Comprensive Peace Agreement required elections in 2010, and the nature of national politics required that the results (overwhelming majorities for the SPLM and President Omer al-Bashir's National Congress Party in the south and north respectively) be more or less agreed in advance. This strange duopoly meant that political challenges in Khartoum and Juba were almost impossible, and real politics got shifted into disputes over administrative/constituency boundaries, posts and nomination processes. This shift revealed Omer al-Bashir's political deftness just as it exposed the SPLM's inexperience. Those who lost out in the nomination process in the south stood as independents and lost. Losers in remote and violent peripheries took to mutiny. The worst of these mutinies took place in two places: one was Murle-land and the second Khor Fulluth, near the strategic junction of the Bahr al-Zeraf and White Nile rivers that was once a front line between the two main factions of the SPLA. John Garang's loyalist general there, George Athor, rebelled after losing the governorship elections (see Chapter 5). Allegedly accepting Khartoum support, he networked the disaffections of other local mutinies in Jonglei in the harried run-up to the 2011 referendum on self-determination that brought the republic of South Sudan into existence. All of South Sudan's mutineers laid down arms for the referendum, but George Athor took them up shortly afterwards. In late 2011, he died in a mysterious shoot-out in Eastern Equatoria.

But the Murle-land rebellion was harder to put down. It was led by David Yauyau, a county official who stood unsuccessfully as an independent for a seat in the Jonglei state legislature in the 2010 elections. Unable to defeat insurgents in Jonglei, the government offered him a generalship in Juba in mid-2011, but within a year he had moved to Khartoum and then returned to Jonglei to restart his rebellion. The persistence of Yauyau's rebellion is linked in part to the persistence of insecurity between raiding groups in Murle-land and other parts of Jonglei, and the government's response to that insecurity.

Arms flowed towards these conflicts in their mysterious way. Juba routinely accused Khartoum of supplying arms to its dissidents, but the Ethiopian border also played a role. Gambella, part of Ethiopia's south-western periphery, had seen several decades of tension that were linked to Sudanese civil wars, but also to the contradictions of official identity politics in a culturally diverse area disconnected from Ethiopia's cultural heartlands. Gambella's identity politics were further complicated by state resettlement of food-insecure populations from those heartlands, and plans to commercialize agriculture in Gambella's hot and fertile plains as a strategy to address national food insecurity (Feyissa 2009; HRW 2012a).

Mapping conflicts – evidence from government records

The most wide-ranging attempt to map conflicts encountered in the course of research for this book comes from the South Sudan Bureau for Community Safety and Small Arms Control

(CSSAC), part of the state ministry of interior. Between January 2009 and November 2011, it listed conflicts in eight of Jonglei state's eleven counties. Reports of violence were verified or partially verified by local CSSAC representatives, government officials or traditional authorities, and although their figures are therefore open to question, the whole dataset sheds light on the geography of conflicts in Jonglei. CSSAC's results were discussed with representatives of many communities and probably underestimate the violence. They do not cover the violence linked to George Athor's rebellion, for example. CSSAC records a single raid by the small Toposa-speaking Jieh ethnic group in Pibor county: it happened in 2011 and it caused two deaths. Several other sources claim that over a thousand people died that year in Jieh raids in Pibor county in an established raiding pattern (humanitarian worker, Pibor, interview 120/2012). Overall, CSSAC records few wet-season deaths, possibly because violence diminishes in the wet season, but also perhaps because monitoring of rural violence becomes much more difficult. In spite of these limitations, CSSAC's data is a record of two main modes of violence – the opportunist raid and the massive attack. It maps these two modes of violence on two front lines – opportunist raids against predominantly Dinka Greater Bor, and reciprocal massive attacks between predominantly Murle Pibor county on the one side, and predominantly Nuer Akobo, Wuror and Nyirol counties.

Massive raids

In 2009, several conflicts erupted all at once. In Malakal, in February, Joint Integrated Units, a temporary force established as part of the Comprehensive Peace Agreement and made up of units of the SPLA and the Sudanese army, fought each other. It was a reminder of the wider context of instability in greater Upper Nile and the availability of and need for weapons. Tax checkpoints in Duk county undermined Lou traders' access to markets – like Murle areas, Lou areas are in the inaccessible Jonglei hinterland.

Murle raiders stole cattle and abducted children in the Lou area of Akobo in January 2009 and Murle-land was subjected to a massive retaliation in March that year. Thousands of Lou youth attacked the Murle town of Likongwele, killing 450 people and stealing children and huge numbers of cattle. In April 2009, Murle raiders attacked Nyandit, south of Akobo town, displacing 16,000 or more of the *payam*'s population and killing several hundred people. Between May and August 2009, armed elements from Lou and Jikainy engaged in cattle raiding, child abduction and trade disruption in areas between Akobo and the Sobat river. In September 2009, armed Lou elements attacked government buildings in Duk Padiet in Duk county, their motivation linked to the obstacles to market access they faced. Two hundred people were reportedly killed in twenty minutes of shooting (ICG 2009; Harrigan 2011: 36).

The eruption of inter-ethnic conflict in 2009 eventually turned into a sustained confrontation between armed elements from two ethnic groups, Lou Nuer and Murle. Jonglei state officials recorded over 2,000 deaths, over 300 abductions, and the theft of over 800,000 cattle in 2009 (Johnson and CSSAC 2012); 2010 was a much quieter year – 147 reported deaths, nearly all in Greater Bor and Pibor. But the insurgencies that started in Jonglei state in the aftermath of the controversial 2010 elections began to affect the area's stability once the 2010 wet season ended. The most lethal were against Pibor in April and June 2011, then Wuror in August 2011, Pibor in December 2011 and Akobo/Nasir in March 2012.

The following figures and tables show the reported losses from raids over three years up to late 2011 (funding for the CSSAC project stopped, so the 2011 figures do not include the deaths in the December 2011 attack on Pibor that is described in the Introduction). The predominantly Murle county of Pibor and the neighbouring, predominantly Lou Nuer counties of Akobo and Wuror had a relatively quiet year in 2010, but devastating raids

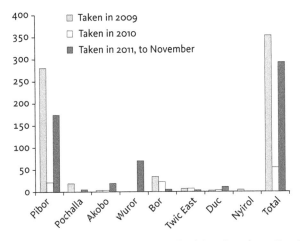

8.1 Reported abductions 2009–11 in eight selected counties of Jonglei (*source*: CSSAC 2012)

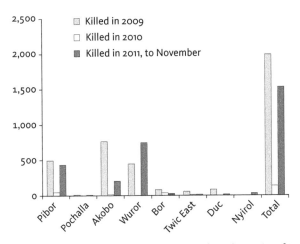

8.2 Reported killings 2009–11 in eight selected counties of Jonglei (*source*: CSSAC 2012)

with many casualties in 2009 and 2011. In contrast, Greater Bor (the predominantly Dinka Bor, Twic and Duk counties) had much lower levels of violence, but no significant reduction of violence in 2010 – CSSAC recorded raids every month except October.

TABLE 8.1 Reported cattle lost to raiding 2009–11 in eight selected counties of Jonglei

	2009	2010	Jan–Nov 2011	TOTAL
Pibor	808,180	2,573	54,800	865,553
Pochalla	646	115	0	761
Akobo	2,158	0	15,975	18,133
Wuror	25,035	200	43,738	68,973
Bor	191	1,535	1,313	3,039
Twic East	25,035	2,306	2,561	29,902
Duk	1,464	935	1,622	4,021
Nyirol	375	173	2,169	2,717
TOTAL	863,084	7,837	122,178	993,099

Source: CSSAC (2012)

In the three years, the predominantly Murle county of Pibor faced the highest number of abductions and cattle thefts.[1] Murle people's vulnerability to abduction and cattle theft is at odds with popular perceptions among non-Murle people. Several non-Murle people interviewed gave credence to the CSSAC figures: attacks on Pibor deployed thousands of people, and their capacity to carry out large-scale abductions or take large numbers of cattle is correspondingly high.

The CSSAC figures suggest the existence of three major conflict zones – regular conflicts with relatively limited losses in Greater Bor, and sporadic major conflicts in Greater Akobo and Pibor. Jonglei had other conflict zones too. CSSAC produced a table of 'inter-tribal' fighting; but it did not include the post-election insurgencies concentrated in the north-west counties of Jonglei – Pigi, Fangak and Ayod counties.

---

1 In an interview, an official involved in the collation of this data stated that the very high figure for cattle losses reported from Pibor in 2009 was based on reports from the district commissioner there, and not a typographical error.

Table 8.2 suggests that conflicts in Pibor, Akobo and Wuror decreased significantly in 2010. Floods that year may have hampered military mobilization, and up to 2,000 kilometres of roads were cleared (Jonglei politician, interview 173/2012), which increased the army's ability to move and may have increased trade (see the section on economy). The elections in April 2010 made local and central government more attentive to local concerns. After the elections, disappointed candidates subsequently mounted violent challenges to the results that were concentrated in the north-west of Jonglei state, which are not represented in this dataset, which aims to give a picture of violence in areas where Murle, Dinka and Nuer people interact.

Opportunistic attacks

Table 8.2 also suggests that conflicts in Greater Bor were very frequent in 2010, occurring during both wet and dry seasons. Why should the contours of the conflict be different in Greater Bor than elsewhere? Raiding in Greater Bor appeared to be smaller-scale and more opportunistic than elsewhere – a few cows or a few killings every week. The effects of these opportunistic attacks were wide ranging, however – whole villages to the east of Greater Bor have been displaced to the banks of the Nile, people feared movement after dark, and rapes and killings devastated individual lives (Harrigan 2011: 32ff.).

TABLE 8.2 Number of raids in eight selected counties of Jonglei in 2010

	Pibor	Pochalla	Akobo	Wuror	Bor	Twic East	Duk	Nyirol
Number of raids	4	2	2	3	5	11	13	1

Source: Johnson and CSSAC (2012)

Interviewees gave two explanations for the geography of conflict in Greater Bor. First, several argued that Dinka society is not organized for raiding – a cultural explanation advanced by colonial observers (Evans-Pritchard 1940a). Raiding is a strategy used by other groups of young people in Jonglei and Bahr al-Ghazal as a means of deterring attacks and gaining cattle. Although Dinka societies in Bahr al-Ghazal developed youth groupings capable of raiding (see Chapter 7), these did not emerge in Greater Bor – there is some evidence of local arrangements to patrol cattle camps and pursue raiders (Harrigan 2011: 50). Partly, this is because of the heavy losses and displacements after the 1991 attack on the area by Riek Machar's faction of the SPLA. Another culturalist explanation is that Dinka herders are less attentive to their cows than Murle and Nuer herders – this explanation may be an expression of the fact that raiders often come from local groups who are more dependent on cattle for their livelihood.

In Murle society, the most cattle-dependent groups are those who live on the western borders of Murle-land, along the seasonal rivers Veveno and Nanaam. Arensen (1992: 30) argues that these groups were a kind of expansionist tip of Murle migration, who would have expanded all the way to the Nile were it not for government restrictions. Arensen may have been reflecting the preoccupation with migration in African studies at the time of his writing – Murle people did not expand into Greater Bor when leading Murle personality Ismail Kony became governor of Jonglei state in 2003; and the presence of bilingual Murle–Dinka speakers in both communities is evidence that many in the two groups are trying to accommodate each other rather than conquer each other. However, cattle dependency in western Murle-land has many consequences. In April 2012, several reports indicated that people who previously had permanent homes on the Nanaam riverbanks were seeking to move west (humanitarian workers in Pibor, interviews 120/2012, 122/2012).

> They are there because of water and grass. Most of them don't want to go to Gummuruk because the pasture and water is insufficient. The fear of big population centres is also part of it. Some want to be far from the government. Because they are

raiders. They want to be away from government surveillance; raiding is a livelihood strategy there. We were there between 1 and 3 April [2012, and Pibor county commissioner] Joshua Kony said, 'I'm going to burn all the houses on the other side if you don't come back to the East side of Nanaam. But if you accept peacefully, it's good.' They accepted, people of West accepted. They said, 'we accept but we need water in Logichar [their original settlement]. We need a small town with police, with water.' (Interview 124/2012)

Many raiders die in raids, and there are some families in Nanaam with no men left, said one interviewee. Some accept loss fatalistically, but others have been led to conclude that it is wrong to continue with raiding, and see it as a harbinger of total destruction for Murle society (interview 124/2012).

Abstracting violence away from social and economic processes, as CSSAC's figures do, conceals motivations. Raiders may be motivated by food crises: food supplies in rural Jonglei are now provided by different, inefficient systems – traditional subsistence systems, market systems, international relief, and looting. Incompatibilities between these systems often create food crises, pushing some people into banditry, which then aggravates existing inefficiencies (humanitarian worker, interview 73/2012; state parliamentarian, interview 141/2012). Economic development is uneven – nascent market systems have been concentrated in state capitals, where state salaries are, and this creates more frustrations about unequal divisions of society's wealth. The following section tries to set out some reasons for the way that different modes of conflict have affected different parts of Jonglei.

The motivations of non-traditional armed groups

The White Army and armed youth groups are not traditional structures – they are examples of how traditional structures are transformed by violent experiences of modernity. Armed youth groups are configured around kinship and locale, so they are not really clandestine – it would be difficult to conceal their organization from village mothers or uncles, especially if organization happens during the wet season, when different generations of rural people live together more closely. But the evidence presented in the previous chapter suggests that they may be more youth-led than the traditional age-set systems, which were directed by elders. To describe the intentions of these different ad hoc groupings is an impossible task. This section sets out some possible interpretations of the political aims of rural male youth with guns over the past twenty years of conflict: defence; conquest; accumulation; or a complex of responses to social and economic transformations around them that are linked to youth politics.

Defence

Rural armed youth in pastoralist communities of South Sudan sometimes describe themselves as community defence forces, or cattle defenders. Military personnel in many societies share this self-perception that they exist to defend society and its values, rather than dominating or destroying it. South Sudan's groups of armed young pastoralists may deter minor attacks but they do not have the capacity to defend villages or cattle camps from many of the attacks they face. One UN military official speculated that the lack of defensive capability was due to a lack of concern for the civilian population: 'Occasionally they deliberately allowed women and children to be overrun by militia ... Are they regarded as a strategic asset to defend? Or not valued that highly?' (interview 14/2012).

Another way of conceptualizing the defensive role of armed youth in Jonglei is to see feuds or wars of revenge as a means to deter hostile acts in a society on the margins of the state. The armed youth do not have the technology or capacity to defend fixed positions, like villages, or even to defend cattle camps. But they can deploy devastating violence against the communities from which their attackers originate. Finally, this inability to defend communities or cattle might not be an indicator of military failure – it might be an indicator of the fact that these groups operate within a semi-autonomous youth sphere, not entirely under the control of, or accountable to, traditional leaders. One local government official stated:

> Why are the community forces weak in defence? Because they don't have organized leadership – when they are in community the direct leaders are traditional leaders. It's when they go out to the bush that they organize themselves. But when they come [to the village] they scatter to the families. They don't have leaderships. These are chiefs who are direct. They are not allowed to sit in one group, to gather like police. You're not allowed to move in uniform. Chiefs cannot allow it and we in authority cannot allow it. (Interview 60/2012)

Accumulation

Senior members of the SPLA interviewed for this book argued that cattle rustling was a major motivation for young people from Nuer society mobilizing to fight. One officer, a former US soldier of South Sudanese origin, emphasized the cultural difference between young Nuer fighters and the educated class to which he belonged: 'These people are open to manipulation around the euphoria that comes from dominating their neighbours, and from acquiring cattle. That's what [rural youth leaders] can manipulate. Educated people have no solutions for the uneducated' (interview 81/2012). Another SPLA officer, who fought in Bor at the time of the 1991 mobilization, commented:

> the political rebels, [Riek Machar's] Nasir faction, could only mobilize the Nuer for cattle raiding [and not for politics]. They knew [Nuer youth] would not join for political motivations. They would not go just to fight the Dinka. But they were told, let us go and raid cattle. (Interview 137/2012)

Ruling elites often depoliticize the actions of unruly youth, and the idea that Nuer or other youth are permanently motivated by cattle accumulation and cattle culture may be a simplification. Cattle-keeping is still an economically rational livelihood strategy in remote parts of Jonglei, because it allows herders to hedge against crop failure. The traditional mechanism for restocking cattle was through marriage, when cattle would be distributed in bridewealth, a sign that two extended families were economically allied. Bridewealth went to the bride's family, and the richest men were those with the most daughters. In the mid-twentieth century, cattle markets also emerged as a mechanism for restocking in Nuer society (Howell et al. 1988: 264ff.; Hutchinson 1996: 56ff.). But during the war, some families faced very heavy cattle losses, and restocking through raiding may have become an attractive option. Raiding brought volatility and unpredictability to herd sizes – large herds could disappear in a single attack. Men with many (raiding) sons might end up with more cattle than men with many daughters. Raiding may have become a restocking strategy, or even a livelihood strategy, but it was one which undermined market access – raided cattle were too recognizable to be sold near their places of origin. So it may have become a self-perpetuating economic strategy. Raiding had many costs associated with it – raiders could die or be wounded in the course of their attacks, and this discouraged attacks on militarily well-organized groups, particularly rural Murle and Lou Nuer groups.

The terms of distribution of cattle taken in raids are important for understanding these accumulatory practices. But distribution protocols vary between different ethnic groups. Nuer booty distribution was described by colonial anthropologists: 'It was recognized that the whole force was jointly responsible for the success of the raid and there was therefore a redistribution of the booty' (Evans-Pritchard 1940a: 128). Some of the spoils were taken by the prophet who sanctioned the raid, and then there was a scramble for the physical possession of the rest, during which clubs but not spears could be used by rival claimants of an animal.

Distribution of raided cattle today is an important determinant of cattle ownership in areas heavily affected by raiding. Cattle ownership is a complex topic in Nilotic societies: individual ownership coexists with family rights of usage and disposal (through sale or nuptial exchange) that are organized by a male household head. For one Nuer commentator, changes to systems of traditional spoils distribution may reflect changes to patriarchal control of cattle. As raids are organized by *bunam*, self-directing youth, younger people may have more power of decision about cattle than before. And looting is now sometimes motivated by a desire to get commodities other than cattle – partly because of the collapse of markets during wartime, people would sometimes loot them from other members of their society (interview 173/2012).

> People raid so they can loot goods. Because people want commodities. If you go to Lou Nuer, when you see someone with a bag, you give him a 'missed call' – that is, shoot and deliberately miss them with a bullet, to make them drop the bag. Then disable the person, gun him down. These days some people will argue, give him a bullet in the head. Because of twenty-one years of war, people don't give value to human life. One of them can't stop to say it's wrong, their minds are corrupt. Commodities have spoilt people, people want things they haven't got. (Jonglei politician, interview 135/2012)

The cattle of the dead are an important consideration: the families of raiders who die in the attack are entitled to part of the spoils from the attack. One observer of recent raiding stated: 'Those who died get more. Leaders get more cows. Big leaders, like [prophet] Dak Kueth, get many. The second way of distribution is by sub-clan. The number of cows you get from raiding belong to sub-clan. Youth leaders distribute within the sub-clan' (humanitarian worker, interview 53/2012). Cattle-raiding distribution systems may be transforming cattle ownership and creating new strategies for accumulation in societies at the edge of the market. Being a part of these strategies may be among the intentions of participants in armed groups.

Murle systems of booty distribution

Ismail Kony conscripted his soldiers from the Titi and Modec age sets, men now in their thirties, forties and even fifties. The people now involved in raiding are from Botonya and Lango age sets. Age sets in Murle society delay marriage by requiring adolescents, the youngest age set, to wait for the marriages of all members of the next age set, in their twenties and thirties, before engaging in courtship themselves. Today, that means that the Lango youngsters are trying to push the next Botonya age set into settling down so that the youngsters can control courtship. 'Pushing' used to mean violent stick fighting, but from the 1980s began to involve guns. In 2005, when the Comprehensive Peace Agreement was signed, the Lango age group was beginning to form, and the violence was memorable – in one case around 2007, an age-set fight finished with the immolation of the victim's corpse (Murle traditions require the dead to be left to scavenging animals and birds).

Murle raiding parties are formed from these age sets. They are generally smaller than Lou Nuer raiding columns, which can number in the thousands. But the pace of violence after 2009 indicates that smaller Murle raiding groups could field enough armed youth to kill hundreds of adversaries and civilians. The age sets are organized loosely and informally, but they relate to the wider Murle social order through members of lineages of spiritual leaders who are known as red chiefs. Each age set in each locale will have a young representative from one of these lineages in the local age-set group: in some cases, a popular or brave youth will be chosen in preference to a young red chief. The age set has the same name across the whole of Murle society, so the leadership of these young red chiefs is very decentralized. Decisions about raiding and booty distribution mostly happen in these young groups. However, responses to massive attacks are likely to be taken by larger sections of the community, with older men involved. Mike Arensen, a researcher based in Jonglei, studied the booty distribution after a particularly big attack by Murle raiders against Lou herders at the Rumyeri pasture near Akobo. He found that the Botonya age set were able to deprive older age sets of a share in booty by intimidation and that people could remember no precedent for this. 'Botonya and Lango are becoming even more brazen about their independence and power … [they] are even trying to prove their independence from the age-set structure' (Mike Arensen, researcher, interview 6/2013). In both Murle and Nuer society, the generational balance of power appears to have shifted youthwards.

Conquest

Both Murle and Nuer migrations are represented in colonial literature in primarily aggressive terms, a representation taken up in secondary anthropological literature (Evans-Pritchard 1940a: 126ff.; Lewis 1972: 22; Kelly 1985). In contrast, Nuer historians and later writers give a more complex account of fragmentations and assimilations through marriage and adoption and negotiation with the radically egalitarian Nuer society, which accords incomers the same rights as established members of the community (Jal 1987; Duany 1992; Johnson 1994). Murle people have fewer post-colonial historians: Andretta (1985) repeats this conquest narrative in the introduction to her anthropological study, while Arensen (1992: 29) argues that traditional conquest narratives may have simplified and idealized a more complex set of interactions.

Some Murle interviewees living in areas that have experienced attacks by columns of armed Nuer youth believed that there was a Nuer conspiracy to occupy Murle land – sometimes, they claim that Dinka leaderships in Bor are instigating these attacks (civil servant in Pibor, interview 115/2012). Most Nuer interviewees did not share this view – they presented their attacks as a reaction to long provocations from Murle people. But one claimed that the massive attack on Pibor in December 2011 was accompanied by a plan for the ethnic cleansing of Murle people, followed by Nuer settlement of the areas. 'Had there not been intervention from the vice-president, the areas would have been settled' (interview 63/2012).

Prophecy and politics

During the disarmament campaigns lasting from 2006 to 2013, the SPLA leadership often gave a depoliticized view of armed youth in Jonglei's hinterland as criminals or cow fanatics. It is difficult for outsiders to build a picture of the political objectives of armed youth, perhaps in part because outsiders are associated with the state and the armed youth may be seeking to evade the state in order to maintain fragile economic interests – this is particularly the case in Murle areas. But in Nuer areas, where armed youth are sometimes linked to prophets, the record of prophetic preaching can be a starting place for understanding political objectives. The White Army was established in the early 1990s, partly in response to the preaching of the prophet Wutnyang Gaarkek (also Gatkek, Gatakek). Wutnyang's life story has the same illustrative qualities as Hassan Ngachingol's. His preaching helped to create the White Army; he joined the SPLA after his prophetic powers left him; and he died an SPLA officer, during the violent 2006 disarmament campaign against the White Army in Wuror.

Nuer prophets have attracted government attention ever since government came to Upper Nile (Johnson 1994). During the Anya-nya 1 rebellion that followed from Sudan's independence, the Khartoum government was able to recruit Nuer prophets to its militias. Sharon Hutchinson and Douglas Johnson, who provide some records of Wutnyang's preaching, both argue that he resisted government attempts to co-opt him. He called for Nuer unity and encouraged Nuer commanders in Anya-nya 2 to join the SPLA.

He mediated truces between Dinka and Nuer communities in the aftermath of the White Army attack on Greater Bor. In Gambella, Ethiopia, he preached on black power during a period of tensions between Nilotic people and Ethiopian highlanders (who distinguished themselves from Nilotic people, seen as black); and in Sudan, he preached for agricultural self-reliance and against relief food; he also preached for South Sudan's separation and helped lead an unsuccessful attack on the garrison town (ibid.: 350; Hutchinson 1996: 338ff.). Gaaluak Deng Garang, then the Khartoum-appointed governor of Upper Nile province, represents his relationship with the prophet more cordially: Wutnyang worked with the government and his mediation missions were part of the government's efforts to manage or reconcile local differences between ethnic communities (Deng Garang 2006: 69).

Wutnyang's preaching addressed many of the elements of the crisis that Nuer young people were living through, and he himself was a young man at the time of his preaching. In 1991, Christianity was not so widespread in Nuer-land, and social acceptance of prophets may have been more widespread. Twenty years later, the prophet Dak Kueth mobilized Lou Nuer youth and some youth from neighbouring communities to fight in Pibor. Many interviewees represented Dak Kueth as a malign social force, a 'Satan' or a *kujur* (a derogatory Arabic term similar to the English term witch doctor). These interviewees were mostly Christian or urban intellectuals with relatively weak connections to rural South Sudan. But Dak Kueth's preaching also had a moral focus. One Presbyterian minister who admired Dak Kueth said:

> Some intellectuals have taken it negatively to condemn prophets ... Personally, when Dak Kueth was leading community to raid I went and talked to him. We realized he had leadership qualities to cement peace-building and we convinced him and he listened to us in August last year and we convinced him not to lead the raid. We found it was useful. He had command. People also came from Gaawar and Lou and Dinka, he

advised them not to go. Others have different opinions, others say Dak Kueth wants to mobilize people to fight government. (Interview 142/2012)

Dak Kueth was from near Pieri, a Wuror county village that was devastated by a Murle attack in August 2011. Most people speaking in public denounced him, but during several private interviews, people who were not his followers gave more nuanced accounts of his preaching and its impact:

> [Interviewee describing a conversation with a young man who took part in the December 2011 attack on Murle areas] I said, what's this about [prophet] Dak Kueth? He said, *all the people call him Computer, because what he says happens.* I said, why don't you listen to church and intellectuals not Dak Kueth? He said, *what are we going to get from that kind of talk? Dak Kueth says where to find cattle and predicts raids of Murle, and predicts casualties. Dak Kueth predicted the Rumyere attack.* (Interview 76/2012)

> [Church official from Dak Kueth's home area] He was actually leading some people before he was possessed by spirit, he was a leader of youth and a hunter, he used to eat animal meat, and he was a brave young man, before the spirit possessed him. This is why the youth like him. He is very brave, he also says that he can find things for them – he says go to that place and you can find everything. (Interview 97/2012)

> [Jonglei politician] Why do youth follow the prophet? He inspires and directs them, give them courage. Dak Kueth was telling them to behave like this, not to do that, when you get cows you divide them fairly, don't fight, don't kill each other or you will die; he said don't steal [each other's] cows. (Interview 61/2012)

> [Former policeman] He's against theft. He said, no drinking of *'aragi* [locally distilled alcohol]. He said if you make *'aragi* the

barrel [you make it in] will explode. Many people like him, but educated people don't like him. Because he opposes the government. He says, why is there no protection? The government is political, but he is not political. (Interview 82/2012)

Several interviewees mentioned that Dak Kueth preached against alcohol misuse too. One (Nuer) observer hostile to recent developments in youth culture argued that rural youth gangs were criminal organizations:

> They even steal cattle from their own family, you sell your wife's cow for alcohol. Most are in village. They can be from seventeen to forty. It's rural criminality. They can go in groups of twenty to thirty and go anywhere and raid some cattle and sell them somewhere else, or give them to other criminals to exchange them on their behalf ... They mostly live around Jikainy and Lou and Gaawar areas, and also in Greater Nasir and greater Ayod. They are motivated by consumer goods, and alcohol. (Interview 80/2012)

This criminality was attributed by some to lack of access to commodities in the Jonglei hinterland – people began looting within their own communities as a result of scarcity of commodities (Jonglei politician, interview 173/2012). Prophetic preaching may have aimed at countering some of the negative social consequences of economic transformation and the undermining of family structures – it is significant that loot distribution and alcohol consumption were both targets of Dak Kueth's condemnation.

Dak Kueth became a prophet around 2009 (Jonglei politician, interview 97/2012). He seems to have aided a process whereby the White Army reconstituted itself as a major force capable of temporary mobilization for tactical goals. He articulated Nuer responses to what were widely perceived as provocative attacks from Murle raiders. After the devastating attacks on his home area of Pieri in August 2011, he was part of local calls for an end to violence, and when the government failed to address local concerns, he helped to mobilize young people for a massive revenge attack on Likongwele and Pibor in December 2011. He was able to use systems of youth organization – the *bunam* system – that operate semi-autonomously on the fringes of traditional structures. He addressed some of the antisocial features of that system, and rationalized its economic function, allowing people to operate in the collapsed economic systems of the Jonglei hinterland. The prophet plays a role in the distribution of looted cattle, and ensures that the families of fatalities receive a share. This may be an attempt to regulate an economic system which has been reshaped by looting.

People with a stake in the market or the government – intellectuals, army officers, clergymen and local government officials do not respond to this preaching – represent the prophet as a Satan or a witch doctor, echoing colonial descriptions. The prophet reflects the uncertainty and violence of a rural order that they no longer inhabit. Likewise, young people involved in pastoralism in Jonglei's hinterland are largely excluded from the market and government structures, and have no ready route on to the government's payroll (unlike members of former Khartoum-aligned militias, who were incorporated into the SPLA). Youth leaders interviewed expressed distrust of the government and its news organs: 'I don't listen to government news. There's government news and there's what the people say. Government news is unreliable' (interview 77/2012). The mutual distrust may reflect the divergence of interests within Nuer society, between those with a stake in the new economic and political order, and those with none.

Armed youth and national politics

Chapter 5 set out some observations about the centralization of economic power in South Sudan's national politics and the persistence of ethnicity as a means for organizing the relationship between the central state and a rural society that is only partially incorporated into the systems of rent and debt and wages that would allow for deeper state penetration. Politicians often invoke ethnic constituencies in order to increase their participation in the state, and urban ethnic associations play an important role in creating or imagining a community of interests between rural and urban kinsfolk. Do messages passing through this network of relationships encourage young men to engage in violence? Some see clear evidence: one politician from a state with many armed young men said, 'Last year someone in the village told me the whole thing, the fighting, is coming from you [the urban population]. If you go there, they can tell you who is involved, encouragement, arms flow. They told me, if you want, we will count the names' (interview 12/2012). Evidence of direct instigation is elusive, although many interviewees were very free with allegations:

> If I'm a politician, how do I get people to fight? For example, in Akobo? The top leaders believe that the Murle are very few. They say to people, *How can you be disturbed by one or two Murle? … Why are you complaining about these small people? We government, there is nothing we can do. Why are you complaining?* Is this statement a kind of incitement? If you say there's a Murle–Dinka problem, they will aggressively tell you, *Your people are disturbing these people.* This kind of statement is taken as a call for revenge. (Anonymous, interview 192/2012)

In Jonglei today, politicians cannot publicly call for revenge, one parliamentary official explained: 'it is not acceptable to people and it's contrary to what government is proclaiming … If you are known as the one creating conflict or bringing people to conflict you will be marked and people will not be with you' (interview 95/2012). Other interviewees argued that aspiring politicians were responsible for instigating violence: publicly calling for peace, but less openly accusing incumbents of failing to safeguard the interests of their community, or even fomenting violence in order to show up incumbents' failures to manage power. One politician said:

With our people today, pressure groups are different from in west. Here you use your tribe to put pressure on the government, killing people, agitating. Use force to demand development. [Politicians say to youth, why can't you deal with the next *payam*, they] are useless, you youth are not even properly organized. So people kill themselves. (Interview 135/2012)

These statements suggest that politicians communicate intensively with their communities. Evidence does not bear this out: politicians spend relatively little time with their constituencies; members of state legislatures are expected to spend three months a year in their constituencies, during the recess. Parliamentary officials discourage all but those nearest Bor from doing so in the current security situation. Politicians may be drawn to inflammatory rhetoric because they are unable or unwilling to transfer resources to their communities – over 80 per cent of national revenues stayed in the national capital, and a similar proportion of state revenues stayed in state capitals. The constituency development funds paid to some members of the National Legislative Assembly do not appear to reach their constituencies – although these funds are only slightly less than a county budget and ambitious politicians could use them to develop an effective clientelist system. The fact that they do not appear to be used to maintain incumbencies in this way raises questions about the depth of communication between politicians and people. One informed observer argued that rural leaderships – prophets and drum chiefs – have more influence on youth participants in violence than city politicians.

Structures of violence

If that observation is correct, more attention needs to be given to rural–urban polarization than to urban–rural instigation. One possible theory explaining the persistence of raiding in Jonglei is that it is a form of political organization by groups excluded from the state – rural youth who are not educated enough to get state posts, and are not able to get army posts because they were not members of the militias formally incorporated into the SPLA. They mobilize around authority figures – prophets and drum chiefs – that are autonomous from official politics, and they are not easily comprehensible within the official political order. These leaders also guide the distribution of spoils. They respond to pressure from city politicians to attend peace conferences – but they do not trust these conferences to deliver peace. One Lou Nuer youth leader expressed his sense of the irrelevance of city politics after a long meeting of the Jonglei State Peace, Reconciliation and Tolerance Committee in Bor. 'This is a peace conference for people in towns' (Sudan Tribune 2012a).

The political objectives of these localized, autonomous youth groupings are hard to discern and are sometimes dismissed by institutions seeking to portray the violent changes in rural South Sudanese society in the language of criminality. They may have begun as a means for defending cattle from raiders through counter-raiding. As weapons were integrated into local patterns of accumulation, raiding became an objective in itself (see Chapter 9). Members of other ethnic communities may see the intent of such groups as conquest – although no raiders have attempted to resettle land whose population they have displaced. Some of the political objectives of the large-scale attacks of the past three years can be read in the preaching of the prophet Dak Kueth. His rules for conducting raiding and exhortations to unity and discipline suggest that young pastoralists, caught up in a raiding economy and with little stake in market or government systems, may be seeking drastic means of rationalizing the violence of their social and economic life. Many people with a stake in the market or the government – officials and urbanized intellectuals – do not respond to these rationalizations and this may be an indication of divisions emerging between rural society and successful urban groups.

Some people argue, however, that urban politicians instigate violence in the periphery because more rigid and antagonistic versions of ethnicity will help them win out in the system of ethnic representation and allocation that has been discussed at length in this book. Fearon and Laitin (2000) set out crisply some of the theoretical requirements for reaching judgements about the social context for ethnic violence, and they argue that 'elite manipulation' arguments fail to explain why 'ethnic publics' follow elite manipulators, and end up paying the costs of the crises that follow. They argue that in coercive or chaotic environments, manipulation can work both ways. Elites may instigate, but some subsections of the 'ethnic publics' may use violence for their own ends. Fearon and Laitin speculate that sections of these 'ethnic publics' who participate in such violence do so out of relatively malign motivations: land grabs; looting; personal revenge; the need of newcomers to prove that they belong, at outsiders' expense.

These motivations may operate in South Sudan too. But this chapter, and the book as a whole, has tried to frame human motivations within South Sudan's spaces and structures within different theories of uneven development (Harvey 2006). The 1983 SPLM/A set out forcefully one theory for the spatial and structural differences that pervade South Sudan: external actors established different patterns of exploitation, development and underdevelopment in the country. This constructivist, and Marxian, explanation is not the only one entertained in this book. Another compelling account of South Sudan's heterogeneous spaces is set out in Paul Howell's work about landscapes, livelihoods and possibilities for development (SDIT 1955; Howell et al. 1988). Howell was a colonial official who went on to work as a development planner, and his detailed and influential work showed how underlying ecological differences have set different pathways to development within South Sudan. His liberal-environmental views, which present development as a primarily technical rather than political task, shape most studies of South Sudanese livelihoods today.

The part played by ordinary rural boys and men in the terrible violence in Jonglei cannot be simply attributed to structural reasons. But uneven economic development creates peripheries, and peripheries are chaotic. Food economies are shaped and reshaped by violence, and they are lived out as impossible balancing acts – farming, herding, fishing, earning wages, queuing for relief and looting. The concluding part of this book looks at South Sudan's cattle economy to address questions about the causes of violence in Jonglei, prospects for an end to that kind of violence, and the way that violence affects everyday calculations and motivations.

PART THREE
SOCIAL TRANSFORMATION

Many liberation movements postpone social transformation until after state capture, and the leaders of South Sudan's liberation struggle set out their intentions to do so early and clearly. Social transformation happened nonetheless, because war exposed people more deeply to the forces around them. The food economies that shaped South Sudanese societies were transformed by looting and expropriation, conscription of youth, war displacement, new markets and new relief systems.

It is difficult to read these changes, for a number of reasons. First of all, the SPLM/A and South Sudan's other major political actors failed to provide people with a means of organizing their response to these changes. Both the SPLM/A and the Khartoum government organized their relationship with South Sudanese people around ethnicity, reworking traditional and neo-traditional authorities or mobilizing ethnic militias to fit their own military, logistical and political needs. Both benefited from the fact that the capacity of traditional authorities to mobilize society is highly localized and, on a national scale at least, relatively weak.

Ordinary people had to improvise responses to the big changes, using the localized, militarized organizational repertoire available. Some resisted incorporation in the state and the market. The raiding groups in the cattle-dependent western edge of Murleland have managed to keep their distance from most markets (other than the arms market). Others sought accommodation with new realities, participating in new institutions such as urban or refugee camp schools, NGO offices or ethnic militias and raiding groups. Both accommodation and resistance pushed many people deeper into the violence. But they also pushed them into an unfamiliar 'organizational repertoire' – one not easily intelligible to outsiders. This part of the book tries to read the changes. Chapter 9 looks at the food economy. Relief systems seem to have drawn people into food markets. But commercialization of the livestock economy is patchy, and reflects differences between provincial centres and hinterlands. Land and water resources are still held in common. But the ethnic and kinship groups which 'own' those resources have been deeply changed by war. Armed men have been empowered, and other social groups have been disempowered, in a way that appears self-defeating for all. Chapter 10 returns, somewhat hesitantly, to the abduction story. It argues that abduction is caught up in changes to gender relations brought on by changing patterns of accumulation and social organization.

9 | RAIDING AND EATING

A transformed food economy

An informal nutritional study conducted in the Jonglei canal zone in the early 1950s estimated that the daily calorific intake in the zone varied between 2,000 kilocalories in the months before harvest, and well over 3,000 kilocalories during the grain harvest (JIT 1954: vol. 1, 244–7, vol. 4, E12). Jonglei had cereal deficits throughout the twentieth century. Colonial records of the tonnage of grain received at river ports between 1930 and 1953 suggest that the area imported grain. But the tonnage was very low. The needs were highest in 1947, when the net import of grain at river stations between Malakal and Bor was 4,648 tonnes. In 1949, South Sudan as a whole exported grain, and the stations between Malakal and Bor exported 654 tonnes (SDIT 1955: 137). Colonial authorities could not mobilize labour from these well-fed people, and they had to raise wages for 'tribal' or forced labour after good harvests (Sudan Government 1955a: 156; 1955b: 179). Most people did not need what money could buy.

Cash use is still limited. A 2009 study found that almost two-thirds of people in Jonglei had not used cash in the previous seven days, one of the lowest rates of cash use in South Sudan (SSCCSE 2010: 150). But money has apparently become essential. A study of food security conducted in 2009 showed something of the new situation. More than half the food in Jonglei was purchased, and food made up 86 per cent of household expenditure in the state. Forty-eight per cent of the population were malnourished, consuming less than 1,730 kilocalories a day, a figure which averages out minimum dietary requirements across a population of adults and children. Hunger in Jonglei was among the deepest in the country – 'depth' of hunger referring to the average number of missing calories in the malnourished population. On average, malnourished people in Jonglei were missing almost 500 kilocalories a day (SSCCSE and CBS 2010: 27, 31, 35, 37). Jonglei's cereal deficit – the mismatch between local supply and demand – was the highest in the country. In 2009/10, Jonglei imported over 100,000 tonnes of grain, more than two-thirds of its grain consumption (FAO/WFP 2010: 20). Its population had probably increased threefold since 1947, when grain imports were under 6,000 tonnes.

The food economy of Jonglei had been repeatedly transformed in the fifty-five years that separated these two surveys. The transformations cannot be summarized simply, and they operated differently in different areas. The substitution of subsistence cultivation of grain by purchased or traded grain was part of it. But some groups, such as the westernmost Murle groups, are almost entirely cattle-dependent, and grain purchase may have meant less there. The switch away from home-grown grain may have been linked to wartime experience of displacement, which pushed people into dependence on relief grain, and may have undermined subsistence systems. Raiding increased dramatically, and became an important part of restocking, once automatic weapons entered the production chain. The response of raided groups varied. Many living near the towns restocked through cash purchase, while many hinterland groups restocked through counter-raiding. Raiding patterns shaped different trajectories of development in the cattle economy and emphasized differences between the state capital and its hinterland. These differences were sometimes apparently patterned around ethnicity, with the ethnic groups of the hinterlands seen as more prone to restocking by raiding. But before examining these apparent patterns, another factor needs to be considered – malnutrition appears to be taking place against a backdrop of plenty.

Hungry people and growing herds

All these changes happened, remarkably, during a period of apparently massive expansion in herd sizes. Overgrazing has become a problem on the lush Nile-side pastures near Bor. Most of this chapter deals with cattle, but the increase in sheep and goat numbers is even more striking (UNEP 2007: 182, 184).

Colonial estimates in the 1950s based on vaccination data found 233,000 cattle in Nuer areas of Jonglei (Howell 1954: 239). A 1972 animal density survey found 1,185,000 cattle in greater Upper Nile – the present-day states of Unity, Upper Nile and Jonglei.

Three recent attempts to enumerate South Sudan's cattle population reached widely varying conclusions. A 2009 survey from the UN's Food and Agriculture Organization based on estimates from a national study gave the lowest figures: 11,735,159 cattle in South Sudan, of which 3,628,120 were in greater Upper Nile, of which 1,464,671 were in Jonglei. State ministries of livestock and fisheries estimates based on vaccination data for 2010 give higher figures: 8,578,000 for greater Upper Nile, of which 2,678,000 were in Jonglei (Table 9.1 gives county estimates). A 2010 study from the Southern Sudan Centre for Census, Statistics and Evaluations based on a survey of 500 households gives an improbably large figure of 11,926,390 for greater Upper Nile, of which 8,487,911 were in Jonglei (MARF/SNV 2010).

The enormous discrepancies between these surveys raise questions about their accuracy. Some highly informed interviewees from north-western Jonglei questioned the assumption that cattle populations are increasing, emphasizing the unreliability of cattle statistics in South Sudan and their own local experiences of cattle loss (veterinarian, interview 35/2012; politician, interview 38/2012). A recent (undated) Jonglei state ministry study of herd dynamics set out below also suggests modest increase: in the herds studied, annual increase was only 1 per cent, much lower than the 11 per cent increase in the study's Kenyan comparators (Ministry of Livestock and Fisheries, Jonglei State 2011: 9). But taken as a whole, the evidence suggests that there has been a significant increase in the cattle population in the past sixty years. Interviewees in Pibor county generally accepted the notion of an increase (humanitarian worker, interview 120/2012). Hunger has appeared out of plenty.

A cattle economy at the margins of the market

If there is an increase in cattle population, the extra cattle are not being sold. The herd dynamics study suggests that the cattle economy there is not highly commercialized. Most herd turnover is made up by dowry transactions. Purchase and sale of cattle makes up a much smaller proportion of turnover, a little more than raiding.

TABLE 9.1 Herd dynamics for an average household with a herd of sixty-five cattle

	Number	Per cent of herd at start of year
At start of year	65	100
Born in last 12 months	14	21.5
Died as calves	6	9.2
Sold	1	1.5
Slaughtered	1	1.5
Given away for dowry	14	21.5
Given to herders	0	0.0
Given away for other reasons	2	3
Bought	6	9.2
Received as dowry/other	10	15.4
Lost through raids/theft	5	7.7
TOTAL	66	101.5

Source: Ministry of Livestock and Fisheries, Jonglei State (2011: 9)

The main commercial markets for cattle are in Bor, Juba and Malakal. A 2010 study found a particularly low concentration of

cattle markets in Jonglei, in spite of its enormous cattle population – only ten markets out of a national total of 167. Cattle-poor
Western Equatoria has twenty-nine (MARF/SNV 2010: 102).

Markets are a relatively recent phenomenon. The twentieth-
century cattle economy in Nuer-land was perceptively described
by the anthropologist Sharon Hutchinson. In the early twentieth
century, exchange was organized around marriage, not markets
– the families of bridegrooms shared wealth with the families of
brides. It was only in the late colonial period that cattle began
to be sold for cash (to pay colonial taxes); or bought for cash
(courts imposed fines in cattle which were then auctioned). After
independence, Nuer people's participation in cattle and labour
markets expanded as Nuer people deepened their connections
to the money economy centred in Khartoum – but they used
the money economy to smooth consumption in hunger seasons
and smooth supply and demand in the more important social
(marriage) exchange system. During the civil war, many South
Sudanese people reconsidered the money economy, which they
had largely resisted during the twentieth century:

> Twenty years ago, the people of South Sudan had started to
> look inwardly into the monetary economy rather than barter.
> [Previously] this monetary economy didn't go far away from
> cattle – sell cattle in order to buy cattle. The other part was
> to sell cattle for school fees, health, trade, to open a shop.
> (Veterinary expert, interview 87/2012)

Interviews in the cattle markets serving Jonglei suggest that
trade volumes are low. A Malakal cattle market official stated that
daily sales averaged about sixty cows, of which forty were from
Nyirol (a predominantly Lou Nuer area) and ten to fifteen
from Nasir (a predominantly Jikainy Nuer area). The market in
Akobo is a collection of Ethiopian butchers' shacks without even
an enclosure, just a few cattle tied to a tree. Pibor market has an
enclosure and volumes there may be slightly higher.

In spite of the low trade volumes reported by some interviewees, several suggested that the appetite for participation in market economies may be spreading. In a relatively hungry season of the year, drovers and traders used their profits to engage in trade rather than to buy grain, according to one cattle market official: 'Nyirol people don't buy sorghum. That's Nasir people. Nyirol people buy clothes, cars, shoes, sometimes in wholesale quantities to sell in Nyirol' (interview 154/2012). This was borne out by a recent study of livestock marketing, which suggested that livestock sales were motivated mostly by a desire for participation in the modern economy: people said they sold livestock to buy food, to pay medical bills and school fees, or to build cattle byres (MARF/SNV 2010: 9).

Many people attribute low trade volumes to the cultural importance of cattle in Murle, Nuer and Dinka society, which makes cattle owners reluctant to sell their animals. Perhaps President Salva Kiir had this cattle culture in mind when, after a particularly bloody sequence of cattle raids in Jonglei in 2012, he upbraided the people of Jonglei for having a cow emblem on the state flag: 'This picture of a cow on your flag should be changed. This cow is killing you' (Radio Miriya 2012).

The research conducted for this study was not comprehensive enough to reach conclusions about the resilience of cattle culture in Jonglei. Nonetheless, it is important to recall that pastoralists are unusually vulnerable to mystification and sentimentalization, and explanations that privilege their cultural attachments should be assessed against other available evidence. In Jonglei, that evidence is more confusing than conclusive. Cattle 'off-take rates' – the proportion of the herd sold or consumed in a year – are apparently lower than in other states in South Sudan, which in turn has lower off-take than many African countries. But off-take rates for sheep and goats – which are the 'petty cash' of the pastoralist economy, easily traded and easily replaced – are also low (MARF/SNV 2010: 9). The reasons for low trade volumes, and the resilience of social exchange, may lie instead in the way that state and market systems simultaneously incorporate and marginalize places like Jonglei. Rural people there have had to shift into the market for food, but having done so, their calorie intake dropped dramatically. They may seek, or be forced to seek, market participation, but those markets are too inaccessible for them because of violence or for other reasons. Market inaccessibility may be linked to the raiding economy, a feature of the Jonglei hinterlands which has transformed traditional systems.

Traditional cattle ownership, exchange and labour systems

In the traditions of Nilotic society, several people can have a stake in a single animal, but only the head of the household has the right to take the animal out of the herd, a kind of 'ownership' right. His wife, and any relatives who have no cattle, have rights in milk, and some of them may trade the cow's milk. His sister's son may hope that the cow will be part of his dowry; his friend may hope the cow will repay a debt; and he may hope to trade it for grain or school fees. And if he divorces his wife, her family will demand the cow back. Restocking often happened in a social framework too. If too many people in the household are living off too few cows, the head of the household may encourage his daughter to marry someone who has collected a bridewealth. Yet he himself may not look after his cows in the dry season: they go to a cattle camp and are looked after by a labour pool of young men drawn from his neighbours or cousins (Iles 1994: 11).

The breakdown of the traditional livestock economy

Many people interviewed for this book spoke about the changes to traditional systems of ownership, exchange, stock management and labour. During the 1990s, households from communities in Greater Bor, Greater Akobo and Nasir faced sudden massive losses to their herds as a result of intercommunal conflicts arising out of political crises in the greater Upper Nile.

Traditional restocking mechanisms broke down in most areas: these methods included family loans of cattle; or exchanging a cow for goats or sheep accumulated through wage labour or cultivation of agricultural surplus. A 1994 study of Dinka and Nuer responses to the crisis found that bridewealth was being turned into cash in many areas and that cultivation and trade were seriously undermined by insecurity. Raiding was seen as a high-risk, high-return restocking mechanism, and unlike the bridewealth restocking system, it favoured families with sons more than families with daughters (ibid.: 18ff.).

Evans-Pritchard (1940a: 128) describes booty distribution after a raid as a scramble organized by the prophet whose revelations had sanctioned it. Some people interviewed for this book argued that booty-distribution practices were changing. Cattle from raids were no longer routinely shared between relatives, which meant that raiders were undermining the cattle ownership rights exercised by the male household head. Young raiders began to feel that the cattle they had risked their lives to steal belonged to them personally, and not to their fathers:

> Now young men and militia men can make decisions about cows and marriage ... In the Nilotic household in the twentieth century, the economy was controlled by the male household head ... Now this time the economy is so destabilized. Not like those days. Men [household heads] are not controlling cows or food crop. If someone goes and raids, that cow belongs to him. Or if you buy a cow with your crop, it belongs to you. It's not shared with your brothers. It's the emergence of individual ownership. A big change in Nilotic society, not necessarily accounted for by market relations. (Agriculturalist, interview 53/2012)

Changes to ownership may be changing labour relations – at least in some cattle-keeping areas. Raiding means that a few individuals can amass large numbers of cows. A person with hundreds of cows needed to find people to look after them. One government minister argued that accumulation of cattle pushed wealthy owners of big herds to cast a wider net among their relations in order to mobilize labour from up to seven generations of relations: 'The increase in cattle is pushing people to a sense of ethnic/lineage affiliation. Lineage previously was defined – up to fifth grandfather, we split up. Now in our family we are paying cousins in sixth or seventh generation [to look after cattle]' (interview 12/2012).

Deepening the lineage system in order to manage a larger herd is one response. Other interviewees argued that wage labour for cattle keepers is emerging: in the past, a cattle owner would give a cow to a relative with an understanding that the relative would look after the animal in return for milk and some contribution to his bridewealth. This extended family system still exists in the hinterland of Akobo. But in more commercialized areas, this system is being replaced by something approaching a labour contract: 'People with big herds give [financial] support to people after one year, or one month. It's near to traditional system, not really pay, but the days are calculated. So it's coming to time and money. That doesn't happen here [in Akobo]. It happens in Warrap and Greater Bor' (agriculturalist, interview 53/2012).

Problems in labour supply for the cattle economy are compounded in some areas by the fact that young people are seeking alternative livelihoods. Several interviewees claimed that the labour force working on cattle was decreasing, and older people were taking more responsibility for cattle camp labour – youth remain indirectly linked to the cattle system, through marriage (veterinary expert, interview 35/2012).

Uneven development in Bor and in the Jonglei hinterlands

During the civil war, South Sudanese people from pastoralist communities began to change systems for cattle labour and ownership; developed new restocking systems based on cash or violence; and changed patterns of accumulation. The bridewealth system was maintained, although its rationale – sharing wealth between two families and between different generations of one family, and insuring against climate risks – was changing. These changes did not happen uniformly across the entire territory of a state like Jonglei, however. Changes to the cattle economy affect Jonglei's state capital and its hinterland very differently.

Bor town – integration into a market economy

Markets have penetrated life in Bor more deeply than in Jonglei's hinterland, in part because of the brutal 1991 experience of displacement. As a probable consequence of that displacement, Bor people increased dependence on the SPLA and used their links with the military to expand into new areas of pasture and control markets in cattle in Equatoria and Bahr al-Ghazal (Walraet 2008). Many Bor people sought education outside Sudan (Jonglei politician, interview 19/2012). Migrants restocked by buying cows, and this deepened Bor communities' experience of the market. On return from displacement, people restocked through purchases from other parts of the state, including Pibor (AU-IBAR 2001).

One of the major changes wrought by the Comprehensive Peace Agreement was the establishment of a large salaried class in Juba, and smaller salaried classes in state capitals such as Bor. These salaries have made educated young people even less inclined towards cattle labour – but (with the partial exception of the SPLA payroll) the vast majority of spending on salaries is concentrated in state capitals. Akobo county's allocation from the 2011 Jonglei state budget, for example, was less than 1 per cent (finance ministry official, interview 36/2012; local government officials, interviews 60/2012, 79/201). In Jonglei, the salaried class lives in an area where there are road and river connections to the national capital; where most educational institutes are found; where markets have spread most widely and where there is a large diaspora. All these factors change the cattle ownership and labour systems – people acquire cattle with cash, and then use distant relatives, or even informally contracted workers, to look after them. Educated people do not want to work full time in the cattle economy because it is laborious and dangerous: as one young man said, 'I don't love cattle work, I don't have a gun and I don't know how to shoot' (interview 83/2012). Politicians and entrepreneurs with foreign properties still maintain large herds as absentee owners, for prestige rather than economic reasons, diverting investment away from production. Powerful absentee owners exercise control over marriage decisions of cattle-poor relatives, and engage in bridewealth bidding wars. The bride-wealth system is becoming less of an economic alliance between families, and more about conspicuous displays of wealth (student, interview 90/2012).

Lou Nuer areas and the functions of the raid

In Bor, new markets and new links with the diaspora are changing the social meaning of cattle. In the Lou Nuer hinterland, mass raiding rather than commercialization is driving changes. Communities sometimes lost entire herds in raids in 2012, as one humanitarian worker described.

> I have seventy-five cows, my family herd is 160. All were lost in the March [2012] attack on Lou Nuer. My father looked after the herd in the *toič* [dry-season pastures] with his son and two daughters, nobody else. It was the second time that my father lost an entire herd, the first was in 1993 or 1994 during the conflict between Jikany and Lou. I rebuilt that herd, and bought the cattle from my salary. My father is distraught and not sure what he is living for, I told him not to despair, and to remember I have a salary and he still has an unmarried daughter. My mother told me to look after my father, because she's afraid he will die. (Interview 72/2012)

The speaker was part of Akobo's tiny salariat and his salary allowed him to plan his way out of these losses. At that year's public peace and reconciliation meetings, many appealed for alternative work in agriculture or in the military. But the government was unlikely to respond to such requests, making counter-raiding an economically rational way to recoup losses.

Massive raids, and the massive herd turnover that they imply, affect notions of ownership. Where previously the patriarch had the sole right to alienate an animal from a herd, today younger raiders have more say over cattle transfers, no doubt partly because of the heavy risks that they have assumed. Sometimes this shift away from patriarchal control is emphatically presented as part of a threatening new rural criminality:

> Criminal gangs are not organized around traditional authorities. They are sometimes against traditional leaders. They even steal cattle from their own family ... The system of the male household head disposing of cattle – that's splitting ... the splitting up of family economy – the criminals are part of this. (Humanitarian worker, interview 80/2012)

So some of the factors driving the commercialization of the cattle economy are socially traumatic. Some interviewees presented the shift away from patriarchal rights in cattle more tentatively – one young man in Akobo explains:

> If father is alive, anything that is bought belongs to the father. In some families, that system is still there. Son might call something his own if he lives in a different house and if he has got it by cultivation or looting. This applies to our generation, after 1992. I have heard about this, but never seen it. (Humanitarian worker, interview 56/2012)

Pibor – access to markets

In the far west of Murle-land, a relatively small number of people were able to maintain an economy that was almost entirely dependent on pastoralism, and a diet which included blood but almost no grain. It is apparently the least monetized economy in Jonglei, and the people who practise it have almost no participation in the consumer economy of radios and pots and pans that has reached many small settlements. These groups are not representative of the whole population of Pibor county. Many of them consume grain, but because it is difficult to grow in the relatively arid Lotilla plains, they have got involved in trade and exchange.

Many Murle people speak Dinka, Nuer, Anuak and Toposa, evidence of a history of interaction with their neighbours (local government official, interview 93/2012). A 'footing' or pedestrian trade with Eastern Equatoria in spears and goats was reported up to the 1970s (associate of Murle traditional leader, interview 15/2012). There was a trade with Nuer people in tobacco, cloth and sorghum. According to some government chiefs (or neo-traditional authorities), this trade continued through the civil war. But after the 2005 Comprehensive Peace Agreement between the SPLM and the Khartoum government, violence increased in Jonglei, and the trade stopped (interview 74/2012). 'Before 2005 there was exchange between Murle [and Lou Nuer people]. If there was a clash, they would escort Lou traders who were in cattle camps to their borders, provide security' (Akobo resident, interview 73/2012).

A study of the food economy of the arid areas of south-eastern Jonglei and Eastern Equatoria conducted between 2000 and 2004 found that more than half of household food came from trade or exchange. 'Exchange' in this study included raiding from neighbours. But many groups, including the poorest groups, depended on petty trade and markets for food and non-food staples (SSCCSE 2006: 97–8). It is not very meaningful, then, to speak of a Murle people as if they have a unified livelihood and common economic interests. Far from it – they are one of the most economically diversified small ethno-linguistic groups in

South Sudan. Boma people are agrarian, and plains people are agro-pastoralist or pure pastoralist. The Murle community has a significant diaspora who now practise urban livelihoods. Hassan Ngachingol's daughter became an air hostess, and Ismail Kony's son plays for the national football team.

In Murle society, there are local differences in the labour and ownership systems of the cattle economy, and paths to development are also different. Some interviewees with experience of Murle cattle-keeping stated that it is organized around relatively small units (abductee, interview 136/2012; government official, interview 180/2012; former local government official, interview 185/2012). Smaller cattle camps may have been a consequence of fears of insecurity during the war; but even before the war, one anthropologist described a herding system based around a homestead – a group of brothers descended from the same father (Andretta 1989). There is no evidence that wage labour is emerging in Murle cattle systems (agriculturalist, interview 112/2012). But smaller cattle-keeping units are likely to face starker problems in mobilizing labour – and these small cattle-keeping units' need for labour may contribute to the problem of abduction, which is discussed in greater detail in the next chapter.

Some of Pibor's history of raiding was set out in the previous chapter. Neighbouring groups, particularly the people of Anyidi in Bor county, believed that the Khartoum government triggered Murle raids just as the 1983 war broke out (Guarak 2011: 648). When Pibor was contested between the SPLA and government forces, the SPLA raided cattle there. After the 1991 SPLA split, Pibor remained under control of John Garang's faction for a year or so, and they apparently encouraged Murle raiders to attack Nuer areas around Akobo and Waat as Jonglei shifted into a war of civilian raiding (Johnson 2003: 114). The raiding continued after Ismail Kony's Brigade took over Pibor.

Before 1983, Murle people would sell cattle in Bor, but after the outbreak of war, the security situation and the 1991 destruction of Bor town prevented Murle from trading in cattle in Bor (Jonglei politician, interview 19/2012). But in 1995, a road to Juba opened, and Murle people began trekking cattle there through Eastern Equatoria (local government official, interview 91/2012). Even when Ismail Kony was installed as the governor of Jonglei, Bor market did not appear to draw Murle drovers.

After the 2005 Comprehensive Peace Agreement, access to markets for people from Pibor county deteriorated. In 2006 or 2007, Murle drovers attempting to reach Juba were getting ambushed. Some Murle traders were trying to work their way into their new order, and some felt that new SPLA checkpoints were undermining their attempts to maintain the Juba trade that they had developed during the war. In 2006, some Murle traders were abducted, and according to one UN official involved at the time, many believed that their abduction was a means of pressuring Ismail Kony to reach a deal with the government (interview 176/2012). Raiding continued in the Bor area, and after some particularly lethal attacks on Bor in 2007 which were attributed to Murle raiders, four Murle patients in Bor hospital were murdered by a mob.

Cross-country cattle drovers are often (mis)taken for cattle rustlers (parliamentarian, interview 38/2012), and perhaps the Juba trade that began in the mid-1990s was in fact linked to cattle rustling. Discussing the links between raiding and markets, veterinary officials said that they believed that raiding had fostered commercialization of the livestock sector and long-distance droving. One government official working in the livestock sector said:

> Raiding is a driver of commercialization. I want to get rid
> of stolen cattle when I steal it. Raided cattle can't be sold in
> Bor, they sell it in their ethnic community or in Juba, but in Bor
> they will be caught. But now some people sell cows for school,
> for rent, house purchase or health services. (Interview 88/2012)

One veterinarian believed that the link between raiding and market participation was most evident in Murle areas:

What I would say is the Dinka now are under less pressure to go and raid for cattle for marriage. And I think with the Nuer it is the same. If you look at the level of development, the Human Development Index, the Nuer and Dinka are almost at par. During the war a big number were able to access formal education in Ethiopia and East Africa. A good number of them are exposed. If they want to marry, they will walk into the bank and buy the animals. But the Murle they don't have the money. (Interview 35/2012)

A transformed society

The food economy that emerged from South Sudan's second civil war kept the people of Jonglei state hungry amid its plenty. The war pitted Jonglei's people against each other, and human-itarian attempts to relieve suffering may even have aggravated social divisions. Humanitarian assistance was channelled through the United Nations, which in turn channelled it through relief agencies under the control of parties to the conflict. Commanders sometimes used the grain to build up ethnic constituencies. The Nuer prophet Wutnyang Gaarkek said: 'This relief has destroyed our relationship with the Dinka and other groups' (quoted in Hutchinson 1996: 342). The wartime food system established commanders as intermediaries with an international system that dealt in grain and logistics, rather than in financial subventions or profits and debts. But the system was transformative: at the end of the civil war, Jonglei became dependent on grain imports and grain markets, and the money system. This complicated economic change is very difficult to describe and explain within the limits of conventional economic theories. Hunger amid plenty is one of the characteristics of capitalism, but Jonglei has not moved into a 'capitalist mode of production', whereby productive resources are privately owned and the majority of people sell their labour to owners. The state recognizes communal ownership of Jonglei's productive resources. At the same time, Jonglei's people are being chaotically drawn into markets, or desperately seeking entry into them. Relief food is implicated in this process. Nowadays, there is not much scholarly concern with understanding the way in which an economy like Jonglei's gets drawn into wider economies, and the way in which local structures of inequality are reconfigured. In 1980s Sudan there were a few attempts at understanding how remote economies like Jonglei's connect or 'articulate' with global systems of production (Akuany 1990: 167; Tully 1988: 5). But this 'articulation school' apparently lost its nerve at the end of the Cold War, and its exponents perhaps were cautious about describing remote and chaotic places with undue precision.

The expansion of the grain market took place at a time of increased raiding. The immediate cause of the newly intensified raiding was the breakdown in security in Jonglei as a result of splits in the SPLA. But raiding acquired its own momentum, and did not end when those splits were reconciled or when the civil war ended. Weapons were incorporated into systems of production. Raids may have represented attempts by people of the hinterland to restock when they were not able to find other means to do so. They may have been attempts to participate in the grain market or to engage with the fast-growing markets that emerged to serve the new salariats in Juba and Bor. People from the hinterlands had less access to those markets than people from Bor, and they experienced that lack of access through ethnicity – Murle access to markets was more complicated than that of other groups. Raiding also influenced the generational and gender orders in the hinterlands, and the next chapter looks at these influences in more detail.

10 | NYABURJOK

Nyaburjok

'Nyaburjok,' said the security man, who had come in without introduction to listen silently in the county official's office. 'Nyaburjok. It was the last age set. It was opened in 2001,' said the county official. It was not proving an easy task to find out what was happening to the Lou Nuer age-set system, which appeared to have been reworked into the *bunam* system. People remembered the names of age sets up to the 1980s, when the sets started to have names like Militia or Koryom (the name of an SPLA battalion). But then memories failed, or contradicted each other. The county official said: 'Before [Nyaburjok] there was militia. There was no age set. They would scarify [young men] and take them to the militia and name the militia after contemporary events' (interview 60/2012).

'It's Nya Bur Jok – nya = daughter, bor = white, jok = white and black. They are ox colours. No, it is not considered age set,' said a group of Presbyterian pastors the next day. They brought the name up in a discussion of Nuer prophets. Like many Jonglei pastors, they distinguished between the nineteenth-century prophet Ngundeng Bong, and prophets arising from twentieth-century war, such as Wutnyang and Dak Kueth, whom they said were deceivers. Nyaburjok, they said, was a group set up by a prophet named Gai Manyong, who preached in Akobo in 2000. Gai was from Ayod, or Fanjak, from one of the Nuer sections on the east bank of the Bahr al-Zeraf, said some other pastors. He said he was a messenger of Ngundeng and that Lou Nuer should migrate east, to the farthest point reached in the great

Nuer migrations that ended in the early twentieth century. He let women go naked and gave people tobacco, and he ended up getting into problems with local people in Akobo and with the government (Akobo was controlled by a pro-Khartoum Southern faction at the time). They killed him, and some of his followers ran away to Pibor (interviews 76/2012, 168/2012).

'Nyaburjok. Those of Gai came in 2001. They attacked people but they didn't kill women. They only stayed for a few days,' said the Murle chief. He was a former SPLA soldier recently appointed by the government as a chief or neo-traditional leader, to the hot seat in Pibor county. It was 2012, just a few months after the devastating December 2011 attacks by people calling themselves the White Army. 'In the recent attacks there were thirty thousand came first time, and ten thousand the second time. Those who came recently called themselves Nyaburjok' (interview 104/2012).

'I think you asked the wrong question about age sets. Our people still have them. Cherekuoth is the name of the current one,' said a friend in Juba from the Eastern Jikainy (interview 187/2012). The conclusions in this chapter are hesitant, and some of them are no doubt based on the wrong questions.

Unruly and mysterious

Nyaburjok is one unruly outcome of the long, harsh processes of peripheralization that have given South Sudan the kind of poverty that cannot quickly be addressed, not even by money. Its name, a compound of daughters and the colour names of cattle, is an expressive one for a raiding group in a society still shaped by bridewealth in cattle. It might hark back to older, euphoric raiding styles, when cattle or girls were the main consideration. But it was a mysterious name too: an age-set name, or a Nuer cult name, that could be taken up a decade later by a huge young raiding party on a killing spree in Pibor county. Lots of people had heard of it and they all had different ideas about what it meant. Perhaps the young raiders of 2011 were exploring its meaning ironically and cruelly – during their attack many women were raped, killed and mutilated and many were abducted too (UNMISS 2012: 15).

Many people in South Sudan report the demise of purification rituals for homicides and the breakdown of customary protections for women and children that appear to have taken place in Nuer and Dinka societies in the twentieth century (Jok and Hutchinson 1999; Hutchinson 2000; UNMISS 2012: 7). At the start of the December 2011 attack on Murle-land then-vice-president Riek Machar flew to meet raiders on their way to Pibor. He reminded them that in Lou Nuer culture, women and children should not be killed (UNMISS 2012: 17). His advice was not heeded. Raiders in Jonglei today may be using the targeting of women and the abduction of children as a means of sending messages to each other. In March 2012, Murle raiders attacked Lou Nuer cattle camps in an area called Wanydeng, in Ulang, part of Upper Nile state. Both Murle and Nuer people interviewed a few months later stated that they believed that the raiders abducted children but did not deliberately kill their mothers or other women (humanitarian worker, interview 63/2012; local government official, interview 93/2012). The Wanydeng incident came at the end of a long sequence of attacks in Pibor, Wuror and Akobo between 2009 and 2011 in which women had been deliberately targeted for killing. Some believed that the shadowy communication between gangs of armed youth through calibrated targeting of women or other groups deemed entitled to special protection was an important development, which might once have been the basis for an eventual dialogue between armed youth (some vigorously rejected this suggestion).

Another form of shadowy communication is that between raiders and victims. Murle raiding groups are often smaller than Lou Nuer columns of attackers, and they may use extreme violence tactically to convince their enemies of the certainty of defeat. Men are often more able to escape this intense violence than women are, and this may increase female casualty rates. It also means that women sometimes have to plead for their lives, with people speaking another language. One interviewee in Pibor county stated that when Murle raiders attacked Nuer women, those women invoked Murle age-set names to plead for their lives:

> When Murle went [to Nuer areas] the women of Nuer would say, *I am a woman of Butot.* They went to kill Nuer, to kill children, Nuer had killed their women and children. Murle arrived and the Nuer youth ran. Women could not run as fast. Nuer women would say – *my man is Butot* or *my man is Titi*, so they would not be killed. (Interview 104/2012)

Jonglei's historical processes may be difficult to interpret, but they are marking gender relations very deeply. Women bargain with ethnic identities as a means of surviving violence. Men send calibrated messages to each other across language divides, by taking or sparing women's lives. Women help to define ethnic and ethical boundaries for communities, in a place where ethnic boundaries are obscurely and deeply connected to the processes of state formation and market development.

Abduction as a gender story

In 2012, many explanations about violence in Jonglei began with allegations about the abduction of women and children, and abduction was a story related to women's fertility. The infertile women of Jonglei's ethnic outsiders appeared to offer a ready explanation for Jonglei's lengthy crisis. This explanation has powerful supporters. In his 2008 interview quoted in the Introduction, President Salva Kiir claimed that Murle people have high rates of infertility linked to sexually transmitted disease, and that this infertility motivates some Murle people to abduct or forcibly adopt children from neighbouring groups. The claims of Murle vulnerability to infertility date back to the colonial era. Systems of abduction/adoption date back even farther. They appear to have been conflated in the latter half of the twentieth century – there is no mention of an abduction–infertility link in colonial literature. That conflation has helped to define Murle people as an ethnic community. The new republic claims to represent its people, but very often it represents them as part of an ethnic community, as minorities. Murle women's alleged frailties have been pitched into that process of representation.

The infertility story, and the Nyaburjok raiders, both seem to point to the way that Jonglei's chaotic processes of incorporation into and marginalization from the state and market systems are played out in daily life, in the relationships between women and men. This chapter looks at the (inconclusive) historical evidence that infertility is an ethnic problem. It then goes on to argue that fertility rates cannot account for the problem of abduction, and that explanations need to be sought elsewhere, in the roles of men and women in a society that is being reshaped by devastating violence – that is, in gender relations.

Evidence of Murle women's predisposition to infertility: the colonial period

With the help of Hassan Ngachingol, the colonial officer B. A. Lewis conducted research in Murle-land in the late 1940s. At the time, Murle leaders argued that the Murle population was in decline, partly because of the spread of sexually transmitted diseases. Murle leaders told Lewis that colonial-era changes to customary-law sanctions against adultery had accelerated their spread (Lewis 1972: 154). Lewis's views were perhaps shaped by a paper on Murle reproduction rates written by Dean A. Smith, a medical professor at the University College of Khartoum (Smith 1955). Smith's paper was a clear and straightforward presentation of inconclusive evidence suggesting that gross reproduction rates in Murle-land were lower than in other parts of the greater Upper

Nile. His questions were thorough and he was reluctant to reach premature conclusions.[1]

Low reproduction rates may be due to low conception rates (infertility or sub-fertility), high rates of abortion or stillbirth, or high infant mortality rates. Infertility, in turn, may be due to one or more of many factors: medical, nutritional, social, genetic and psychological. One medical factor was gonorrhoea. Gonorrhoea and chlamydia are two medical conditions that affect the ability to conceive (syphilis does not affect fertility, but it is linked to stillbirth: Rashida Ferrand, London School of Hygiene and Tropical Medicine, interview 188/2012). Smith's Murle informants described a disease called *karongmal* which Smith confidently translated as gonorrhoea. Gonorrhoea had been brought by soldiers from the north (probably a reference to the Anglo-Egyptian army's pacification of Murle-land between 1908 and 1912) and other diseases had come from Italian soldiers in Ethiopia, they said. Some men he spoke to believed that colonialism had overturned customary rules on adultery that punished women severely, part of a wider set of concerns that Smith reported about the impact of colonialism on the sexual discipline of youth. Other informants discussed a Murle traditional practice allowing married women to seek male lovers if they could not conceive with their husbands, and complicated and intimate courting rules that give some outsiders the impression of a radically liberated sexual order.

Smith's informants were very conscious of the history of infertility, and Smith had a historical turn of mind too. He speculated that infertility may have been caused by the shock of pacification: '... what might roughly be described as "failure of the tribal will

---

1 The gross reproduction rate is the average number of *daughters* born to a group of women if they survive until the end of childbearing years. The gross fertility rate is the average number of *both sons and daughters* born to the same group in the same period. Sons and daughters are a measure of a population's growth; daughters are a measure of population's capacity to reproduce itself.

to live." This might arise, for instance, from general demoraliza-
tion following a crushing defeat, from disintegration of tribal
institutions and customs, from a failure to adapt to changing
conditions, increased sophistication and new values' (1955: 5).

Perceptions of infertility affected policy. In 1958, Pibor district's first Sudanese commissioner carried out a campaign against
venereal disease (Lewis 1972: 15). Contemporaneous literature
from other areas of Sudan shows that these concerns were not
unusual – people worried about population decline in Western
Bahr al-Ghazal (Santandrea 1964: 319ff.), and about colonially
sponsored changes to gender orders and sexual relations in Western Equatoria (Reining 1966: 64).

Smith's report was based on sketchy research, and he called for
a more careful survey. The 1955/56 census brought new evidence
that shed light on Murle fears of infertility. The census surveyed
samples of the population: sampling methods were believed to be
more accurate than enumeration. It classified people by membership of 'tribal group or nationality group', and by main language
spoken at home; and it provided several fertility indicators. Census
officials acknowledged that for cultural reasons their account of
fertility may have been inaccurate: 'There was one problem that
[the sampling method] could not solve – the tendency of the
head of the household, because of a prevalent superstition, to
underestimate the number of his children' (PCO 1956: vol. 1, 7).
However, the census results allow for rough comparative analysis
of fertility rates among different ethnic groups.

There were twenty-five census areas in South Sudan. Pibor
census area corresponds approximately to the present-day counties of Pibor and Pochalla. Census officials classed the main
tribal group of Pibor census area as 'Didinga-speaking Eastern
Southerners (Nilo-Hamitic)' – that is, Murle. This group made up
78.7 per cent of the population of the census area. Seventeen per
cent of Pibor census area were classed as 'Other Nilotic' – that is,
the Anuak population of Pochalla. 'Tribal' classification did not

correspond always and exactly to language use. In Pibor census area, 82.5 per cent of the population spoke Teso at home (at the time, Murle and Didinga were not classed as Surmic, but as a variant of the Teso language of Uganda and Eastern Equatoria). In Bor census area, 99.7 per cent of the population were classed tribally as Bor Dinka and exactly the same percentage spoke Dinka at home. Pibor census area was represented in the census as ethnically heterogeneous, predominantly a Murle–Anuak mix, and this complicates ethnic comparisons.

There were several fertility measures in the 1955/56 census. Four are reviewed here:

- gross reproduction rates
- average sizes of completed families – the families of women who had passed childbearing age
- the number of children had by women who had passed child-bearing age
- the number of children under five per 1,000 women of child-bearing age.

Upper Nile province shared with Bahr al-Ghazal province the highest gross reproduction rate in Sudan. Present-day Jonglei state (which corresponds closely to the census areas of Pibor, Zeraf Valley, Lau Nuer and Bor) had very high gross reproduction rates, and Bor was the highest of the twenty-five census areas in South Sudan. Pibor was the exception: its gross reproduction rate was below the Sudanese average. Only four census areas in South Sudan had lower gross reproduction rates than Pibor: Malakal town (the capital of Upper Nile province) and three census areas in Western Equatoria. The lowest rates in all Sudan were in Zande East, and they are given in the table below, as a comparison.

At the end of their childbearing years, most mothers in Pibor census area – 58.1 per cent – had three children or fewer. Almost a quarter – 22.9 per cent – had three children. This contrasted with other Upper Nile census areas. Eighty per cent of mothers

TABLE 10.1 Ethnicity and fertility in the 1955/56 census

Census area, 1955/56	Gross reproduction rate	Average size of completed families	Percentage of women past childbearing age who have no children	Number of children under 5 per 1,000 women of childbearing age
Sudan	2.4	4.7	9.6	902.3
Upper Nile	2.7	5.5	2.3	1,001.2
Pibor	1.7	3.4	3.4	763.8
Zeraf Valley	2.9	5.8	2.0	928
Lau Nuer	3.2	6.5	1.2	1,045.9
Bor	2.8	5.5	2.4	1,198.7
Zande East	1.2	2.4	42.5	415.2

Sources: PCO (1958: vol. 9, 58–60; 1957: vol 8, 58–60; 1957, vol. 6, 58–60; 1957, vol. 4: 58–60; n.d.: vol. 2, 52–4)

in Upper Nile province as a whole had four or more children at the end of their childbearing years. But it also contrasted with Zande areas, where the census found that as many as 42.5 per cent of women had no children at the end of their childbearing years. The reasons for the results in Pibor or Zande East census areas may have been pathological – but the pathologies may not have been the same. In Pibor, many women had fewer children, and in Zande East many women had none.

The census supports some of the concerns about fertility that had been raised by Smith, but it does not allow for emphatic conclusions about links between ethnicity and fertility. And it is difficult to argue that the concerns about fertility have affected population growth. In 1955/56, the total population of Pibor, Zeraf Valley, Lau Nuer and Bor was 395,650, and the population of Pibor census area was 53,061. The 2008 census enumerated 1,358,602 people in Jonglei state, and 214,676 people in Pibor and Pochalla counties. These figures can be used as the basis for a very rough estimate of population growth rates. The 2008 population of Pibor/Pochalla was 4.04 times greater than that of the 1956 Pibor census area. The 2008 population of Jonglei state was 3.43 times greater than that of the 1955/56 Pibor, Zeraf Valley, Lau Nuer and Bor census areas together. The problems in making such comparisons are self-evident, but nonetheless, the gross reproduction rates recorded in 1955/56 seem to have played out unpredictably.

The question of infertility in Zande-land received some scholarly attention during the colonial period. Anne Retel-Laurentin conducted studies of fertility in the Zande areas of present-day Central African Republic, then under French rule. Her work linked infertility to social and cultural factors, such as premarital sexual liberty and instability of marital unions, which are themselves linked to the fear of infertility and may contribute to the spread of sexually transmitted diseases that affect fertility. She also linked infertility to sexually transmitted diseases: gonorrhoea and syphilis affected most men in French-administered Zande-land. Sleeping sickness – prevalent in Zande-land and also in the Boma plateau of Murle-land – is also linked to infertility. But she argued that medical factors were secondary, and that the least fertile African societies were the ones that had been most exposed to the social dislocations brought about by colonialism and its wars (Retel-Laurentin 1974). The problem of infertility in Zande areas persisted after the end of colonialism. A 1995 Central African demographic study found that 26.2 per cent of women from the Nzakara-Zande ethnic group in the 40–49 age group had never given birth to a living child: 'women from ethnic Nzakara-Zande are most affected by infertility. [This] confirms the situation that was observed in colonial times by Anne Retel-Laurentin, in the 1959–1960 Demographic Study, and in the censuses of 1975 and 1988' (DSDS 1995: 55).

Evidence from the 1970s

South Sudan's population was uncounted or undercounted in the 1973, 1983 and 1993 censuses, and it is not possible to use these as a basis for local comparisons of ethnicity and fertility. The 1979 *Sudan Fertility Survey* did not cover South Sudan (Department of Statistics 1979: vol 1, 11). But discussion of Pibor fertility rates reappeared in the South Sudan literature that began to appear after the 1973 peace deal and the establishment of the Southern Regional Government. Arensen's study of Murle language and society was based on fieldwork begun in the 1970s. Arensen (1992: 40) argues that venereal diseases spread by the sexual practices of young people had led to female infertility (in an unpublished 2012 article, Arensen argued that venereal diseases were spread in the 1960s from a garrison of 'Arab soldiers'). An unpublished study in Pibor in the late 1970s based on 500 interviews in four locations found high rates of infertility, and high rates of secondary infertility, which means that a woman has not been able to complete a pregnancy after having had one or more children – post-partum infection may have been a cause (CPI 2008).

Recent evidence

The Swiss humanitarian organization Medair conducted studies on the prevalence of sexually transmitted diseases in Likongwele *payam*, an administrative subdivision of Pibor county, in 2003 and 2004. A 2004 survey of 401 females and 116 males in 2,099 households found an overall syphilis infection rate of 11.4 per cent; and a female gonorrhoea infection rate of 7.0 per cent (it was not possible to survey chlamydia infection rates). Compared with rates in selected African countries, these rates were slightly above average. Study authors estimated Likongwele's population at 20,000, of which 600 were people of Nuer origin. Nuer participants had slightly higher rates of syphilis infection – 16.0 per cent. This may have been due to sample design.

A separate 2003 Medair study of knowledge, attitudes and practices regarding sexual health, conducted in 500 households, found that 10 per cent had no children (Dyment 2004). More recent and more informal studies have found higher syphilis infection rates (anonymous, interview 123/2012). Syphilis testing for pregnant women is common because it is medically useful: syphilis increases the risk of stillbirths, and specialists often check for it. So medical staff may have a picture of syphilis rates among pregnant women but not of other diseases – doctors cannot ethically administer medical tests that might help correlate fertility and ethnicity just because that happens to be a hot political topic.

All these studies linking infertility to ethnicity are suggestive but inconclusive. Possible causes for low reproduction rates – such as stillbirths, abortions and infant mortality; or poor obstetric health services; or limited access to health services in a barely monetized and widely scattered population; or misunderstandings about the process of conception; or the frequent casual sexual partnerships arising from the sexual or generational segregation periodically imposed by the pastoralist lifestyle – have been identified but not examined in depth (Smith 1955; Akuei and Jok 2011: 35ff.; Juba politician, interview 12/2012). Sexually transmitted diseases, infertility and/or low reproduction rates are interlinked problems faced by the people of Pibor county, but to attribute the problem of abduction to disease or infertility is an unduly mechanistic explanation of a complex social phenomenon, and to attribute it to infertility is careless. The reasons for abduction should be sought elsewhere.

Reasons for abduction

Abduction denotes an unexpectedly wide range of behaviours, including trafficking, taking war captives, extralegal adoption, or stealing children for their labour or affection. Nuer, Dinka, Anuak and Murle communities in Jonglei have practised these behaviours at different historical periods. The tables in Chapter 8 suggest that Murle children were more likely than any other children to be taken captive in the conflicts of 2009 to 2011, although abductions of Murle children are invariably represented as revenge for prior abductions by Murle raiders. Murle raiders, in turn, appear to be responding to a demand for children in Murle society. There are several possible explanations for that demand. Chapter 9 discussed briefly the evidence that Murle herders work in smaller groups, which are drawn from specific age sets in relatively small groups of homesteads, rather than from a wider lineage. A shortage of sons may present an individual homestead with a critical problem.

The most cattle-dependent Murle groups, who live in the far west of Murle-land, may be more predisposed to abduct. Chapter 8 argued that there may be different front lines and different modes of attack in Jonglei – a war of massive attack between Murle and Nuer raiders, and a war of pinprick attacks between Murle raiders and Dinka populations of Bor, Twic and Duk. The neighbours of the most cattle-dependent Murle groups suffered small, opportunistic attacks from raiders seeking cows and children. The persistence of raiding in these Dinka areas is sometimes attributed to a stereotype of Dinka passivity. Perhaps it is also linked to the situation of women in those areas.

Abduction and the changing status of childless women

An old barren Murle woman who had adopted a child who was sold to her for 100 cows (for which her husband had toiled) by abductors just before her husband's death said, 'this is my beloved adopted son; I will not leave him; I will stay with him until I die with him and his home will be my home. What he has cost me, he should also cost [his parents] to redeem their son.' The child told her to claim her cows from the people whom she paid and to forget about him, but she insisted that she would remain with him. The old woman stayed with the boy until she died of old age in 2002 while staying with his family. (Harrigan 2011: 22)

Abduction/forced adoption may be driven by the burdens or stigmas of widowhood or lack of sons which are borne by women; or by other features of the understudied South Sudanese gender order. Medair's respondents in their studies of Likongwele found that women not bearing children bore a social stigma and were at risk of abandonment (Dyment 2004: 5).

One interviewee argued that the burdens of childless Murle women are getting heavier. Women marry into Murle sections and their daughters marry out of them: they want a son in order to have a permanent ally in the section. Having children is an important part of women's contribution to society, and childless women are seen as having failed in that contribution: an unpopular childless woman might even face divorce. In addition to these established features of Murle society, one interviewee observed significant changes in gender orders. Murle society, like other societies in Jonglei, allowed for the lawful marriage of two women for the purpose of procreation. A childless woman could pay the bridewealth for another woman, who would conceive with a man – but the children would be the legal heirs of the childless woman, and the mother would be her legal wife. The Murle version of this system is called *allawan-ci-ngaawo*, and it has disappeared, partly because of pressure from children of these unions. The system is also on the decline because some fathers do not want to give up their children, and chiefs support their claims:

> Maybe because now, the man might claim the children and the chiefs may support this right. So the whole lady is losing. Because she's getting old, no sons. Woman can then divorce the woman and marry the father.
>
> *Why do the chiefs support male claims?* Because they are borrowing another culture from other people. In the old culture of Murle, if you divorce your wife with children, she goes with children. But there is something new, borrowed from Bor, whereby the man when you divorce your wife the children remains with the man ... Now the chiefs why [do they] support [the father]? They don't want to leave the sons in a divorce, they are very careful for themselves in case one of the wives get divorce. (Former local government official, interview 192/2012)

This change to the gender order puts more pressure on women to have children, and when they communicate their anxieties to young men in their circle, the young men may read that as a demand for abductees. Are women more anxious now than they were, say, before the 1983–2005 civil war, when, according to the limited available evidence, abduction was less widespread? The local government official's remarks quoted above raise many questions for future research. If women face new risks of sonlessness from divorce, might that push them towards more reckless means of acquiring sons? Are changes to women's rights regarding their children linked to the changing role of men in the increasingly important cattle-raiding economy?

Fertility and men

There probably was a drop in reproduction rates in 1980 but it was nothing to do with fertility or women. A rinderpest outbreak that year killed so many cows in Pibor county that many men were unable to find bridewealth to marry (Andretta 1985: 54 describes it as a drought). There are still bachelors from the Moden age set, which came of age at that time.

> In 1980 many animals died in a rinderpest outbreak in Pibor. This disease wiped out a lot of animals of the Moden age group – it created a lot of bachelors. Now they started others, they came to town and became military, police, because all the animals they died. These young men, they all joined Ismail Kony's Brigade. They got food and money. They married from other tribes, Shilluk ladies and Equatorian ladies, for fewer cows. (Veterinarian, interview 119/2012)

In 1980, some Murle men were unable to reproduce because they did not have cattle and could not marry. That crisis was resolved by urbanization, made possible by war – war created work in towns, and opened new marriage possibilities, and war also offered new means of acquiring cattle. Ismail Kony's Brigade was armed by the government and could mobilize that firepower for raids. Raids led to cattle accumulation which in turn led to an increase in polygyny among commanders: 'Ismail Kony did no development ... But Ismail Kony's people were taking more and more wives. They took some people's wives to be their wives ... But they never took wives from other age sets' (researcher, interview 124/2012).

Polygyny tends to be practised by older and more powerful males (Ismail Kony married over forty wives) and it can help to deepen their authority over younger males, who may have to postpone marriage because of the reduction in the numbers of available women; and also because more powerful males are able to control access to cattle for bridewealth. Murle society is fairly polygynous – the 1956 census found that 27 per cent of adult males were polygynous and a later study found that 33 per cent had married more than one wife. Murle traditions manage the intergenerational tensions of polygyny through the institution of the age set, which displaces competition over women to the two youngest age groups; also through levirate marriage – marriage of a widow to her dead husband's brother. The brothers-in-law of widows with children have an interest in remarriage because this simplifies inheritance rights. Polygyny creates many young widows, and the younger sons of widows had responsibility for them (PCO 1957: vol. 8, 46; Andretta 1983: 99–103).

But childless widows have much weaker bargaining power. 'Childlessness for Murle women is a pitiful state,' wrote Andretta in 1983. The childless widows she came across ended up being looked after by co-wives of their former husbands, or becoming concubines (wives without bridewealth) or diviners. Perhaps the raiding economy has changed things for widows and patriarchs, allowing Murle men the possibility of acquiring cattle or women without going through a patriarch or taking a concubine.

Dependence and resistance

Abduction is obscurely linked to fertility and to Murle culture, but directly linked to conflict and to conflict-driven shifts in social and economic life in Jonglei. These shifts are not easy for outsiders, or indeed for local people, to read. A cattle economy has been reshaped by new systems of food that have drawn people into dependence on relief, markets and raiding. This dependence may vary between richer and poorer groups, but also between groups that are remoter from or nearer to new centres of wealth. The differences are not 'ethnic' in substance, but they are experienced ethnically, because raiders come from hinterland areas associated with particular ethnic groups. The changes come in unruly and mysterious garb, and that makes it difficult for people to organize responses to them, and difficult for outsiders to read those responses. On the face of it, the changes have made young men desperate and violent, weakening them in the face of the external forces surrounding them, but perhaps empowering them vis-à-vis members of their own societies. Perhaps the childless widows are feeling more beleaguered than they did before.

CONCLUSION: SLOW LIBERATION

The Jonglei vantage point

Khartoum slave traders and Ethiopian gunrunners began to make inroads into Jonglei in the late nineteenth century. Ever since, it has been a place of resistance. Its young men have been routinely presented as troublemakers, and some of them have got into a lot of trouble. This book has tried to explain its dramatic story, using some of Jonglei's many thoughtful bright voices.

Multilingual; muddy and remote; mutinous and divided against itself: Jonglei exemplifies South Sudan. One of the main arguments of this book is that South Sudan is also an exemplary place – a place to learn lessons about the way that post-colonial states and societies work. It was incorporated harshly, and early, into the international system, and that system's stark spatial and social inequalities. That incorporation shaped the history of the state in South Sudan – and that state is not an exceptional one. It represents an extreme example of the weaknesses of the post-colonial state. External forces imposed the state on South Sudanese society, and the state has long been economically dependent on those forces. It has also long been economically autonomous from the productive forces of South Sudanese society. Its cities and its barracks have changed everything for everyone, but the state has never organized its relationship with South Sudanese people around their economic interests. Instead, it has resorted to a mix of ethnically structured systems of coercion and of patronage to manage its relationships with society.

The nature of oppression often shapes the nature of resistance. This book has argued that South Sudan's would-be liberators were not able, in the course of their long struggle, to rethink the relationship between state and society. The SPLM/A structured their relations with society around ethnicity. They sometimes separated themselves from ordinary people through predation and manoeuvres to control relief food. They constantly postponed liberation until after victory, or until after the creation of a New Sudan, or until after independence. South Sudanese society was not liberated, but transformed by local, national and international wars, local and global economic crises and a new, local and malnourished food economy. The liberation movement took power only after it reoriented itself towards diplomacy and won powerful allies; and only after South Sudan's enormous natural resources had found their way to international markets for the first time. The SPLM government has been built on rents from those natural resources. Like its poorer predecessors, the new government in Juba is economically autonomous from society, and dependent on external forces. And when the SPLM took power, Jonglei's liberation was once again postponed.

Crises in 2012 and 2013

The research for this book was mostly completed in 2012, and it was mostly written in 2013. At the end of 2013, a political crisis in Juba spread to Jonglei and turned into a political wildfire which has at the time of writing reached across the whole of greater Upper Nile. It was not the first time that a crisis has mutated into something much worse in Jonglei, but this crisis mutated faster than any previous one.

How did it happen? South Sudan and Sudan share an oil infrastructure, but after South Sudan's secession failed to reach an agreement on sharing oil revenues, and in late 2011 the SPLM decided to shut down oil production. Ninety-eight per cent of the Juba government's revenue came from oil exports. The Khartoum government was less dependent on oil revenues than its southern neighbour, but Sudan's more complex economy was more exposed to the enormous shock that the shutdown would bring. President Salva Kiir was inclined to compromise, but he was outmanoeuvred by SPLM leaders hostile to Khartoum, who saw the shutdown as an opportunity to bring down the government there through economic pressure, and replace it with a government more open to the SPLM's vision of the future. These anti-Khartoum politicians were associated with John Garang and his vision of a transformed New Sudan. Some may have thought that this self-inflicted crisis was a step forward for national sovereignty, replacing South Sudan's dependence on Khartoum with direct dependence on international markets. The crisis might even be a means for the state to deepen its penetration of everyday life by extracting taxes from society, rather than living off its oil rents. South Sudanese politicians had long mythologized the resilience of the general population, and many thought that ordinary people could survive a period of total austerity. And proponents of the shutdown calculated that South Sudan had enough reserves to finance Juba's expensive military patronage network, which could survive longer than Khartoum's more precarious but better-managed patronage system – Khartoum would fall before Juba. Reserves lasted longer than many expected, and when they ran out, the government borrowed against future oil earnings. At the end of 2013, the finance minister reportedly said that the country had borrowed over US$4 billion, mostly from oil companies (*Gurtong*, 21 November 2013). The army still got paid.

TABLE C1 South Sudan's military budget, 2011–13

	2011	2012	2013
GDP, South Sudanese pounds (billion)	52.5	36.0	48.2
GDP, US dollars (billion)	17.5	12.2	13.5
GDP growth (per cent)	1.4	−52.9	32.1
Defence budget, South Sudanese pounds (billion)	1.6	2.4	2.5
Defence budget, US dollars (million)	533	819	714

Source: IISS (2014: 460), which gives a low-end estimate of military spending

The crisis in Jonglei

Tension with Khartoum may even have helped unify the SPLA and give it a military purpose: the two parties stumbled into a brief shooting war in April 2012, from which both quickly withdrew. At the same time, the massive attacks in Jonglei died down. A capable and astute SPLA general named Peter Gatdet was appointed to lead a disarmament campaign that was aimed at all communities involved in the fighting of the previous few years. His forces were not much bigger than the Lou Nuer armies of massive attack, but the general was clever about co-opting Lou Nuer youth leaders, and as the 2012 wet season got under way, raiding subsided.

The disarmament campaign faltered in August 2012, when the Murle rebel leader David Yauyau launched a new mutiny. He had first mutinied in May 2010, after failing in an electoral bid for a state parliamentary seat (see Chapter 8). In response to his second rebellion, the SPLA began a counter-insurgency campaign in Pibor county. According to human rights observers, the SPLA killed villagers, looted villages and sent thousands of people into displacement. About 100,000 Murle civilians were displaced, some moving to Kenya or Ethiopia (HRW 2013). Raiding returned. Between 30 September 2012 and 8 February 2013, the UN mission in South Sudan documented thirty-six deaths from forty-six cattle raids in the predominantly Dinka counties of Bor, Duk and Twic East. More deaths occurred in Murle and Lou Nuer hinterlands. In February 2013, at the height of the dry season, several thousand Lou Nuer pastoralists were moving their cattle to Sobat river grazing areas. At least eighty-five of them were killed in a raid near Wangar, in the far north of Akobo county (UNMISS 2013). Over three hundred died in a raid on Pibor in July the same year (Reuters 2013a). Several thousand cattle were reportedly lost. The economic basis of raiding had not been addressed by disarmament or counter-insurgency.

December 2013: the army splits

The Juba government resumed oil production in April 2013. But it was not holding its nerve. Salva Kiir faced two main challenges: one came from his deputy, Riek Machar, who publicly announced his intention to stand against him in presidential elections. The other came from the group of John Garang loyalists who had pushed Salva Kiir towards confrontation with Khartoum. There was little political common ground between the two groups, but Salva Kiir ineptly brought them together. He could have sent his enemies off, one by one, to glamorous diplomatic postings; he could have given them, one by one, other unrefusable offers. Instead, in July 2013, he dismissed en masse Riek Machar and the Garang loyalists. The sackings did not lead to an immediate crisis. Instead, the sacked politicians and party officials prepared a challenge against the president through SPLM structures. In December 2013, the political crisis came to a head. Led by Riek Machar, the sacked officials challenged Salva Kiir in the SPLM politburo and then staged a walkout. That evening, fighting broke out in the barracks of the presidential guard in Juba. The president said that there had been an attempted coup. The president's opponents said that he had ordered the disarmament of Nuer members of the presidential guard. The next day, elements from the army rounded up and killed Nuer soldiers and Nuer community members. Overnight, Salva Kiir had dismantled his biggest political achievement, the Juba Declaration of 2006, which at vast cost brought former adversaries (many of them from Nuer communities of greater Upper Nile) on to the army payroll, and backed Juba's political and diplomatic campaign for independence with credible force. A report from the (official) South Sudan Human Rights Commission set out the events soberly:

> South Sudan is a multi-ethnic society comprised of more than 60 different ethnic communities. Such reality should have been reflected at least in the establishment of key national institutions

including the army. The Sudan People's Liberation Army (SPLA), the national army, absorbed former ethnic militias in 2005 following the Comprehensive Peace Agreement and subsequently continued to absorb more tribally based armed groups. The process of absorbing the large number of ethnic armed groups basically resulted in Nuer-led armed groups constituting a tribal majority in the SPLA. Some of these troops continued to maintain loyalty to their ethnic Nuer Commanders including Riek Machar. On the other hand, the SPLA also consists of professional soldiers mainly from Dinka tribe and other tribes including also Nuer who are loyal to Salva Kiir as the legitimate Head of State and Commander-in-Chief of the SPLA. Therefore, when the political dispute within the SPLM translated into fighting, consciously or unconsciously, the two groups found themselves in opposite sides fighting each other and trading accusations and counter-accusations, mainly that the Dinka massacred Nuer in Juba … and that the Dinka were massacred in Bor, Akobo, Bentiu, and Malakal. Initial reports of ethnic massacres seem to have been the reason why at the early stage the conflict quickly assumed an ethnic dimension although the two fighting forces deny this. (SSHRC 2014: 4)

Jonglei's new mutiny

The 1955 Torit mutiny led to an insurgency which took eight years to reach Jonglei. The 1983 mutinies that marked the start of the second civil war took place in Jonglei – but it took the mutineers several months before they began capturing territory. In 2013, the speed of events was shocking. The massacres in Juba were revenged in brutal attacks on Dinka civilians in Akobo three days later. Sacked Garang loyalists were arrested in Juba as Riek Machar fled to Jonglei. Defecting rank and file joined a mutiny that started in Jonglei three days after the massacres in Juba. Peter Gatdet, the commander of Jonglei's disarmament campaign and the Pibor counter-insurgency, led the mutinies. A former Sudanese army officer, he had fought on the Iraqi side during the Iran–Iraq war and then joined the SPLA. After the 1991 split in the SPLA, he joined Riek Machar's faction and fought on different sides of the war of militias that ensued. He was more than a warlord – his defections were often astutely timed and prefigured the strategic shifts of more senior figures. Within days, he captured Bor, using forces reportedly made up of defecting soldiers and some or other incarnation of the 'White Army' – the young men of the ethnically structured raiding economy of the hinterland. His forces wreaked destruction on Bor's government buildings and the big market of shops that had flourished in the preceding years, when the hinterland had been engulfed in violence. No journalists dared go there, but satellite pictures showed that most of the market's corrugated iron shops had been razed (*Think Progress*, 15 January 2014). Local authorities estimated that 300 people drowned trying to swim across the Bahr al-Jebel, and over two thousand died in the fighting (UNMISS 2014: 28). The civil war's rapid onset and cruelty, and the power of supposedly defunct politicos to summon up an apocalypse from Jonglei's contradictions, astonished even the most pessimistic analysts of South Sudan.

National unity and national memory

'Long live the unity of South Sudan,' said the president to a press conference the day after the crisis began. He was wearing his general's uniform and he spoke in code:

> Let me reiterate my statement during the opening of the NLC [National Liberation Council of the SPLM] meeting few days ago in which I said that my government is not and will not allow *the incidents of 1991* to repeat themselves again. This *prophet of doom* continues to persistently pursue *his actions of the past* and I have to tell you that I will not allow or tolerate such incidents once again in our new Nation. (*Gurtong*, 16 December 2013, emphasis added)

Salva Kiir was referring to the 1991 Bor massacre, when forces under the ultimate command of Riek Machar killed or displaced almost the entire Dinka population of the east bank of the Nile in Jonglei. The 1991 attack was widely seen as an attack against a Dinka population by Nuer raiders ('prophet of doom' is a reference to Nuer traditions of prophecy). In a national crisis, he chose to remind his audience of national divisions. So did Peter Gatdet: two days after the speech, he and his forces re-enacted the 1991 attack on Bor. The outrages of the periphery turned out to be lodged in the memories of politicians and generals at the centre of the state. The ferocious attack and the deep reconsideration of their pastoralist system which it brought about was also lodged deep in Dinka cultural memories:

> Wutnyang [White Army prophet Wutnyang Gaarkek] took my
>   cows from me, oh!
> Our cattle have gone
> A gourd of cow's milk was left on the ground
> A gourd from my bright cow
> A gourd of cow's milk was left on the ground
> The Nuers played like hyenas
> Famine came to the village where a gourd of the cow's milk
>   had been left on the ground
> A gourd from my bright cow
> A gourd of cow's milk was left on the ground.
> (Akoy Tiemraan Mayom Deng Chol, quoted in Impey 2013)

This song was composed in the immediate aftermath of the attack. It was still being sung two decades later, long after Wutnyang's prophetic powers had left him, after he had died as an SPLA officer fighting in the violent disarmament campaigns against the White Army. Angela Impey's work on Bor Dinka songs argues that they offer alternative processes of public disclosure for unresolved or suppressed memories of the past (ibid.: 76).

Before the 2013 crisis, politicians tried to intervene in those memories. Riek Machar was using trips to Bor to deliver apologies for his role in the attack: his repentance may have been an attempt to start a dialogue with alienated Dinka constituencies as part of his prospective presidential candidacy. At a meeting of the Committee for Community Peace, Reconciliation and Tolerance of Jonglei State in Bor on 3 April 2012, Riek Machar opened up an awkwardly politic discussion of memory and forgiveness before a silent audience of people from across the state. He was then vice-president, and he shared the stage with Kuol Manyang, then Jonglei's governor, who in 1991 had led the SPLA's harsh counter-attack against Riek Machar's forces:

> *Riek Machar:* Some of the things we must reconcile includes legacy of [the 1991] split. One particular area was affected. Twic to Bor, the civil population got affected. Death, displacement, looting ... As my part as the leader of the other part of the SPLM that split I have responsibility and that responsibility it's only me who recognizes it. I said, look I want to apologize to those that lost their kins during that split. To those who got displaced, because displacement is not an easy thing. To those who lost property ... I ask your forgiveness ... I think we should start the process of reconciliation ...

> *Kuol Manyang:* Dr Riek has apologized many times, I think Dinka Bor should respond. Myself as a person has accepted the apology. I'm saying it now but I accepted it long ago although I didn't say it. I'm asking anyone who has bitterness in himself or herself to leave it to God. All that was done by Mandela, Truth And [Reconciliation], these are foreign to our cultures. These Europeans who come and tell us you must reconcile, they are foreign. Irish and British, when will they reconcile? Dr Riek, thank you very much for that. We too have done wrong. Any wrong we have done to Nuer, we are also sorry. (Near-verbatim transcript)

This reconciliation meeting took place against the backdrop of massive attacks by Murle and Nuer raiders on each other's communities. In a process where Murle responsibility for Jonglei's violence was repeatedly emphasized, here was an acknowledgement of a prior conflict that had undermined relationships between different ethnic communities across the state. For some Murle people, 'Nuer–Dinka' rapprochement was seen as an ethnic conspiracy. Dinka people are colluding with Nuer people to attack Murle people, and to postpone addressing their own differences, they argued: 'People blame Murle [for the crisis in Jonglei] because Bor Dinka and Nuer have joined together. Bor said, let's get the people together to kill Murle' (neo-traditional leader, interview 104/2012). Another view is that the violence in Jonglei was a covert divide-and-rule policy masterminded by 'Dinka':

> Dinka incited Nuer to attack Murle. Dinka hate Nuer more than Murle. But Nuer–Murle war kills Nuer. It helps keep Dinka ascendancy. After the peace agreement, Murle asked for a separate state … with Nuer. Some Nuer MPs agreed with it, some had reservations. When Dinka saw the emergence of a Murle–Nuer coalition, they saw it as a threat. (Government official, interview 93/2012)

These Murle interviewees both saw the Murle role in Jonglei's order as a means for larger groups to avoid past memories. Nuer and Dinka people were pitched into a split between SPLA leaders in 1991, and then on to opposite sides of Khartoum's long war for control of the oilfields of greater Upper Nile. They were part of the costs of the 2006 Juba Declaration – the cost of suppressed memories.

Was there a vengeful Dinka conspiracy to postpone or forestall a reckoning with Nuer people, as the government official above angrily suggests? One of the arguments of this book is that the chaos and violence that have beset relations between Nuer and Dinka and Murle people are partly an outcome of patterns of uneven development. Politicians and ordinary people may engage in ethnic scheming, but the kind of unified Nuer power and unified Dinka power envisaged by the angry government officials are both illusions. But they are useful or necessary illusions for a small minority group that is caught up in the process of scapegoating: Murle people were being represented as a tiny group threatening Jonglei's stability with 'their' violence and 'their' venereal diseases. Chapter 3 argued that the notion of 'minorities' emerged alongside the notion of representative government in the 1970s. Minority talk was a way for the population, which had been organized around ethnicity and generally excluded from the state, to start making claims on it. Perhaps the state also needed minorities. In the 1980s, the Khartoum government used minority talk in South Sudan to set people against each other, part of an effort to reshuffle its alliances in the shadow of a financial crisis. In 2005, the Juba government set itself a different task – to build national unity around a well-fed army. Perhaps the SPLM preferred to use Murle people as a kind of cultural margin or boundary for this national unity. As the movement granted itself amnesties and moved towards a state-constructed national future, perhaps it was easier to keep the periphery busy with Murle scapegoats and local violence than to turn back and face the accumulated contradictions of decades of war which had thoroughly undermined the social and economic bases of life in Jonglei and across the South Sudanese periphery. And because the SPLM failed to turn back and reflect, the raids and counter-raids of Nuer and Murle young men and the crisis in Nuer–Murle relationships may have turned into a rehearsal for a much bigger war, which erupted in December 2013.

The state rolls forward

One of the many unexpected revelations that came from the tragic turn to violence in December 2013 was the speed with which the government in Juba moved to consolidate alliances

TABLE C2 GDP and GNI, East African countries (current USD)

	GDP (million)	GDP per capita	GNI per capita	GNIpc/ GDPpc
South Sudan	13,227	1,546	984	0.6
Burundi	1,611	189	160	0.8
Ethiopia	29,717	350	380	1.1
Kenya	31,409	769	780	1.0
Rwanda	5,628	548	540	1.0
Tanzania	23,057	527	530	1.0
Uganda	17,011	503	490	1.0

Source: NBS (2011a)

with other states. This was easier than might have been predicted, because its neighbours were invested in the stability of the Juba government. As the SPLA split in two, the government drew on the support of the Ugandan army to secure its capital and the road linking it to the Ugandan border. In January the Juba government concluded a rapprochement with Khartoum, even briefly considering a reoccupation of South Sudan's oilfields by the security forces of its erstwhile adversary. Juba had blamed every other South Sudanese mutiny of the past nine years on Khartoum, regardless of the many local contradictions that each mutiny reflected. When the big mutiny arrived, Khartoum's interest in the stability of South Sudan's government became very visible. The oil shutdown contributed to a sharp contraction in the Sudanese economy. The International Monetary Fund pushed the economically weakened government to withdraw fuel and other subsidies, and when the government finally complied in September 2013, government security forces shot dead over two hundred anti-austerity demonstrators in the capital (IMF 2012; Radio Dabanga, 29 September 2013).

In January 2014, it felt as if South Sudan's state had come of age. Its leaders sought pragmatic alliances and used foreign debt to shore up their internal position. But South Sudan's international position is an unusual one. Not because it is so dependent on rents, but because so much of its rent gets taken out of the country. Chapter 3 described the expatriation of South Sudan's rents as the difference between its gross domestic product (the total value of goods and services produced in a country) and its gross national income (the income received from production of goods and services as salaries or profits – the money that stays in the country). The National Bureau of Statistics undertook just such a comparison in 2011, before South Sudan tried to reduce Sudan's share of South Sudan's oil rents. Other countries are also living off South Sudanese rents – and this shaped regional responses to the crisis.

Distributing rent

Sudan gets a share of South Sudan's oil rents because it owns the pipeline that takes South Sudanese oil to East Asian markets. Other neighbours did not get a direct cut, but they were able to benefit from South Sudan's huge oil rents through the country's open and lopsided trading arrangements. South Sudan can afford to buy commodities internationally, but it has nothing but piped oil to export: the lorries bringing goods to Juba from East Africa often return empty. Landlocked South Sudan's import bill was 40 per cent of gross domestic product in 2010 (NBS 2011a). This huge import bill is another expression of the way that Juba's oil rents are distributed regionally.

Trade with Ethiopia is negligible. Trade with Sudan is subject to intense political fluctuation. But trade with Uganda is significant for both countries: South Sudan is Uganda's biggest African export destination. In the three years from 2005, when the autonomous government of South Sudan was set up, exports increased tenfold, from about $60 million to over $600 million. In the same period, Kenyan exports more than doubled, to about $150 million worth (ADB 2013: 50ff.). Crises in South Sudan disrupt Sudan and Uganda's shares in South Sudan's oil rents, and that is one reason that both countries backed the government in Juba in December 2013. This joint support surprised many observers, because of the history of antagonism between the two countries, and it prevented the possibility of the crisis turning into a regional war (staging a regional war is an unexceptional fate for a peripheral country like South Sudan). Instead, the crisis integrated South Sudan into the regional interstate system. It maintained the state's economic autonomy vis-à-vis the productive forces of its own society. And it deepened the state's complicity in South Sudan's ethnic divisions.

In spite of Sudanese/Ugandan support, Juba was not able to convince its international partners of its version of the events of December 2013 – that Riek Machar and others had mounted a coup against a legitimate government. It was also not able to recapture the areas of Jonglei and greater Upper Nile that fell so quickly to the rebels. Instead, it negotiated directly with rebels. In March 2014, the government signed a peace agreement with David Yauyau, which created an autonomous zone in Jonglei called the Greater Pibor Administrative Area, to be administered by a nominee of his South Sudan Democratic Movement – Cobra Faction. In May 2014, Salva Kiir and Riek Machar signed a cessation-of-hostilities agreement in person. The agreement (which did not immediately end the fighting) called for negotiations on the composition of a transitional government of national unity – a political reconciliation constructed around the oil-backed payroll. Liberation has been postponed again, this time until the restoration of the status quo ante.

The periphery and the future

Jonglei, Upper Nile and Unity states are often seen as the Nuer homelands. When the rebellion spread across them in December 2013, they were the hungriest places in South Sudan, according to the United Nations. Compared to the rest of the country, those three states had higher levels of severe food insecurity, the highest cereal deficits, and very high dependence on markets for staple food (WFP/FAO 2014).

Jonglei exemplifies a set of changes that affect other areas of South Sudan. Food insecurity is linked to the way that communities have been drawn into dependence on food markets which they cannot afford. New patterns of accumulation have failed to meet human needs, and have made society a more destructive place rather than a more creative one. These destructive patterns are most clearly seen in the way that technology is reshaping production – the gun, not the tractor, is the way that old systems of subsistence are 'modernized'. The war in Jonglei receives attention because it is cruel, intractable and has continued for the better part of the last fifty years. It has completely reshaped society, economic life and youth aspiration, and created new groupings of armed youth, drawing them into the struggles between Juba politicians. If those politicians do manage to reconcile, they will not be able to wish away these unruly youngsters. The armed young men live in a world where crisis is the rule, not the exception, and their astonishingly rapid mobilization is an eloquent expression of local attitudes to crises in general, and may also be an expression of their judgement on the systems set up in Juba and Bor.

For the pragmatists running the negotiations between the Juba government and the rebels, peripheral contradictions could be ignored for just a little bit longer, until the status quo ante is restored. Colder pragmatists might argue that the state could withdraw altogether from Jonglei's hinterlands, and other peripheries, and manage a slow dirty war with all the resources that states have at their disposal – a bit like the Khartoum government's war in Darfur. But one of the lessons of Sudan's nineteenth and twentieth centuries was that the country's future was decided at the periphery. Its natural resources and its hungry and subordinated people have a powerful historical force.

BIBLIOGRAPHY

Names beginning with Al- come under A and those beginning with El- come under E

Abdelhay, Ashraf Kamal (2007) 'The politics of language planning in the Sudan: the case of the Naivasha language policy', Unpublished PhD thesis, Edinburgh University, Edinburgh.

ADB (African Development Bank) (2013) *South Sudan: A Study on Competitiveness and Cross-Border Trade with Neighbouring Countries*, Tunis.

African Rights (1995) *Facing Genocide: The Nuba of Sudan*, London: African Rights.

— (1997) *Food and Power in Sudan: A Critique of Humanitarianism*, London: African Rights.

Ahmad, Ja'far Karar (2005) *al-hizb al-shiyū'ī al-sūdānī wa al-mis'ala al-janūbīya 1946–1985* [The Sudanese Communist Party and the Southern Question 1946–1985], Khartoum: Khartoum University Press.

Akol, Lam (2007) *Southern Sudan: Colonialism, Resistance and Autonomy*, Asmara: Red Sea Press.

— (2009) *SPLM SPLA: Inside an African Revolution*, Khartoum: Lam Akol/Khartoum University Printing Press.

Akuany, Deng Dongrin (1990) 'The political consequences of uneven development in Sudan: an analysis of political struggles, with special reference to the Sudan People's Liberation Movement and the Sudan People's Liberation Army (SPLM/SPLA)', Unpublished PhD thesis, Hull University, Hull.

Akuei, Stephanie Riak and Joseph John Jok (2011) *Child Abduction in Jonglei and Central Equatoria States*, London/Nairobi: Rift Valley Institute.

Al-Gaddal [al-Qaddāl], Muḥammad Sa'īd (1986) *al-siyāsah al-iqtiṣādīyah lil-dawlah al-mahdīyah* [The economic policy of the Mahdist state], Khartoum: Khartoum University Press.

Alavi, Hamza (1972) 'The state in post-colonial societies: Pakistan and Bangladesh', *New Left Review*, I(74).

Ali, Abbas Ibrahim Muhammad (1972) *The British, the Slave Trade and Slavery in the Sudan 1820–1881*, Khartoum: Khartoum University Press.

Ali, Musaddeg Ahmed El haj (1987) 'The redivision of the Southern Sudan', in Al-Agab Ahmed al-Teraifi (ed.), *Decentralization in Sudan*, Khartoum: Khartoum University Press.

Alier, Abel (2003) *Southern Sudan: Too Many Agreements Dishonoured*, Khartoum: Abel Alier.

Amin, Samir (1972) 'Underdevelopment and dependence in black

Africa – origins and contemporary forms', *Journal of Modern African Studies*, 10(4).

Andretta, Elizabeth Hain (1983) 'Aging, power and status in an East African pastoral society', in Jay Sokolovsky and Joan Sokolovsky (eds), *Aging and the Aged in the Third World: Part II, Regional and Ethnographic Perspectives*, Studies in Third World Societies, publication no. 23, Williamsburg, VA: College of William and Mary.

— (1985) 'A reconsideration of the basis of group cohesion among the Murle of the Southern Sudan', PhD thesis, University of Pennsylvania, Philadelphia, PA.

— (1989) 'Symbolic continuity, material discontinuity, and ethnic identity among Murle communities in the Southern Sudan', *Ethnology*, 28(1).

Arensen, Jonathan E. (1992) *Mice are Men: Language and Society among the Murle of Sudan*, Dallas, TX: International Museum of Cultures.

— (2012) 'Contemporary issues facing the Murle', Paper delivered at a conference in Nairobi organized by AECOM.

Arou, Mom K. N. (1989) 'Ethnic conflicts in Southern schools after the establishment of regional government', in Sayyid H. Hurreiz and Elfatih A. Abdel Salam (eds), *Ethnicity, Conflict and National Integration in the Sudan*, Institute of African and Asian Studies, Khartoum: Khartoum University Press.

AU-IBAR (African Union/Interafrican Bureau for Animal Resources) (2001) *Rinderpest Eradication Strategy in the East and West Nile Ecosystems*, Nairobi

AUPD (African Union High-Level Panel on Darfur) (2009) *Darfur: The quest for peace, justice and reconciliation. Report of the African Union High-Level Panel on Darfur*, AU reference PSC/AHG/2(CCVII), Addis Ababa: African Union.

Ayoker, Kunijwok Gwado (1983) *State and Development in the Black Sudan*, Khartoum: Development Studies and Research Centre, University of Khartoum.

Badal, Raphael Koba (1976) 'The rise and fall of separatism in Southern Sudan', *African Affairs*, 75(301).

— (1977) 'British administration in Southern Sudan', PhD thesis, School of Oriental and African Studies, London

— (1986) 'Oil and regional sentiment in the South', in Muddathir Abd Al-Rahim et al. (eds), *Sudan since Independence: Studies of the Political Development since 1956*, Aldershot: Gower.

— (2006) *Local Traditional Structures in Sudan: A base for building civil society for the promotion of peace and reconciliation*, Nairobi: Life and Peace Institute.

Bader, Christian (2000) 'Notes sur les Balé du sud-ouest de l'Éthiopie', *Annales d'Éthiopie*, 16.

Beachey, R. W. (1967) 'The East African ivory trade in the nineteenth century', *Journal of African History*, 8(2).

Bender, M. Lionel (2000) 'Nilo-Saharan', in Bernd Heine and Derek Nurse (eds), *African Languages: An Introduction*, Cambridge: Cambridge University Press.

Benjamin, Walter (1968) *Illuminations*, trans. Harry Zohn, New York: Schocken Books.

Berger, Carol (2010) 'Southern Sudan's Red Army: the role of social process and routinised violence in the deployment of underaged soldiers', Unpublished PhD thesis, University of Oxford.

Birkbeck Hill, George (ed.) (1885) *Charles Gordon in Central Africa 1874–1879*, London: De La Rue.

Bjørkelo, Anders (1989) *Prelude to the Mahdiyya: Peasants and Traders in the Shendi Region 1821–1885*, Cambridge: Cambridge University Press.

Bok, F. (2003) *Escape from Slavery: The true story of my ten years in captivity and my journey to freedom in America*, New York: St Martin's Press.

Bradbury, Mark, John Ryle, Michael Medley and Kwesi Sansculotte-Greenidge (2006) *Local Peace Processes in Sudan: A Baseline Study*, London/Nairobi: Rift Valley Institute.

Chanie, Paulos (2007) 'Clientelism and Ethiopia's post-1991 decentralisation', *Journal of Modern African Studies*, 45(3).

Clapham, Christopher (1989) 'The state and revolution in Ethiopia', *Review of African Political Economy*, 44.

Clarence-Smith, William G. (2008) 'Islamic abolitionism in the western Indian Ocean from c. 1800', Paper given at the conference 'Slavery and the Slave Trades in the Indian Ocean and Arab Worlds: Global Connections and Disconnections', Yale University, New Haven, CT.

COI (Commission of Inquiry) (1956) *Report of the Commission of Inquiry into the Disturbances in the Southern Sudan during August, 1955*, Khartoum: Republic of the Sudan.

Collier, Paul and Anke Hoeffler (2001) *Greed and Grievance in Civil War*, Washington, DC: World Bank Development Research Group.

Collins, Robert O. (1960) 'Patrols against the Beirs', *Sudan Notes and Records*, 41.

— (2008) *A History of Modern Sudan*, Cambridge: Cambridge University Press.

Comyn, D. C. E. ff. (1911) *Service and Sport in the Sudan: A record of the administration in the Anglo-Egyptian Sudan with some intervals of sport and travel*, London: John Lane/Bodley Head.

Cordell, Dennis D. (1985) *Dar al-Kuti and the Last Years of the Trans-Saharan Slave Trade*, Madison: University of Wisconsin Press.

— (2010) 'African historical demography in the postmodern and postcolonial eras', in Karl Ittman, Dennis D. Cordell and Gregory H. Maddox (eds), *The Demography of Empire: The Colonial Order and the Creation of Knowledge*, Athens: Ohio University Press.

CPI (Child Protection International) (2008) 'The Save Yar Campaign: background for July 28, 2008 briefing', Minneapolis, MN: Child Protection International.

Craig, G. M. (ed.) (1991) *The Agriculture of the Sudan*, Oxford: Oxford University Press.

Crazzolara, J. P. (1950) *The Lwoo: Part I, Lwoo Migrations*, Verona: Missioni Africane.

CRSP (Committee for the Redivision of the Southern Provinces) (c. 1975) *Final Report*, Juba: Higher Executive Council.

CSSAC (Community Safety and Small Arms Control Bureau) (2012) A group of reports on the situation in Jonglei summarized by Douglas H.

Johnson in a paper entitled 'Jonglei losses', based on official reports.

Daly, M. W. (1986) *Empire on the Nile: The Anglo-Egyptian Sudan, 1898–1934*, Cambridge: Cambridge University Press.

Davis, Mike (2002) *Late Victorian Holocausts: El Niño Famines and the Making of the Third World*, London: Verso.

De Waal, Alex (2004) 'The politics of destabilisation in the Horn, 1989–2001', in Alex de Waal (ed.), *Islamism and Its Enemies in the Horn of Africa*, Bloomington: Indiana University Press.

Deng, A., B. Deng, B. Ajak and J. A. Bernstein (2005) *They Poured Fire on Us from the Sky: The true story of three Lost Boys of Sudan*, New York: Public Affairs.

Deng, Francis (1973) *Dynamics of Identification: A Basis for National Integration in the Sudan*, Khartoum: Khartoum University Press.

— (1995) *War of Visions: Conflict of identities in the Sudan*, Washington, DC: Brookings Institution.

— (2005) 'African Renaissance: towards a new Sudan', *Forced Migration Review*, 24: 6–8.

Deng, Lual (2013) *The Power of Creative Reasoning: The Ideas and Vision of John Garang*, Bloomington, IN: iUniverse.

Deng, Luka Biong (2010) 'Livelihood diversification and civil war: Dinka communities in Sudan's civil war', *Journal of Eastern African Studies*, 4(3).

Deng Garang, Gaaluak (2006) *al-nahr wa al-rijāl* [The river and the men], Book apparently published by the author while he was federal minister of animal resources and fisheries, Khartoum.

Department of Statistics (1979) *The Sudan Fertility Survey, Principal Report*, Khartoum: Ministry of National Planning, Democratic Republic of the Sudan.

Dhal, Abraham Matoc (2002) *Local Government Financing in the Southern Sudan*, Khartoum: Khartoum University Press.

DJAM (Darfur Joint Assessment Mission) (2012) *DJAM Update: Budget Trends and Fiscal Management*, www.darfurconference.com/sites/default/files/files/6, accessed 6 September 2014.

DSDS (Direction des Statistiques Démographiques et Sociales) (1995) *Enquête Démographique et de Santé, 1994–95*, Bangui: Division des Statistiques et des Études Économiques, Ministère de l'Économie, du Plan et de la Coopération Internationale, République Centrafricaine.

Duany, Wal (1992) 'Neither palaces nor prisons: the constitution of order among the Nuer', Unpublished PhD thesis, Indiana University, Bloomington, IN.

Dyment, Wendy (2004) *Lekuangole STD Intervention: Final Report, December 3, 2003–February 28, 2004*, Unpublished Medair report.

Ehret, Christopher (1982) 'Population movement and culture contact in the Southern Sudan, c. 3000 BC to AD 1000: a preliminary linguistic overview', in John Mack and Peter Robertshaw (eds), *Culture History in the Southern Sudan*, Nairobi: British Institute in Eastern Africa.

— (2002) *The Civilizations of Africa: A History to 1800*, Oxford: James Currey.

El-Battahani, Atta (2009) *Nationalism and Peasant Politics in the Nuba*

Mountains Region of the Sudan, *1924–1966*, Khartoum: Khartoum University Press.

Emin Pasha (1888) *Emin Pasha in Central Africa: Being a Collection of His Letters and Journals*, ed. G. Schweinfurth, F. Ratzel, R. W. Felkin and G. Hartlaub, London: George Philip and Son.

Evans-Pritchard, E. E. (1940a) *The Nuer: A Description of the Modes of Livelihood and Political Institutions of a Nilotic People*, Oxford: Clarendon Press.

— (1940b) *The Political System of the Anuak of the Anglo-Egyptian Sudan*, London: London School of Economics.

— (1963) 'The Zande state', *Journal of the Royal Anthropological Institute of Great Britain and Ireland*, 93(1).

— (1973) 'Fifty years of British anthropology', *Times Literary Supplement*, 3722, 6 July.

Fahmy, Khaled (1998) 'The era of Muhammad 'Ali Pasha, 1805–1848', in M. W. Daly (ed.), *The Cambridge History of Egypt*, vol. 2, Cambridge: Cambridge University Press.

— (2002) *All the Pasha's Men: Mehmed Ali, his army and the making of Modern Egypt*, Cairo: American University in Cairo Press.

Fanon, Frantz (1963) *The Wretched of the Earth*, New York: Grove.

FAO/WFP (Food and Agriculture Organization/World Food Programme) (2010) *Special Report: FAO/WFP Crop and Food Security Assessment Mission to Southern Sudan*, Rome.

Fearon, James D. and David D. Laitin (2000) 'Violence and the social construction of ethnic identity', *International Organization*, 54.

Feyissa, Dereje (2009) 'A national perspective on the conflict in Gambella', in Svein Ege, Harald Aspen, Birhanu Teferra and Shiferaw Bekele (eds), *Proceedings of the 16th International Conference of Ethiopian Studies*, Trondheim: NTNU.

— (2011) *Playing Different Games: The paradox of Anywaa and Nuer identification strategies in the Gambella Region, Ethiopia*, New York: Berghahn.

Ga'le, Severino Fuli Boki Tombe (2002) *Shaping a Free Southern Sudan: Memoirs of our struggle 1934–1985*, Loa: Loa Catholic Mission Council.

Garang, Joseph [Ukel] (1971) *The Dilemma of the Southern Intellectual: Is It Justified*, Khartoum: Ministry of Southern Affairs.

Garang de Mabior, John (1981) 'Identifying, selecting, and implementing rural development strategies for socio-economic development in the Jonglei Projects Area, Southern Region, Sudan', PhD thesis, Iowa State University.

— (1994) *This Convention is Sovereign: Opening and Closing Speeches by Dr John Garang de Mabior to the First SPLM/SPLA National Convention*, SPLM Secretariat of Information and Culture.

Gardner, Leigh (2012) *Taxing Colonial Africa: The Political Economy of British Imperialism*, Oxford: Oxford University Press.

— (2013) 'Fiscal policy in Belgian Congo in comparative perspective', in Ewout Frankema and Frans Buelens (eds), *Colonial Exploitation and Economic Development: The Belgian Congo and the Netherlands Indies compared*, Abingdon: Routledge.

Garfield, Richard (2007) *Violence*

and Victimization after Civilian Disarmament: The Case of Jonglei, Geneva: Small Arms Survey.

Geertz, Clifford (1973) *The Interpretation of Cultures*, New York: Basic Books.

Ghai, Yash (2008) 'Devolution: restructuring the Kenyan state', *Journal of Eastern African Studies*, 2(2).

Giegler Pasha (1984) *The Sudan Memoirs of Carl Christian Giegler Pasha*, ed. Richard Hill, London: British Academy/Oxford University Press.

Graeber, David (2011) 'The divine kingship of the Shilluk: on violence, utopia and the human condition, or, elements for an archaeology of sovereignty', *Hau: Journal of Ethnographic Theory*, 1(1).

— (2012) *Debt: The First 5,000 Years*, New York: Melville House.

Gray, Richard (1961) *A History of the Southern Sudan 1839–1889*, Oxford: Oxford University Press.

Groenendijk, Cathy and Jolien Veldwijk (2011) *'Behind the Papyrus and Mabaati': Sexual Exploitation and Abuse in Juba, South Sudan*, Juba: Confident Children out of Conflict.

Guarak, Mawut Achiecque Mach (2011) *Integration and Fragmentation of the Sudan: An African Renaissance*, Bloomington, IN: AuthorHouse.

Gurtong (2013a) 'Minister says oil money is for loan repayment, no salaries', by Waakhe Simon Wudu, 21 November, www.gurtong.net/ECM/Editorial/tabid/124/ctl/ArticleView/mid/519/articleId/13867/Minister-Says-Oil-Money-Is-For-Loan-Repayment-No-Salaries.aspx, accessed 29 March 2014.

— (2013b) 'Full statement by President Salva Kiir on attempted coup', 16 December, www.gurtong.net/ECM/Editorial/tabid/124/ctl/ArticleView/mid/519/articleId/14151/Full-Statement-by-President-Salva-Kiir-on-Attempted-Coup.aspx, accessed 13 March 2014.

Harrigan, Simon (2011) *South Sudan: Waiting for Peace to Come: Study from Bor, Twic East & Duk Counties in Jonglei*, Local to Global Protection (L2GP).

Harrigan, Simon and Nikodemo Arou Man (2005) 'Traditional authority in South Sudan, Upper Nile Team B – case study 15 Jan–13 Feb 2005: Pibor County, Pocalla County & Twic (E) County', Report with no bibliographic information.

Harvey, David (2006) *Spaces of Global Capitalism: Towards a Theory of Uneven Geographical Development*, London: Verso.

Hashimoto, Eri (2013) 'Prophets, Prophecies, and Inter-communal Conflict in Post-independence South Sudan', *Nilo-Ethiopian Studies*, 18.

Henin, R. A. (1958) 'Modes of living in Sudan', in *The Population of Sudan, Report on the Sixth Annual Conference*, Khartoum: Philosophical Society of Sudan.

Hill, Richard (1959) *Egypt in the Sudan, 1820–1881*, Oxford: Oxford University Press.

Hodgkin, Thomas (1956) *Nationalism in Colonial Africa*, London: Frederick Muller.

Holt, P. M. (1977) *The Mahdist State in the Sudan*, Nairobi: Oxford University Press.

Howell, P. P. (1954) *A Manual of Nuer Law*, Oxford: Clarendon Press.

Howell, Paul, Michael Lock and Stephen Cobb (1988) *The Jonglei Canal: Impact and Opportunity*,

Cambridge: Cambridge University Press.

HRW (Human Rights Watch) (1994) *Sudan: The Lost Boys, Child Soldiers and Unaccompanied Boys in Southern Sudan*, New York.

— (2003) *Sudan, Oil and Human Rights*, New York.

— (2012a) *'Waiting Here for Death': Forced Displacement and 'Villagization' in Ethiopia's Gambella Region*, New York.

— (2012b) *'What will happen if hunger comes?' Abuses against the Indigenous Peoples of Ethiopia's Lower Omo Valley*, New York.

— (2013) *'They are killing us': Abuses against civilians in South Sudan's Pibor County*, New York.

Hutchinson, Sharon E. (1996) *Nuer Dilemmas: Coping with Money, War and the State*, Berkeley: University of California Press.

— (2000) 'Nuer ethnicity militarized', *Anthropology Today*, 16(3).

IBRD (International Bank for Reconstruction and Development) (1969) *Current Economic Position and Prospects of the Republic of the Sudan*, Report MA-6, Washington, DC.

— (1973) *Report of a special mission on the economic development of Southern Sudan*, Report no. 119a-SU, Washington, DC.

ICG (International Crisis Group) (2009) *Jonglei's Tribal Conflicts: Countering Insecurity in South Sudan*, Juba/Nairobi/Brussels.

IDMC (Internal Displacement Monitoring Centre) (2010) 'Sudan: durable solutions elusive as southern IDPs return and Darfur remains tense. A profile of the internal displacement situation', Geneva: Norwegian Refugee Council.

Ignatiev, Noel (1995) *How the Irish Became White*, London: Routledge.

IISS (International Institute of Strategic Studies) (2014) *The Military Balance*, London: IISS.

Iles, Karen (1994) *Feasibility Study for Restocking Displaced Dinka and Nuer Peoples in Southern Sudan*, UNICEF OLS HHFS programme, Nairobi.

IMF (International Monetary Fund) (2012) *Sudan: Selected Issues Paper*, IMF Country Report no. 12/299, November, Washington, DC: IMF.

Impey, Angela (2013) 'The poetics of transitional justice in Dinka songs in South Sudan', in María-Ángeles Alaminos Hervás (ed.), *Special Issue on Sudan and South Sudan*, Discussion Paper no. 33, Madrid: Unidad de Investigación sobre Seguridad y Cooperación Internacional, University of Madrid.

IRI (International Republican Institute) (2011) *Survey of South Sudan Public Opinion, September 6–27, 2011*, Washington, DC.

Jal, Gabriel Giet (1987) 'The history of the Jikany Nuer before 1920', Unpublished PhD thesis, School of Oriental and African Studies, London.

JIT (Jonglei Investigation Team) (1954) *The Equatorial Nile Project and Its Effects in the Anglo-Egyptian Sudan*, 6 vols, London: Sudan Government.

Johnson, Douglas H. (1981) 'The Fighting Nuer: primary sources and the origins of a stereotype', *Africa*, 51(1).

— (1986) 'On the Nilotic frontier: imperial Ethiopia in the Southern Sudan, 1898–1936', in Donald Donham and Wendy James (eds), *The Southern Marches of Imperial Ethiopia: Essays in History and*

Social Anthropology, Cambridge: Cambridge University Press.

— (1988) 'The great drought and famine of 1888–92 in northeast Africa', in Douglas H. Johnson and David M. Anderson (eds), *The Ecology of Survival: Case Studies from Northeast African History*, London: Lester Crook Academic Publishers.

— (1989) 'The structure of a legacy: military slavery in northeast Africa', *Ethnohistory*, 36(1).

— (1993) 'Prophecy and Mahdism in the Upper Nile: an examination of local experiences of the Mahdiyya in the Southern Sudan', *British Journal of Middle Eastern Studies*, 20(1).

— (1994) *Nuer Prophets: A History of Prophecy from the Upper Nile in the Nineteenth and Twentieth Centuries*, Oxford: Clarendon Press.

— (1997) 'The Sudan is *sui generis*', *Sudan Studies*, 20.

— (1998) 'The Sudan People's Liberation Army and the problem of factionalism', in Christopher Clapham (ed.), *African Guerrillas*, Oxford: James Currey.

— (2003) *The Root Causes of Sudan's Civil Wars*, Oxford: James Currey.

Jok, Jok Madut (1999) 'Militarization and gender violence in South Sudan', *Journal of Asian and African Studies*, 34: 427–42.

— (2001) *War and Slavery in Sudan*, Philadelphia: University of Pennsylvania Press.

— (2005) 'War, changing ethics and the position of youth in South Sudan', in Jon Abbink and Ineke van Kessel (eds), *Vanguard or Vandals: Youth, politics and conflict in Africa*, Leiden: Brill.

Jok, Jok Madut and Sharon Elaine Hutchinson (1999) 'Sudan's prolonged second civil war and the militarization of Nuer and Dinka ehnic identities', *African Studies Review*, 42(2).

Kafi, Mohammed Haroun (1988) *The Kachipo, People and Land: A relief and development proposal for this forgotten, neglected and underdeveloped people and land*, Nairobi: Kapoeta Research Branch, Sudan Relief and Rehabilitation Association.

Kapteijns, Lidwien and Jay Spaulding (1982) 'Precolonial trade between states in the Eastern Sudan, ca 1700–ca 1900', *African Economic History*, 11.

— (1991) 'History, ethnicity and agriculture', in G. M. Craig (ed.), *The Agriculture of the Sudan*, Oxford: Oxford University Press.

Karim, Ataul, Mark Duffield, Susanne Jaspers, Aldo Benini, Joanna Macrae, Mark Bradbury, Douglas Johnson, George Larbi and Barbara Hendrie (1996) *Operation Lifeline Sudan: A Review*, United Nations, no bibliographic information.

Karshoum, Hussain Ibrahim (2004) *Operation Lifeline Sudan and State Sovereignty: A documentary study*, Khartoum: Khartoum University Press.

Kathish, Hathashil Masha (1901) *Jehovah-Nissi, the Life of Hatashil Masha Kathish*, n.p.

Kelly, Raymond Case (1985) *The Nuer Conquest: The structure and development of an expansionist system*, Ann Arbor: University of Michigan Press.

Khalid, Mansour (1990) *The Government They Deserve: The role of the elite in Sudan's political evolution*, London: Kegan Paul International.

Kiir Mayardit, Salva (2008) 'Opening

statement', SPLM 2nd National Convention, Juba, 15–20 May, www.cmi.no/sudan/doc/?id=993, accessed 6 September 2014.

Komey, Guma Kunda (2007) 'The denied land rights of the indigenous peoples and their endangered livelihood and survival: the case of the Nuba of the Sudan', *Ethnic and Racial Studies*, 31(5).

KSMSD (Khartoum State Ministry for Social Development) (2004) 'The Mygoma story: setting a standard for de-institutionalization in Sudan', Unpublished report produced in partnership between KSMSD, Khartoum Council for Child Welfare, UNICEF, Hope and Homes for Children and Médecins sans Frontières, Khartoum.

Kuol, Monyluak (1997) *Administration of Justice in the (SPLA/M) Liberated Areas: Court Cases in War-torn Southern Sudan*, Oxford: University of Oxford Refugee Studies Programme.

Lagu, Joseph (2006) *Sudan, Odyssey through a State: From Ruin to Hope*, Omdurman: MOB Centre for Sudan Studies.

Leonardi, Cherry (2007) '"Liberation" or capture: youth in between "hakuma" and "home" during civil war and its aftermath in Southern Sudan', *African Affairs*, 106(204).

— (2013) *Dealing with Government in South Sudan: Histories of Chiefship, Community and State*, Woodbridge: James Currey.

Lewis, B. A. (1972) *The Murle: Red Chiefs and Black Commoners*, Oxford: Clarendon Press.

Lewis, M. Paul (ed.) (2009) *Ethnologue: Languages of the World*, 16th edn, Dallas, TX: SIL International, www.ethnologue.com/.

Lienhardt, Godfrey (1961) *Divinity and Experience: The Religion of the Dinka*, Oxford: Clarendon Press.

— (1982) 'The Sudan: aspects of the South Government among some of the Nilotic peoples, 1947–52', *Bulletin (British Society for Middle Eastern Studies)*, 9(1).

Lindqvist, Sven (2002) *A History of Bombing*, London: Granta.

Lloyd, David Tyrrell (1978) 'The pre-colonial economic history of the Avongara-Azande c 1750–1916', Unpublished PhD thesis, University of California, Los Angeles.

Lowrey, William O. (1996) 'Passing the peace ... people to people: the role of religion in an indigenous peace process among the Nuer people of Sudan', Unpublished PhD thesis, Union Institute Graduate School, Cincinati, OH.

Mahmud, Ushairi (1983) *Arabic in the Southern Sudan: History and spread of a Pidgin-Creole*, Khartoum: FAL Advertising and Printing.

Malok, Elijah (2009) *The Southern Sudan: Struggle for liberty*, Nairobi: Kenway Publications.

MARF/SNV (Ministry of Animal Resources and Fisheries/Stichting Nederlandse Vrijwilligers) (2010) *The Livestock Sector in Southern Sudan: Results of a Value Chain Study of the Livestock Sector in Five States of Southern Sudan covered by MDTF with a Focus on Red Meat*, Juba.

Markakis, John (1979) 'Garrison socialism: the case of Ethiopia', *MERIP*, 79.

Marshall, Jaqueline (2006) *Literacy, Language, Non-Formal Education and Alternative Learning Opportunities in Southern Sudan*, 2nd revision, 18 September, Hamburg: UNESCO Institute of Education.

Marx, Karl (1963) *The Eighteenth Brumaire of Louis Bonaparte*, New York: International Publishers.

Mawut, Lazarus Leek (1995) 'The Southern Sudan under British rule 1898–1924: the constraints reassessed', Unpublished PhD thesis, Durham University, Durham.

McCallum, Judith (2013) 'Murle identity in post-colonial South Sudan', Unpublished PhD thesis, York University, Toronto.

McColl, Storrs (1969) 'The rise of a provisional government in Southern Sudan', Paper presented at University Social Sciences Council Conference, University of East Africa, Nairobi, 8–12 December.

McKinnon, Sara L. (2008) 'Unsettling resettlement: problematizing "Lost Boys of Sudan" resettlement and identity', *Western Journal of Communication*, 72(4).

McMichael, Gabriella (2010) 'Land tenure and property rights in Southern Sudan: a case study of informal settlements in Juba', in Sibrino Forojallah (ed.), *Land Tenure Issues in Southern Sudan: Key Findings and Recommendations for Southern Sudan Land Policy*, Washington, DC: USAID.

Meillassoux, Claude (1970) 'A class analysis of the bureaucratic process in Mali', *Journal of Development Studies*, 6(2).

Mercer, Patricia (1971) 'Shilluk trade and politics from the mid-seventeenth century to 1861', *Journal of African History*, 12(3).

Ministry of Livestock and Fisheries, Jonglei State (2011) *Strategic Plan*.

Mitchell, Timothy (2002) *Rule of Experts: Egypt, techno-politics, modernity*, Berkeley: University of California Press.

Mkandawire, Thandika (2001) 'Thinking about developmental states in Africa', *Cambridge Journal of Economics*, 25.

— (2002) 'The terrible toll of postcolonial "rebel movements" in Africa: towards an explanation of the violence against the peasantry', *Journal of Modern African Studies*, 40(2).

MOFEP (Ministry of Finance & Economic Planning) (2011) *Approved Budget*, Juba: Government of South Sudan.

NBS (National Bureau of Statistics) (2011a) 'Release of first Gross Domestic Product (GDP) and Gross National Income (GNI) figures for South Sudan by the NBS', Press release, Juba, 11 August, www.ssnbs.org/storage/GDP%20 Press%20 release_11.08.11.pdf, accessed 21 February 2014.

— (2011b) *South Sudan Cost-to-Market Report: An Analysis of Check-points on the Major Trade Routes in South Sudan*, Juba.

Nhial, A. and D. Mills (2004) *Lost Boy No More: A true story of survival and salvation*, Nashville, TN: B & H Publishing Group.

Nugud [Nuqud], Muhammad Ibrahim (2003) *'alāqāt al-riqq fil-mujtama' al-sūdānī, al-nasha', al-simāt, al-iḍmiḥlāl, tawthīq wa-ta'līq* [Relations of slavery in Sudanese society: its establishment, characteristics and disappearance. Documents and commentary], Khartoum: Azza.

Nyaba, Peter Adwok (1997) *The Politics of Liberation in South Sudan: An insider's view*, Kampala: Fountain.

— (2001) 'The disarmament of the Gel-Weng of Bahr El Ghazal and the consolidation of the Nuer–

Dinka peace agreement 1999', Nairobi: New Sudan Council of Churches/Pax Christi – Netherlands.

— (2005) 'Righting the past wrongs against the African people: time for Arab restitution of the Nile Valley, Red Sea and Indian Ocean slave trade', in Kwesi Kwaa Prah (ed.), *Reflections on the Arab-led Slavery of Africans*, Cape Town: Centre for the Advanced Studies of African Society.

— (2011) 'The challenges of state and nation building in South Sudan', in Riek Machar et al., *State Building and Development in South Sudan*, Nairobi: African Research and Resource Forum.

Nyombe, Bureng G. V. (1997) 'Survival or extinction: the fate of the local languages of the Southern Sudan', *International Journal of the Sociology of Language*, 125.

— (2007) *Some Aspects of Bari History: A Comparative Linguistic and Oral Tradition Reconstruction*, Nairobi: University of Nairobi Press.

Ochalla-Ayayo, A. B. C. (1980) *The Luo Culture*, Wiesbaden: Franz Steiner Verlag.

Oduho, Joseph and William Deng (1963) *The Problem of the Southern Sudan*, London: Institute of Race Relations/Oxford University Press.

O'Fahey, R. S. (1982) 'Fūr and Fartīt, the history of a frontier', in John Mack and Peter Robertshaw (eds), *Culture History in the Southern Sudan*, Nairobi: British Institute in Eastern Africa.

Office of Refugee Resettlement (2003) *Annual Report to Congress*, Washington, DC.

Ohrwalder, Joseph (1892) *Ten Years'*

Captivity in the Mahdi's Camp, ed. F. R. Wingate, London: Sampson, Low, Marston and Co.

Owen, Roger (1981) *The Middle East in the World Economy, 1800–1914*, London: I. B. Tauris.

Pamuk, Şevket (1987) *The Ottoman Empire and European Capitalism, 1820–1913*, Cambridge: Cambridge University Press.

Pankhurst, Richard (1967) 'Tribute, taxation and government revenues in nineteenth and early twentieth century Ethiopia (Part I)', *Journal of Ethiopian Studies*.

Pantuliano, Sara, Margie Buchanan-Smith, Paul Murphy and Irina Mosel (2008) *The Long Road Home: Opportunities and obstacles to the reintegration of IDPs and refugees returning to Southern Sudan and the Three Areas. Report of Phase II: Conflict, urbanisation and land*, London: Overseas Development Institute.

PCO (Population Census Office) (1956) *First Population Census of Sudan 1955/56*, First interim report, Khartoum: Ministry of Social Affairs, Republic of Sudan.

— (n.d.) *First Population Census of Sudan 1955/56*, Second interim report, Khartoum: Ministry of Social Affairs, Republic of Sudan.

— (1957) *First Population Census of Sudan 1955/56*, Fourth and sixth interim reports, Khartoum: Ministry of Social Affairs, Republic of Sudan.

— (1958) *First Population Census of Sudan 1955/56*, Eighth and ninth interim reports, Khartoum: Ministry of Social Affairs, Republic of Sudan.

Petherick, John and Katherine Harriet Petherick (1869) *Travels in Central*

Africa, and Explorations of the Western Nile Tributaries, London: Tinsley Brothers.

Poggo, Scopus (2009) *The First Sudanese Civil War: Africans, Arabs and Israelis in the Southern Sudan, 1955–1972*, New York: Palgrave Macmillan.

Radio Dabanga (2014) 'Sudanese doctors report 210 dead in Khartoum during demonstrations', www.radiodabanga.org/node/56633, accessed 29 March 2014.

Radio Miriya (2012) 'President Kiir rebukes the Jonglei cow emblem', www.radiomiraya.org/news-202/south-sudan/8022-president-kiir-rebukes-the-jonglei-cow-emblem.html#gsc.tab=0, accessed 21 March 2014.

Reining, Conrad C. (1966) *The Zande Scheme: An Anthropological Case Study of Development in Africa*, Evanston, IL: Northwestern University Press.

Retel-Laurentin, Anne (1974) *Infécondité en Afrique noire: maladies et conséquences sociales*, Paris: Masson.

Reuters (2013a) 'Over 300 killed, thousands uprooted in bout of South Sudan fighting', by Andrew Green, 8 August, www.uk.reuters.com/article/2013/08/08/uk-southsudan-fighting-idUKBRE9770TF20130808, accessed 29 March 2014.

— (2013b) 'In landlocked South Sudan, one road is a lifeline – and a bottleneck', by Ulf Laessing, 30 August, www.reuters.com/article/2013/08/30/us-africa-investment-southsudan-idUSBRE97T0GT20130830, accessed 29 March 2014.

Rodney, Walter (1981) *How Europe Underdeveloped Africa*, Washington, DC: Howard University Press.

Rolandsen, Øystein H. (2005) *Guerilla Government: Political Changes in the Southern Sudan during the 1990s*, Uppsala: Nordiska Afrikainstitutet.

Rondinelli, Dennis A. (1981) 'Administrative decentralisation and economic development: the Sudan's experiment with devolution', *Journal of Modern African Studies*, 19(4).

Rowe, John A. and Kjell Hødnebø (1994) 'Rinderpest in the Sudan 1888–1890: the mystery of the missing panzootic', *Sudanic Africa*, 5.

Ruay, Deng D. Akol (1994) *The Politics of Two Sudans: The South and the North 1821–1969*, Uppsala: Nordiska Afrikainstitutet.

Sanderson, G. N. (1985) 'The ghost of Adam Smith: ideology, bureaucracy and the frustration of economic development in the Sudan, 1934–1940', in M. W. Daly (ed.), *Modernization in the Sudan: Essays in honor of Richard Hill*, New York: Lilian Barber.

Sanderson, L. and N. S. Sanderson (1981) *Education, Religion and Politics in Southern Sudan 1899–1964*, London: Ithaca Press.

Santandrea, Stefano (1964) *A Tribal History of the Western Bahr El Ghazal*, Bologna: Editrice Nigrizia.

— (1980) 'Ndogo ethonological texts (Sudan): with translation and commentary', *Anthropos*, 75.

Saul, John (1974) 'The state in post-colonial societies: Tanzania', in Ralph Miliband (ed.), *Socialist Register*, London: Humanity.

Schweinfurth, Georg (1874) *The Heart of Africa: Three years' travels* and adventures in the unexplored regions of Central Africa from 1868 to 1871, London: Sampson Low, Marston, Low and Searle.

Scott Villiers, Alistair and Acuil Malith Banggol (eds) (1991) An Investigation into Production Capability in the Rural Southern Sudan: A Report on Food Sources and Needs, Nairobi: United Nations Lifeline Sudan.

SDIT (Southern Development Investigation Team) (1955) Natural Resources and Development Potential in the Southern Provinces of the Sudan, London: Sudan Government.

Seekers of Truth and Justice (2004) The Black Book: Imbalance of Power and Wealth in Sudan, Anonymous publication often attributed to the Darfurian Justice and Equality Movement, English translation available at www.sudanjem.com/sudan-alt/english/books/black-book_part1/book_part1.asp.htm, accessed 25 September 2013.

Seligman, C. G. and B. Z. Seligman (1932) Pagan Tribes of the Nilotic Sudan, London: Routledge.

Seneca (1972) Natural Questions, Books IV–VII, trans. Thomas H. Corcoran, Cambridge, MA: Harvard University Press.

Serels, Steven (2012) 'Feasting on famines: food insecurity and the making of the Anglo-Egyptian Sudan, 1883–1956', Unpublished PhD thesis, McGill University, Montreal.

Sikainga, Ahmed A. (1996) Slaves into Workers: Emancipation and Labor in Colonial Sudan, Austin: University of Texas Press.

Skedsmo, Arild, Kwong Danhier and Hoth Gor Luak (2003) 'The changing meaning of small arms in Nuer society', African Security Review, 12(4).

Smith, Dean A. (1955) 'The Murle: report of a preliminary enquiry into reproduction rate', Unpublished typescript, Khartoum: Department of Physiology, Faculty of Medicine, University College.

Southall, Aidan (1970) 'The illusion of tribe', in Peter C. W. Gutwind (ed.), The Passing of Tribal Man in Africa, Leiden: Brill.

— (1975) 'Nuer and Dinka are people: ecology, ethnicity and logical possibility', Man, New Series, 11(4).

Spaulding, Jay (1982) 'Slavery, land tenure and social class in the northern Turkish Sudan', International Journal of African Historical Studies, 15(1).

— (1985) The Heroic Age in Sinnār, East Lansing: African Studies Center, Michigan State University.

Spencer, Paul (1998) 'Age systems and modes of predatory expansion', in Eisei Kurimoto and Simon Simonse, Conflict, Age and Power in North East Africa, Oxford: James Currey.

SPLM (Sudan People's Liberation Movement) (1983) Manifesto, no bibliographic information, available at Palace Green Library, Durham University, Durham, Medu* 17/3/PRE.

SSCCSE (Southern Sudan Centre for Census, Statistics and Evaluations) (2006) Southern Sudan Livelihoods Profile: A Guide for Humanitarian and Development Planning, Nairobi: SSCCSE and Save the Children UK.

— (2009) Statistical Yearbook for Southern Sudan, Juba.

— (2010) Statistical Yearbook for Southern Sudan, Juba.

SSCCSE and CBS (Central Bureau of Statistics) (2010) *Food and Nutrition Security Assessment in Sudan: Analysis of 2009 Baseline Household Survey*, Khartoum: Food Security Technical Secretariat of the Ministry of Agriculture.

SSHRC (South Sudan Human Rights Commission) (2014) *Interim Report on South Sudan Internal Conflict, December 15, 2013–March 15, 2014*, Juba.

Stiansen, Endre (1993) 'Overture to imperialism: European trade and economic change in the Sudan in the nineteenth century', Unpublished PhD thesis, University of Bergen, Bergen.

Sudan Government (1955a) *Report on the Administration of Sudan in 1950/51*, Khartoum.

— (1955b) *Report on the Administration of Sudan in 1951/52*, Khartoum.

Sudan Informazioni News Agency (serial) Milan.

Sudan Tribune (2012a) 'Jonglei peace deal may not stop violence', 4 May, www.sudantribune.com/spip.php?article42491, accessed 25 September 2013.

— (2012b) 'Pigi county commissioner resigns over community disturbances', 22 June, www.sudantribune.com/spip.php?iframe&page=imprimable&id_article=43013, accessed 27 February 2014.

Suret-Canale, Jean (1971) *French Colonialism in Tropical Africa, 1900–1945*, New York: Pica.

Swart, Morrell F. (1998) *The Call of Africa: The Reformed Church in America Mission in the Sub-Sahara, 1948–1998*, Grand Rapids, MI: Wm B. Eerdmans.

Takana, Yusuf (2008) 'The politics of regional boundaries and conflict in Sudan: the South Darfur case', Sudan Working Paper no. 2, Bergen: Chr. Michelsen Institute.

Thelwell, Robin (ed.) (1978) 'Aspects of language in the Sudan', Occasional Papers in Linguistics and Language Learning no. 5, Coleraine: New University of Ulster.

Think Progress (2014) 'PHOTOS: viewing the South Sudan crisis from space', by Hayes Brown, 15 January, www.thinkprogress.org/security/2014/01/15/3163821/photos-viewing-south-sudan-crisis-space/, accessed 23 May 2014.

Thomas, Edward (2010) *The Kafia Kingi Enclave: People, Politics and History in the North–South Boundary Zone of Western Sudan*, London: Rift Valley Institute.

Toledano, Ehud (1998) 'Social and economic change in the "long nineteenth century"', in M. W. Daly (ed.), *The Cambridge History of Egypt*, vol. 2, Cambridge: Cambridge University Press.

Tornay, Serge (1980) 'The Omo Murle enigma', in D. L. Donham and Wendy James (eds), *Working Papers in Society and History in Imperial Ethiopia: The Southern Periphery from the 1880s to 1974*, Cambridge: African Studies Centre.

Trenchard, Hugh (1929) 'The fuller employment of air power in imperial defence', AIR 2/1560 ROYAL AIR FORCE: General (Code B, 67/1), London: National Archives.

Tully, Dennis (1988) *Culture and Context in Sudan: The Process of Market Incorporation in Dar Masalit*, Albany: State University of New York Press.

Tvedt, Terje (1994) 'The collapse of the state in Southern Sudan after the Addis Ababa Agreement: a study of internal causes and the role of the NGOs', in Sharif Harir and Terje Tvedt (eds), *Short Cut to Decay: The case of Sudan*, Uppsala: Nordiska Afrikainstitutet.

— (2004) *The River Nile in the Age of the British: Political Ecology and the Quest for Economic Power*, London: I. B. Tauris.

UNEP (United Nations Environment Programme) (2007) *Sudan: Post Conflict Environmental Assessment*, Nairobi.

UNICEF (United Nations Children's Fund) (2013) *State of the World's Children Report: Children with Disabilities*, New York.

UNMISS (United Nations Mission in South Sudan) (2012) 'Incidents of inter-communal violence in Jonglei State', Juba.

— (2013) 'Report on the 8 February 2013 attack on Lou Nuer pastoralists in Akobo West Sub-County, Jonglei State', Juba.

— (2014) 'Interim report on human rights crisis in South Sudan, report coverage 15 December 2013 to 31 January 2014', Juba.

Wai, Dunstan (1981) *The African–Arab Conflict in the Sudan*, New York: Africana Publishing.

Wakoson, Elias Nyamlell (1984) 'The origin and development of the Anya-Nya Movement 1955–1972', in Mohamed Omer Beshir (ed.), *Southern Sudan: Regionalism and Religion*, London: Ithaca Press.

Walraet, Anne (2008) 'Governance, violence and the struggle for economic regulation in South Sudan: the case of Budi County (Eastern Equatoria)', *Afrika Focus*, 21(2).

Wawa, Yosa (2008) *Southern Sudanese Pursuits of Self-Determination*, Kisubi: Marianum Press.

Weitour, Gabriel Gai Riam (2008) *Christian–Muslim Relations in Sudan: A study of the relationship between church and state (1898– 2005)*, Khartoum: Azza House Publishers and Distributors.

WFP/FAO (World Food Programme/ Food and Agriculture Organization) (2014) 'South Sudan conflict reverses progress on food security', Joint press release, 7 March, www.wfp.org/news/news-release/ south-sudan-conflict-reverses-progress-food-security, accessed 28 March 2014.

White, Benjamin Thomas (2011) *The Emergence of Minorities in the Middle East: The Politics of Community in French Mandate Syria*, Edinburgh: Edinburgh University Press.

Willis, C. A. (1995) *The Upper Nile Province Handbook: A Report on Peoples and Government in Southern Sudan, 1931*, ed. Douglas H. Johnson, Oxford: British Academy.

World Bank (1987) *Sudan: Problems of Economic Adjustment*, vol. I, Report no. 6491-SU, Washington, DC: World Bank.

— (2003) *Sudan: Stabilization and Reconstruction, Country Economic Memorandum*, Report no. 24620-SU, vols 1 and 2, Washington, DC.

— (2007) *Sudan: Public Expenditure Review, Synthesis Report*, Report no. 41840-SD, Poverty Reduction and Economic Management Unit, Africa Region.

— (2009) *Sudan: The Road toward Sustainable and Broad-Based Growth*, Report no. 54718, Washington, DC.

— (2012) *Devolution without Disrup-*

tion: Pathways to a successful Kenya, Washington, DC.

— (2013) 'South Sudan overview', www.worldbank.org/en/country/southsudan/overview, accessed 30 July 2013.

Yongo-Bure, Benaiah (1989) 'Economic development of the Southern Sudan: an overview and a strategy', Bremen: University of Bremen Sudan Economy Research Group.

Young, John (2006) *The South Sudan Defence Forces in the Wake of the Juba Declaration*, Geneva: Small Arms Survey.

— (2007) *The White Army: An Intro-duction and Overview*, Geneva: Small Arms Survey.

Zeleza, Paul Tiyambe (1993) *A Modern Economic History of Africa*, vol. 1: *The Nineteenth Century*, Dakar: CODESRIA.

— (2002) 'The challenges of writing African economic history', in George Clement Bond and Nigel C. Gibson (eds), *Contested Terrains and Constructed Categories: Contemporary Africa in Focus*, Boulder, CO: Westview.

Zewde, Bahry (1987) 'An overview and assessment of Gambella trade (1904–1935)', *International Journal of African Historical Studies*, 20(1).

INDEX

abduction, xi, 1, 3–6, 27, 51, 203, 211, 220, 256, 272; and gender, 263–4, 273–6; and labour, *see* labour: and abduction; and language, 45; as a way of sending messages to enemies, 262; as coercive assimilation, 7; history of, 11–13, 71, 179; in 2009–11, 218–20

Addis Ababa agreement (1972), *see* peace agreements: Addis Ababa agreement

age sets, 224, 275–6; and churches, *see* churches: opposition to age sets; and labour, 272; and militias, 159, 180, 197, 202, 260; and SPLM, *see* SPLM: and age sets; as elder-led systems, 197; Dinka age sets, 205; Murle age sets, 159, 198–202, 228, 263, 272; Nuer age sets, 190, 194–9, 260–1; social functions of, 47

Aja (ethnic group), 52

Akobo (settlement, county), 72, 73, 98, 131–3, 135, 140, 150, 172, 174, 177, 179, 184, 185, 191, 193, 196, 203, 209, 210, 212, 214, 217–21, 229, 235, 247, 249, 251–4, 255, 256, 260–2, 281, 283; and Anuak, *see* Anuak/ Anywaa: and struggle for Akobo

Akol, Lam (politician), 186

alcohol: and prophetic preaching, 232–3; trade with Ethiopia, 75–6

Alier, Abel (politician), 92, 101, 102, 135, 137

Amum, Pagan (politician), 185–6

Anglo-Egyptian condominium, ix, 68–9, 84, 90, 106, 170, 265, *see also*

Britain: occupation of Egypt; and slavery, 56

Anuak/Anywaa (ethnic group), 3, 33, 42, 48, 49, 140, 151, 181, 185, 196–8, 208, 266–7; and abduction, 272; and first civil war, 78, 170, 171, 172; and struggle for Akobo, 131–2, 177, 178, 196; and weapons, 76, 78; identity, 51; relations with Murle people, 70–2, 74, 255

Anya-nya, 2, 178, 187, 190, 198, 230

Anya-nya (armed group), 87, 155–6, 172, 177, 178, 192; and administration, 176; and Murle people, 175, 178; and post allocation, 94–5, 184–5; and prophets, 172–3, 230; combat, 170; political aims, 108–19, 170; provisions, 112; weapons, 78

Anyang, Gabriel (protagonist), 1, 4–7, 9, 16, 17, 45

Anyidi (settlement), 71–2, 183, 184, 256

Arabic, 6, 18, 28, 103, 171, 191, 231; and churches, 46; and 'detribalization', 46; and projects for national identity, 11, 13, 86; and SPLA, 46–7; and urban migration, 45–7

Arabs, 108, 174, 183, 270; and Arab-ness as a basis for national identity, 13, 55, 79, 86, 107, 110; and 'settler colonialism', 108; and slavery, 18, 59, 80; and War Against Terror, 12; as 'national bourgeoisie', 109; 'Real Arabs', 31

armed forces of Sudan: and National Guard, 172–7, 182, 184; and torture, 171; attacks on local people's food supplies, 113; Bor mutiny 1983, 185, 187; colonial period (Sudan Defence Force), 77–8, 93, 116, 164; Early colonial period (Egyptian army), 68, 77, 265; Joint Integrated Units, 217; post-colonial (Sudanese [People's] Armed Forces), 110, 111, 113, 129, 153, 170, 179, 190, 198, 203, 204, 284; southern command and integration of Anya-nya, 177, 183–4

Athor, George (general and rebel), 137, 165, 215–17

Atuot (ethnic group), 41

austerity, 133, 139, 280, 289; and British rule, 91; and fostering instability, 133; and Islamism, 24

Ayod (settlement), 191, 209, 215, 220, 233, 260

Bahr al-Ghazal: province/region, viii, ix, 40, 42, 44, 50, 67, 70, 90, 98, 137, 157, 204, 205, 206, 222, 252, 267; Western Bahr al-Ghazal district/state, 39, 44, 48, 266

Bahr al-Jebel (river), 5, 34, 36, 42, 73, 75, 140, 184, 192, 284

Bahr al-Zeraf (river), 75, 140, 172, 209, 215, 260

banks: Islamic banks and Gulf capital, 107

Bany, William Nyoun (SPLA commander), 183, 205

Bari (ethnic group), 40, 65

Belgian colonialism, ix, 84, 90

Benjamin, Walter, 109, 125

Bin Laden, Osama, 179

Blue Nile (state), 15, 18, 48, 57, 63, 77, 170, 189

Boma (plateau and settlement), 36, 37, 181, 185, 186, 187, 199, 200, 256, 270

Bong, Ngundeng (prophet), 72, 73, 260

Bor (town, county and Dinka area to the east of Bahr al-Jebel), 4, 6, 7, 10, 11, 13, 71, 102, 135, 140, 150, 159, 168, 173, 198, 236, 237, 243, 245,

246, 249, 251, 267, 269, 274, 292; 1983 mutiny, 178, 182, 185; 1991 attack on, 8, 9, 161, 190, 191–2, 193, 194, 202, 203, 205, 210, 213, 225, 231, 285, 286; attacks on Bor after 2007, 212, 217–22, 257, 272, 281, 283, 284; Bor's market economy, 251, 252, 256, 257, 259; diaspora, and return, 148, 152, 153, 204, 211; links with Murle areas, 71, 72, 183, 184, 185, 186, 188, 222, 256

borders/boundaries, administrative: and ethnicity, 44, 59, 92, 96, 98, 99, 127, 130–8, 151, 158, 160, 162, 164, 179, 185, 214, 215, 263

bridewealth, 36, 275, 276; economics of, 148–9, 151, 226, 249, 251, 252, 253, 261; monetization of, 148, 250; of peace, 16; social functions of, 8, 48, 57, 200, 273

Brigade (also called Pibor Defence Force) 182, 187, 198, 199, 201, 202, 205, 207, 211, 256, 275

Britain, 74, 97, 286; free trade agreements, 61–2, 66, 67; occupation of Egypt, 61, 68

British colonial officials, 71, 77; and Adam Smith, 23; and slavery, 69

British colonialism, 1, 95, 97, 106, 109, 112, 116, 156, 169, 183, 193; early administration and violence, 71, 74–7, 84, 91, 108, 177, 182; reluctance about Southern development, 84, 85, 86; revenues from, 90

Budgets, see finances, Sudanese public

bunam (youth groups), 196–9, 227, 234, 260

Burun (ethnic group), 77

cattle, 5, 6, 8, 16, 28, 34, 36, 57, 137, 148, 149, 173, 181, 195, 196, 200, 209, 210, 238, 241, 244, 252, 255, 256, 257, 275; and bridewealth, see bridewealth; and early exchange,

65, 76; and labour, *see* labour: and
cattle economy; and raiding, 1, 9,
10, 27, 30, 58, 59, 72, 166, 179, 182,
183, 184, 186, 189–94, 201, 203,
206, 208, 212–15, 218, 220, 222,
224–7, 233–4, 237–9, 243–59, 261,
262, 272, 274, 276, 281, 285; blood
cattle, 96–7; cattle diseases, 73,
131, 184; herd sizes and dynamics,
245–9; markets, 80, 211, 226,
246–8, 254; ownership of, 148,
249–51, 254
Central African Republic, 269, 270
Chaung, Gier (politician), 137–8
chiefs, *see* traditional authorities,
neo-traditional authorities, chiefs
China, 25, 85, *see also* East Asia
Choul, Abdalla (Anya-nya 2 leader),
198
Choul, Abel (Anya-nya administrator),
176
Choul, Gordon Kong (militia leader),
208
Christians/Christianity, 29, 46, 57, 127,
149, 231
churches, 46, 150, 232; as places to get
education, 7; opposition to age
sets, 195, 201
class, 20, 25–7, 85, 86, 114, 117, 118, 122,
125, 155, 235, 252, *see also* elites,
government posts
closed districts (1930), ix, 23, 24, 84,
85, 90, 106–8, 170
Committee for the Redivision of
Southern Provinces (1974), 98,
130–1
Comprehensive Peace Agreement
(2005) *see* peace agreements:
Comprehensive Peace Agreement
Comyn, D. C. E. ff. (colonial official),
72
Congo, 41, 83, 176, *see also* Zaire

Dar es Salaam school, 25, 114, 116, 117,
119, *see also* dependency theory
Darfur, ix, 15, 67, 68, 88, 101, 119, 121,

128, 164, 169, 170, 292; pre-colonial
state, 48
debt, 20, 24, 91, 249, 258, 289;
compound interest and slavery,
66, 106; creation of debt zone, 18,
57, 64, 79, 96, 107, 234; debt crisis
of 1970s and 1980s, 88, 100, 103,
123, 132, 179; used to subordinate
Egypt, 61, 66
Deng Garang, Gaaluak (politician),
207, 231
dependency and dependency theory,
22, 67, 85, 104, 105; definition
and critique of theory, 25–7,
113–25; John Garang's ambivalence
towards theory, 115
development: and austerity, 133; and
clientelism, 139, 144; and ethnicity,
146, 160; and future, 208; and
liberation movements, 106–24, 157,
275; and pessimism, 82, 84; and
the developmental state, 130; and
violence, 54–6, 236; construction
of underdevelopment, 60–7;
development indicators in Khor
Fulluth/Pigi, 137; history of
development policies, 49, 50,
82–105, 128, 171, 176; theories of
development, 21–30; uneven 10,
16, 17, 18, 20, 30, 38, 52, 54, 55,
58, 59, 70, 75–8, 79, 80, 115, 145,
146, 160, 223, 238, 239, 251–8, 287;
unipolar Sudanese model, 180
Dhal, Abraham Matoc (scholar), 105
diaspora, 1, 3, 252, 253, 256; and urban
politics, 127, 147–59
Didinga (ethnic group), 40, 44, 181,
266, 267
Dinka (ethnic group), 3, 4, 5, 8, 9, 13, 29,
41, 42, 74, 80, 88, 96, 97, 140, 157,
176, 188, 198, 211, 213, 217, 219, 221,
229, 248, 258, 262, 281, 283–7; Agar,
157, 206; and 1991 attack on Bor,
10, 150, 161, 187, 192–3, 202–3, 225,
285–7; and abduction/assimilation,
13, 36, 42, 272–3; and age sets, 195;

and bridewealth, 201, 250; and militias, 205–6, 222; Apuk, 97; Bor, 71, 72, 135, 152, 180, 183, 192, 206, 213, 285, 287; Chiech, 206; Dinka plurality in South Sudan, 101–2, 129; Ghol, 152, 192, 209, 215; lack of unified identity, 192, 288; Luaic, 137, 153, 206; Nyaraweng, 152, 192, 209; relations with Luo and Shilluk people, 41, 62, 99, 135–8; relations with Murle people, 70–2, 133, 172, 182–3, 187, 202, 204, 221, 229, 235, 255; relations with Nuer people, 36, 42, 51, 74, 132, 190, 192, 204, 208–9, 221, 231, 258; Rut, 137, 152; Ruweng, 137, 152; songs, 285; Thoi, 137, 152; traditional food economy, 33; Twic, 152, 192, 205, 213, 215, 219–21, 272, 281, 286

disarmament: attempt to disarm Bor garrison in 1983, 183; civilian disarmament in 1970s, 183; disarmament of Anya-nya, 177; in Jonglei after 2005, 11, 14, 15, 37, 206–10, 211–13, 230, 281–3, 285

displacement and returns, *see* migration: displacement and returns

Duk (county), 150, 152, 173, 188, 192, 205, 209, 213, 217–21, 272, 281

Duk Padiet (settlement), 192, 218

Dukey (militia), 205

East Asia: economic relations, 2, 27, 180, 290

economic history, 18, 32; and ecology, 34–7

economic theory: and idealization of history, 22–4, 54, 63, 79, 114, 120; and modernization, 24; neo-classical theory and violence, 24, 25

education, 28, 52, 154, 196; and diaspora, 150, 208, 252, 258; and government employment, 93, 94, 175; and promotion of

Arabic national identity, 86, 107, 171; and rebellion, 175, 188; Bor College High, 147–9; John Garang Memorial University, 148; regional and ethnic differences in educational participation, 7, 10, 11, 50, 115, 172

Egypt, ix, 18, 37, 56, 57, 77, 79, 84, 97, 106, 146; economic history of, 61–8, 118

Egyptian nationalism, 94; Army, 61, 63–5, 67, 164

elections, 103, 165, 282; 1953 elections, 93, 94; 1978 elections, 99; 2010 elections, 162–3, 214–16, 218, 220–1

elites, 111, 180, 207; bureaucratic and commercial elites of Khartoum, 87; military-bureaucratic elites, 116, 118; South Sudanese elite relations with other groups, 158, 225, 238; South Sudanese elite reticence, 124; South Sudanese elites and war, 9, 118; South Sudanese state elites, 93, 103, 105, 110, 111–12, 119, 123, 126; Sudanese elites and inequality, 18, 80; Zande elites and labour, 48, 49

Emin Pasha (Turkiya official), 85, 90

Engels, Friedrich, 116–17

Equatoria, viii, ix, 23, 34, 36, 39, 40, 46, 50, 66, 70, 78, 85, 90, 98, 99, 101, 105, 108, 152, 170, 181, 204, 216, 247, 252, 255, 257, 266, 267, 275

Ethiopia, ix, 34, 41–4, 51, 70–3, 75–8, 83, 84, 191, 193, 198, 206, 208, 216, 231, 247, 258, 265, 278, 281; and SPLM/A, 111–13, 185–7, 189; clientelism, 144; land tenure and revolutionary possibility, 113; socialist-military, regime, 9, 120, 179; tax system, 90, 92; trade with South Sudan, 289, 290

ethnicity, 30, 33–52, 61, 74, 77, 96, 98–105, 212, 278; and Anya-nya theories of liberation, 114; and borders, *see* borders/boundaries, administrative; and conflict, 84, 99, 123, 150, 218; and fertility, *see* fertility and infertility, human: and ethnicity; and gender, *see* gender: and ethnicity; and language, migration, see language: and migration, ethnicity; and livestock economy, 244, 251; and manipulation of ethnic publics, 127, 128, 238–9; and militias, *see* militias: and ethnicity; and payroll, *see* payroll; and posts, *see* government posts; and state relations with rural people, 19, 22, 104, 127, 167, 234; and statistics, 28; and towns, *see* towns: urban ethnic associations; definition used, 19, 33; difficulty of correlating with fertility, 4; ethnic competition for state posts, 129, 144; ethnicity-first explanations, 3, 17, 194; may conceal social difference, 7, 20, 25; military mobilization around, 9, 182; pre-colonial experiences of ethnicity, 59; regional differences amount to ethnic differences, 10, 20, 98, 146

famine: in Bor, 1990, 4, 285; in Sudan, nineteenth century, 69, 91
Fangak (settlement), 137, 220
Fashoda (settlement), viii, 48, 90
fertility and infertility, human: and abduction, 4, 263–4, 276; and ethnicity, 4, 268–72; and men, 275; histories of, 264–73; Nyandit cult of, 72
feuds, 190, 214–15, 224
finance, global systems: and the end of modernization, 100; Egypt and, 61ff; financialization of slave raiding, 18, 65–7, 75, 82, 90, 106; incorporation of South Sudan, 57; international credit markets and development, 24, 26, 91
finances, Sudanese public, 105; and

crises, 133; and SPLA, 164–5, 280; budgets, 10, 20, 21, 28, 82–5, 87, 236; budgets after 2006, 83, 128, 138, 140–4; budgets and ethnicity, 130; colonial, budgets, 89–93; failure to finance or execute budgets, 95, 100; local budgets, 127, 139, 252; oil, *see* oil: and exports, and peripheral investment, as rent, twentieth-century budgets
financial crises: 1929, 91; 1970s and 1980s, 24, 99, 100, 102
firearms, guns, rifles, weapons, 5, 6, 9, 11, 14, 57, 62, 75, 76, 77, 78, 96, 165, 171, 172, 174, 178, 179, 183, 186, 187, 189, 199, 201, 204, 206, 207, 209, 212, 217, 224, 228; as adjuncts to production, 27, 166, 194, 237, 244, 259; as vectors of modernization, 75
flood plain, 33, 34, 36, 38, 39, 41, 42, 43, 47, 50, 58, 70, 73, 75, 76, 80, 86, 115, 178, 184, 190
Food and Agriculture Organization, 245
food and food economy, 8, 9, 30, 36, 44, 69, 112, 242, 291–2; and famines, *see* famine; and humanitarian/relief supplies, 8, 112, 121–3, 154, 223, 231, 239, 241, 242, 244, 258, 259, 276, 279; and markets, *see* markets and market penetration: food markets; and provisioning of soldiers, 112, 113, 157, 176; cuisines and food commodification, 126; hunger and plenty, 44, 160, 188, 244, 246, 247, 258; incorporation of Jonglei food economy into money system, 8–9, 11, 123, 223, 243–59, 292; nutrition studies, 244
French colonialism, ix, 61, 84, 90, 108, 269, 270
French Revolution, 56

Ga'le, Severino Fuli Boke Tombe (official), 155–6

Gaarkek, Wutnyang (prophet), 191, 230–1, 258, 260, 285

Gai Tut, Samuel (Anya-nya 2 commander), 173

Gambella (town), 208, 216, 231

Garang, John (politician), 9, 10, 114, 115, 117, 118, 119, 120, 121, 122, 123, 124, 149, 157, 161, 162, 164, 186, 187, 188, 190, 191, 192, 205, 215, 256, 280, 282–3

Garang, Joseph Ukel (politician), 108, 109, 113–14

Gatdet, Peter (general and militia commander), 281, 283, 285

Gatwich, Simon (militia commander), 209

Gayein, Kennedy (SPLA commander and politician), 187, 202

gender, 27, 30, 36, 52, 153, 242, 259, 263–74; and ethnicity, 263; linguistic gender, 41

Gessi, Romolo (Turkiya official), 90

Goldscheid, Rudolf, 141

Gondokoro, 60, 64, 65

government posts, 6, 7, 10, 11, 16, 20, 21, 30, 46, 70, 83, 87, 93–4, 99, 101–5, 115–16, 129, 130, 131, 138, 139, 140, 142, 144, 148, 158, 160, 162, 167, 169, 171, 175, 213, 215, 223, 237, 252, 253, 259, 282, 290

government revenues, 89, 90

governments, 100; Southern Regional Government (1973), ix, 21, 87, 93–105, 110, 121, 128, 135, 136, 185, 270; Coordinating Council in Southern Sudan (1997), x, 132; Government of Southern Sudan (2005), x, 2, 52, 89, 127, 133; Government of National Unity (2005), 2

gross domestic product, 25, 82, 83, 132, 280, 289, 290; and gross national income, 82, 83, 289, 290

haras al-watani, Al-, see armed forces of Sudan: and National Guard

Ibrahim, Su'ad (politician), 120

Industrial Revolution, 56

infertility, *see* fertility and infertility, human

Ironstone plateau, 34–8, 58

Islam, 95, 170, 172; and abolitionism, 66; and law, 57, 64; and legitimation of slavery, 18, 57, 59, 75; and money, 95; and projects for national identity, 11, 86, 170, 171

Islamic banks, 107

Islamism/Islamists, 1, 24, 25, 100, 109, 179, 180

Jakor (chief), 176

Jalle (*payam* in Bor county), 8, 147

Jieh (ethnic group), 181, 217

John Garang Memorial University, *see* education: John Garang Memorial University

Joint Integrated Units, *see* armed forces of Sudan: Joint Integrated Units

Juba (town), ix, 2, 10, 11, 13, 14, 15, 20, 30, 37, 46, 47, 60, 62, 83, 89, 103, 110, 127, 128, 129, 130, 133, 137, 138, 141–5, 146, 153, 155, 157, 158, 159, 163, 169, 183, 204, 207, 208, 209, 210, 215, 216, 246, 252, 257, 259, 261, 272, 279, 280, 282, 283, 287, 288, 289, 290, 291, 292

Juba Declaration (2006), 46, 163, 207, 209, 211, 282, 287

Kachippo (ethnic group), 153, 181

Kathish, Hatashil Masha (missionary and writer), 29, 80

Kelai, Deng (militia leader), 205, 213

Kenya, 10, 41, 43, 83, 92, 106, 111, 147, 149, 152, 245, 281, 289, 290

Khartoum Peace Agreement (1997), *see* peace agreements: Khartoum Peace Agreement

Khor Fulluth/Pigi (county), 137–8, 164, 180, 215

Kidepo valley, 181

Kiir (hero of Jikainy origin stories), 42
Kiir Mayardit, Salva (president), 3, 10,
    14, 15, 53, 157, 162, 186, 187, 248,
    263, 280, 282, 283, 285, 291
Kireru, John (intellectual), 171
Kon, Peter Bol (SPLA commander),
    210
Kony, Ismail (militia leader and
    politician), 140, 187, 198–205,
    211–12, 222, 223, 228, 256, 257, 275
Kordofan and Nuba Mountains, ix, 15,
    18, 63, 79, 88, 113–14, 121, 128, 170,
    189; land and mechanized farming,
    113
Kueth, Dak (prophet), 227, 231–3, 260
Kuic, Ruei (prophet), 172

labour, 96, 106, 118; and abduction,
    256, 272; and bridewealth, 36,
    57; and cattle economy, 5, 200,
    249–53, 256; and identification
    with tribes, 96; and international
    economy, 26, 85; and lineage, 251;
    forced, 11, 48, 49, 56, 57, 60, 61,
    63, 91, 95, 96, 99, 112, 243, see also
    slavery; reservoirs of, 106, 108, 122;
    self-organization of labour, 114;
    waged labour and labour markets,
    20, 91, 107, 152, 157, 247, 258
Lado, Lokurnyang (South Sudan
    Liberation Movement leader) 185
Lado enclave, ix
Lagu, Joseph (politician), 101, 102
land, 19, 20, 44, 59, 61, 64–6, 68, see
    also Ethiopia: land tenure and
    revolutionary possibility and
    Kordofan and Nuba Mountains:
    land and mechanized farming; and
    revolutionary possibility, 112–15,
    118; and subterranean resources,
    140; kinship and access to, 96,
    134, 242; land registration and
    disputes, 133, 135, 151, 238; raiders
    do not settle, 237; state's inability
    to refashion land tenure, 107
language, 6, 7, 11, 13, 19, 31, 33, 34,
    39, 40, 41, 47, 50, 51, 52, 59, 71,
    72, 75, 101, 123, 126, 127, 129, 149,
    164, 171, 180, 181, 196, 237, 263,
    266, 267, 270; and exogamy, 44–5;
    and migration, ethnicity, 39–47;
    multilingualism and development,
    84
Leer (settlement), 205
Likongwele (settlement), 152, 218, 234,
    271, 273
Lokurungole, Lado (translator), 185
Longarim/Boya (ethnic group), 44, 181
Lost Boys, 147, 149, 150, 152, 191
Luo (ethno-linguistic group), 39–41,
    44, 45, 48, 131, see also Shilluk and
    Anuak/Anywaa (ethnic group)

Machar, Riek (politician), 9, 10, 126,
    132, 139, 141, 147, 161, 162, 190, 191,
    193, 195, 197, 203–5, 208, 213, 222,
    225, 230, 262, 282–6, 291
Madi (ethnic group), 40, 155–6
Mahdi, Muhammad Ahmad Al-
    (religious leader), 56, 68, 106
Mahdiya (1885), viii, ix, 91, 106; and
    slavery, South Sudan, 56, 91;
    history, 67–9; theory of liberation,
    21, 22, 106
Majangir (ethnic group), 71
Malakal (town), 132, 135, 136, 152, 171,
    204, 208, 217, 243, 246, 247, 267,
    283
malnutrition, see food and food
    economy
Manyong, Gai (prophet), 260
markets, and market penetration,
    6, 7, 10, 11, 29, 37, 46, 49, 57, 62,
    64, 69, 70, 80, 178, 234, 241, 263;
    access and conflict, 206, 213,
    217, 218, 226, 227–8, 234, 237,
    243–59, 284; and cattle, see cattle:
    markets; and creation of social
    and spatial difference, 29, 223;
    evasion, 6, 50, 70, 241; export
    markets, see oil: and exports, and
    peripheral investment, as rents;

food markets, 8, 9, 91, 242, 243–59, 292; global markets, 20, 24, 25, 38, 60, 61, 75, 264, 279, 280, *see also* finance, global systems; idealized markets, 23, 54; in labour, 27; in land, 64

marriage, 5, 8, 11, 49, 57, 173, 192, 200, 201, 226, 228, 229, 247, 250, 251, 253, 258, 273, 275, 276; and bridewealth, *see* bridewealth; and childlessness/sonlessness, 27, 273–4, 276, 277; bachelors, 275; polygyny, 200, 275–6; widowhood, 5, 200, 273, 276–7; woman–woman marriage, 273–4

Marx, Karl, 116

Marxism/Marxists, 22, 25, 27, 108, 114, 116–17, 120, 238; theory of liberation, 22

Medair (NGO), 271, 273

Mehmed Ali (viceroy of Egypt), 61, 63–5

migration, 33, 39, 41–7, 70, 145; and language, 39; displacement and returns, 5, 10, 41, 45, 46, 65, 68–9, 113, 131, 145, 148, 149, 150–5, 182, 190, 196, 200, 204, 206, 212, 213, 216, 221, 222, 237, 241, 242, 244, 252, 276, 281, 285, 286; refugees, 10, 53, 62, 65, 103, 104, 112, 147, 149, 152, 184, 202, 213, 241

militias, 9, 10, 17, 163, 190, 192, 194, 195, 202–9, 224, 284, *see also* South Sudan Defence Forces; aligned with Khartoum government, 9, 14, 134, 137, 163, 164, 165, 179, 182, 184, 195; and age set, *see* age set; and cattle economy, 250; and colonial periods, 30, 65, 77, 78; and Dinka people, *see* Dinka: and militias; and ethnicity, 30, 160, 161, 167–8, 172–7, 190, 198, 241, 283; and prophets, *see* prophets, and prophecy: and militias; and traditional authorities, 19; Arabic-speaking pastoralists and, 11;

incorporation into SPLA, 46, 164, 182, 212, 234, 237; Other Armed Groups, 163, 180, 207

minorities: and representative government, 95–102, 264, 288; construction of, 13, 14, 21, 95–102; 'minority clique', 115, 119; scapegoating, 13, 288

modernization, 24, 100, 115, 120, 179; weapons as vector of, 75

money and monetization, 70, 91, 148, 150, 162, 179; and mainstream economics, 22, 23, 54; and slavery, 62; and spread of taxes, 79; and towns, 107, 144–6; coercion as an alternative incentive to, 64, 65; difficulty of monetizing South Sudanese economy, 64, 106; living without money, 56–7, 244, 247, 255, 271; miracle of, 5–7; monetization and periphery, 7, 16, 18, 20, 22, 23, 27, 57, 91, 92, 95, 96; monetizing bridewealth, *see* bridewealth

monopoly: British monopoly system in Ethiopia, 76; Egypt's monopoly system and slavery, 18, 60–4, 65, 66, 106; Mahdist monopoly in South, 68; Shilluk monopoly system, 62

Murle, 50, 140, 153, 169–77, 180–5; abduction and infertility allegations, 3–7, 12, 14–15, 260–77; age sets, 199; and Ethiopian slave trade, 75; and SPLM/A, 186, 187; assimilation, 71; bridewealth and diaspora, 151; conflict after 2007, 211–35; disarmament, *see* disarmament; diverse livelihoods, 6, 34, 36–7; ecological isolation, 8, 202; language, 40–4; markets, *see* markets: access and conflict, evasion; migration, 44–5, 70–1; militias, *see* militias: aligned with Khartoum government, incorporation into SPLA; raiding, *see* raids and raiders; relations with Dinka and Nuer people, 71–4, 135, 172, 183, 185, 193, 202–5; situation after 2012, 281, 287, 288; societal resistance and modernity, 202

Nanaam (river), 5, 6, 36, 222–3
Nasir (town), 126, 156, 169, 203, 206, 207, 208, 218, 225, 233, 247, 248, 249
National Congress Party, 1, 163, 204, 215
National Guard, *see* armed forces of Sudan
national memory, 284–8
nationalism, Sudanese, 84, 95, 124
Negritude, 108, 114
neo-traditional authority, *see* traditional authorities, neo-traditional authorities, chiefs
Ngachaluk, Ngachigak (SPLA commander), 185
Ngachingol, Hassan (administrator), 167, 169–77, 182, 183, 231, 256, 264
Ngalam (agrarian Murle people), 6, 37
Nganley (protagonist), 5
Nimeiri, Jaafer (president), 100, 109, 136, 178–9
Northern Nile valley, 17, 22, 59, 64, 65, 69, 79, 87, 91, 107, 109
Nuba mountains, *see* Kordofan and Nuba Mountains
Nuer, 33, 36, 88, 126, 133, 140, 178, 180, 187, 190, 291; age sets, *see* age sets: Nuer age sets; and abduction, 12–14, 267–71; and gender and raiding, 260–3; and migration, 42–4, 70, 131; and militias, *see* militias: aligned with Khartoum government, incorporation into SPLA; and National Guard, *see* armed forces of Sudan: and national guard; and pacification, *see* pacification/subjugation; Bor attack, *see* Bor: 1991 attack on;

conflict after 2007, 211–37; crisis of 2013–14, 281–8; diaspora and education, 151–60; disarmament, *see* disarmament; Dok, 190, 205; Eastern Jikainy (Gaajak), 42, 77, 126, 130, 131, 134, 156, 157, 191, 193, 195, 202, 207, 208, 218, 233, 247, 261; Gaawar, 152, 172, 191, 192, 198, 209, 215, 231, 233; identity, 51–4; Lak, 152, 191; language, 39–41, 72; Lou (Gun, Mor), 73, 131, 133, 140, 151–3, 158, 173, 180, 191–3, 195, 198, 202–5, 207–10, 239, 247, 253, 255, 260, 262, 281; Nuer civil war, 192–4; prophets, *see* prophets and prophecy; raids after 2007, 3, 5, 8, 9, 10, 11, 12; refugees in Pibor, 202; relations with Anuak, *see* Anuak/Anywaa: and struggle for Akobo; relations with Dinka, and Murle people, 70–4, 132, 135, 196, 203, 204; Thiang, 152; transformations in cattle economy, 245, 247–9, 250, 253–4, 256, 258; White Army, *see* bunam and youth groups, armed: White Army
nutrition, *see* food and food economy
Nyandit (settlement and fertility cult), 72, 218
Nyikang (Shilluk culture-hero), 41
Nyingore, Paul (Anya-nya leader), 171
Nyirol (county), 133, 191, 209, 210, 217, 219–21, 247, 248

oil, 2, 10, 11, 15, 16, 21, 25, 82, 83, 128, 133, 139, 140; 2012 production shutdown, 89, 143, 208, 279–82, 289; and elites, 121; and exports, 180; and peripheral investment, 141; and separatism, 92, 136; and war, 161, 179; as rent, 87–9, 138, 145, 146, 161, 290, 291
Okiech, Edward Amum (chief), 172
Omo valley, 43
Operation Lifeline Sudan, 121
Organization of African Unity, 108, 111

Other Armed Groups, *see* militias: Other Armed Groups
Ottoman Empire, sultan, ix, 57, 61, 63, 64, 67
Ottoman-Egyptian Sudan, *see* Turkiya

pacification/subjugation, 54, 75–8, 84, 91, 167, 177, 182, 265
payroll, 83, 99, 105, 128, 129, 139, 141, 143, 144, 145, 160, 163, 164, 168, 234, 252, 282, 291
peace agreements: Addis Ababa agreement (1972), 87, 92, 94, 99, 100, 102, 105, 109, 110, 155, 177, 178, 183, 185; Comprehensive Peace Agreement (2005), x, 1, 2, 11, 15, 16, 30, 82, 93, 126ff, 141, 152, 162, 206–10, 211ff, 213, 217, 228, 252, 255, 257, 283; Khartoum Peace Agreement (1997), x, 161, 204, 207
periphery, 7, 9, 11, 15, 30, 35, 37, 38, 53, 86, 92, 105, 126, 128, 129, 141, 143, 170, 180, 190, 216, 238, 239, 261, 285, 288, 291; and elections, 215; and the future, 291–2; as transmission zone for debts and crises, 66, 88, 100, 139; centre allies with periphery, 87; ethnicity and peripheral governance, 128, 132–4, 141; periphery defeats the centre, 67–9; raid and neglect as peripheral governance, 18, 20, 57, 78, 79, 80, 81, 95; theories of change and peripheries, 22–7, 55, 106–24; urban ethnic associations and periphery, 147, 156, 158, 163
Petherick, John, 74
Pibor (county, river) 1, 2, 3, 4, 6, 14, 36, 37, 42, 70, 71, 72, 135, 140, 152, 153, 152, 159, 167–77, 180–4, 185, 187, 199–204, 207, 211, 212, 217–23, 230, 231, 234, 246, 252, 254–7, 261, 262, 266–75, 281, 283; Greater Pibor Administrative Area, 291
Pibor Defence Force, *see* Brigade
Pieri (settlement), 173, 232, 233

Pochalla (settlement), 78, 132, 140, 170, 171, 172, 176, 178, 180, 182, 185, 198, 219–21, 266, 269
political charter (1996), 204
polygyny, *see* marriage: polygyny
primordialism, 50–2
Property, 9, 189, 197, 206, 286; institutionalization of private property, 25, 54, 116–18; private property and land, 64
prophets and prophecy, 68, 72, 73, 80, 104, 172, 191, 226, 227, 236, 237, 250, 258, 260, 285; and militias, 230–4

Qaeda, Al-, 179

race and racial oppression, 16, 17, 22, 30, 79, 84, 92, 95, 104, 107, 108, 115, 117, 118; and language, 41; Anya-nya and, 108, 123; construction of, 31, 41, 45, 56–60; definition, 19
radio, 214, 248, 255
raids and raiders: and abduction, *see* abduction; and armed youth groups, *see* youth groups, armed; and cattle, *see* cattle: and raiding; and commercialization, 257; and creation of periphery, 18, 276; and gender and generational difference, 201, 273–6; and slavery, *see* slavery: slave raiding; and spread of commodities, 227; as rehearsal for 2013 civil war, 288; early twentieth-century raids, 71–2, 77–8, 182, 197; pre-colonial raids, 42, 48, 91; raiding economy, 11, 28, 144, 191, 199, 201, 208, 243–59, 281, 284; raids and civil war, 179, 183–7, 192–4, 203–6, 285; raids and raiding after 2007, 3, 4, 7, 12, 27, 30, 37, 135, 158, 211–37, 261–4, 281, 287
reconciliation: between opposing SPLA factions after 1991, 162, 179; during 2013 civil war, 291; in Jonglei after 2005, 16, 237, 254,

286–7; national reconciliation after 2005, 164, 165

Red Army, 149, 191, 198

Red chiefs, *see* traditional authorities, neo-traditional authorities, chiefs

Red Sea, 79

referendum on self-determination (2011), x, 2, 52, 55, 152, 154, 216

refugees, *see* migration: refugees

roads: as vectors of government authority and development, 10, 18, 37, 38, 50, 58, 66, 70, 72, 86, 141, 146, 221, 252, 257, 289; clearance as a means to create traditional authority, 99

Rumbek (town in Lakes state), 37, 41, 48, 63

salaries, *see* government posts

scarification, 192, 195, 260

Selim (navigator), 37

sheep and goats (livestock), 245, 248, 250

Shilluk, viii, ix, 157, 185, 275; and slavery, 62–5; conflicts with other groups, 99, 135–8; grain exports, 69, 91; language, 40, 45; migration, 41, 48; National Guard, 172; pre-colonial state, viii, 48, 56, 62

single-party systems, 147, 159, 161, 162, 163

Sinnar sultanate, ix, 48, 57, 60, 62, 64

slavery: abolition, ix, 56, 66–8, 90; and abduction, *see* abduction: history of; and administration of periphery, 79, 90, 95; and labour, 56, 57, 60–1, 63–5, 68, 69, 79, 91; and revolutionary theory, 109; and urbanization, 58; financialization of slave trade, *see* finance, global systems: financialization of slave trading; in Jonglei, 72–6; pre-colonial, *see* Darfur *and* Shilluk: pre-colonial state, Sinnar sultanate, Zande: pre-colonial state; race, religion and

ideology of, 18, 56–9, 70, 95, 103; slave armies, 67, 78, 96, 177; slave narratives, 29, 80; slave raiding, ix, 18, 22, 56–9, 62–8, 70–4, 77, 78, 145, 146; slave trade, 11, 31, 37, 38, 42, 46, 52, 57, 60, 64, 69, 84, 106, 108, 123, 278

Smith, Adam (economic theorist), 23

Sobat (river), 5, 34, 36, 42, 73, 76, 77, 91, 126, 131, 136, 137, 169, 191, 193, 214, 218, 281

South Africa, 106, 119

South America, 120

South Sudan Defence Forces, 207

South Sudan Democratic Movement/ Cobra Faction, 291

South Sudan Human Rights Commission, 282

South Sudan Liberation Movement or Front, 185

Southern Policy (1930), 45, 46, 86, 92

Southern Regional Government (1973), *see* government: Southern Regional Government)

SPLM/A, Sudan People's Liberation Movement/Army, 2, 11, 13, 51, 83, 209, 255, 288; 1983 manifesto, 105, 110–24, 141, 238; 1991 split, 9, 121, 149, 150, 189, 190, 286–7; 1994 convention, 122–4; 2013 split in SPLA, 47, 282, 283, 289; 2013 split in SPLM, 282–4; and 1983 civil war, 178–210; and age sets, 159, 201, 202; and ethnicity, 129, 134, 159, 161, 163–6, 186, 279; and Nuba areas, 114; and Red Army, *see* Red Army; and self-determination, 123; and social transformation, 7, 10, 112, 114, 121–2, 147, 241, 252, 256, 257, 261; formation, 110, 185–6; SPLA after 2006, 14, 46, 167, 211–37, 281; SPLA slogans, 189; SPLM in government (see elections), 2, 127–8, 279, 280

state: and ethnicity, *see* ethnicity: and state relations with rural people

and ethnic competition for state posts; dependence/autonomy of, 21, 88, 89, 92, 93, 103, 113, 121, 123, 145, 291; governments, *see* governments; patronage and clientelism, 88, 94, 105, 121, 138, 139, 140, 144, 164, 204, 236, 278, 280; pre-colonial states, viii, ix, 48, 56–7, 62–4, *see also* Darfur *and* Shilluk: pre-colonial state, Sinnar
stateless societies, 47–50, 54
subjugation, *see* pacification/ subjugation
subventions, *see* transfers to states
Sudan African National Union, 108
Sudanese Armed Forces, *see* armed forces of Sudan
Sudanese Communist Party, 108, 109, 119, 120; and Maoism, 113; and South Sudan, racism, 22
Sudanization commissions, 93, 97, 116, 167, 169
Sudd (swamp), 37, 48, 60, 75, 85
Sudd Institute, 143

Tanzania, 41, 114, 116, 289
tax, 59, 64, 71, 74, 77, 78, 90, 92, 96–7, 145, 217
Teetadol (military HQ), 176
Tenet (ethnic group), 44, 181
Thiik, Gir (chief), 97, 99
Thijok, Maker (chief), 173, 176
Tholomuthe, John (intellectual), 171
Tonga (settlement), 136
Tonga, Steven Babanen (politician), 169, 171
Tonj (town), 37
Toposa (ethnic group), 3, 40, 43–5, 181, 217, 255
towns, 86, 107; and accumulation, 20; urban ethnic associations, 147, 154–9, 180, 235; urbanization rates, 37, 46, 139, 145, 146, 154, 160, 237, 275
traditional authorities, neo-traditional authorities, chiefs, 19, 47–9, 58, 59, 71, 72, 78, 96, 97, 99, 102, 112, 133,

134, 147, 155–6, 160, 171–3, 175–6, 183, 196, 201, 202, 206, 209, 217, 225, 228, 236, 237, 241, 254, 255, 261, 274
transfers to states, 20, 21, 30, 82, 89, 105, 132, 139, 141–6, 258
tribe/tribalism: and economic policy, 23, 96, 243; and Southern Policy, *see* Southern Policy; definitions, 19, 33, 56, 58, 59, 106, 197, 212, 220; tribalization, detribalization and retribalization, 46, 86, 99, 102, 107, 134, 194
Turco-Egyptian Sudan, *see* Turkiya
Turkana, Lake, 34, 43
Turkiya, viii, ix, 1, 17, 56–69, 78, 79, 82, 85, 90, 128; Turkiya districts, ix

Uganda, 82, 83, 92, 155, 267, 289–91
United Nations, 82–3, 121, 224, 257, 258, 281, 291
United States, 10, 121, 147, 149, 151, 180; treaty with Sudan (2002), 12
Upper Nile: Greater Upper Nile, province and later region, ix, x, 2, 40, 41, 50, 60, 98, 99, 136, 139, 150, 164, 171, 179, 189, 204, 212, 217, 230, 231, 245, 249, 267; oil, 2, 87, 112, 178; state, x, 135, 144, 157, 163, 191, 207, 212, 262
urban ethnic associations, *see* towns: urban ethnic associations
urbanization, *see* towns: urbanization rates
Uror, *see* Wuror

Veveno (river), 222

Waat (settlement), 173, 256
Walgak (settlement), 173
Warrap (state), 97, 135, 176, 251
Wau (town in Western Bahr al-Ghazal state), 37
West African economies, 107
White Army, *see* youth groups, armed
White Nile, Turkiya district, ix; river,

4, 5, 8, 10, 34, 37, 42, 48, 56, 62, 63, 74, 85, 91, 136, 215
widowhood, *see* marriage: widowhood
World Bank, 64, 82; and global crisis of 1980s, 100; and mechanized farming, 113; economic theories of, 24–5
World Food Programme, 154
Wuror (county), 133, 135, 191, 209, 210, 212, 217–18, 230, 232, 262

Yauyau, David (rebel commander), 216, 281, 291
Youth groups, armed: armed youth in 1983 civil war, 149, 157, 168, 180, 186, 188, 189, 203, 205–6, 241, 260; armed youth in 2013 civil war, 10, 11, 281; armed youth in Jonglei after 2005, 1, 2, 3, 7, 15, 19, 30, 144, 166, 213, 218, 222–3, 262, 263, 279, 292; armed youth in Pibor, 198–202; disarmament, *see* disarmament: in Jonglei after 2005; targeting of young men, 171, 174, 188–9; White Army, 13, 154, 190–7, 203, 207, 209–10, 212, 223, 230–3, 261, 284, 285
Yuai (settlement), 173, 210
Yut, Gony (prophet), 172

Zaire, 92
Zande (ethnic group, state): infertility studies, 267–70; language, 40–1; pre-colonial state, viii, 48–50, 56